Ethical
Dilemmas of
Development
in Asia

Ethical Dilemmas of Development in Asia

Edited by
Godfrey Gunatilleke
Neelan Tiruchelvam
Radhika Coomaraswamy
Marga Institute

LexingtonBooks
D.C. Heath and Company
Lexington, Massachusetts
Toronto

Library of Congress Cataloging in Publication Data
Main entry under title:

Ethical dilemmas of development in Asia.

1. Asia—Economic conditions—1945–   —Addresses,
essays, lectures.   2. Economic development—Moral and
ethical aspects—Addresses, essays, lectures.
3. Civil rights—Asia—Addresses, essays, lectures.
I. Gunatilleke, Godfrey.   II. Tiruchelvam, Neelan.
III. Coomaraswamy, Radhika.
HC412.E695–1983   330.95'0428   81–47964
ISBN 0–669–05147–0

Copyright © 1983 by D.C. Heath and Company

Published simultaneously in Canada

Printed in the United States of America

International Standard Book Number: 0–669–05147–0

Library of Congress Catalog Card Number: 81–47964

Contents

Preface

During 1979–1980, the Marga Institute, Sri Lanka, and The Asia Society, New York, jointly sponsored seminars and research dealing with ethical dilemmas of development in Asia. Seven national workshops and two regional seminars were held to consider the problem of human rights in the context of development from the perspective of Asian scholars, policymakers, and others directly involved in the development process. One hundred twenty-one persons from eleven countries—Korea, People's Republic of China, the Philippines, Indonesia, Malaysia, Singapore, Thailand, Sri Lanka, India, Bangladesh, and Nepal—participated. Specialists from a wide variety of fields, ranging from political economy to religion and philosophy, gathered in workshops in seven countries to identify relevant ethical issues. These discussions varied considerably but generally attempted to weigh the social, economic, and political consequences of current development strategies in terms of the human costs often entailed. These meetings laid the groundwork for the two regional seminars that treated the problem in cross-cultural perspective. The first was held in Kathmandu, 16–19 December 1979, and the second in Mt. Lavinia, Sri Lanka, 15–17 July 1980.

The project had two interrelated objectives. The first involved the elaboration of a normative framework against which specific ethical dilemmas and choices could be measured. Some elements of the framework were drawn from the model of another development, increasingly recognized by scholars and policymakers as an alternative to conventional approaches. It was felt that the framework should also embody ethical ideals from the cultural and religious traditions of Asian societies. The second objective was to undertake case studies that would examine empirically ethical dilemmas of central importance to the developmental experience of specific countries. These studies would contribute to a refinement of the normative framework.

The frame of reference of the project, its substantive focus, and specific components were discussed at the national workshops organized by the individuals and institutions in Asia collaborating in the project. These meetings often resulted in sharp clashes of views between participants and helped to refine the concepts and methodologies of the case studies. They were also extremely valuable in initiating critical questioning of the development strategies pursued in each of the countries and in affirming the need to evolve an ethical consensus that would constrain and humanize the process of societal change. In some of these countries, themes relating to the ethics of development received the critical attention of concerned scholars and policymakers for the first time.

In others, the project added a new dimension and provided impetus to ongoing debates about the need for alternative models and styles of development.

The project envisaged one of its principal objectives as initiating a dialogue among scholars and policymakers to increase awareness of the need for an ethical system that would structure and guide the development process. The national workshops and regional seminars that were held constitute an initial step in meeting this objective. The individuals and institutions that have participated in the project can serve as the basis of a network for ongoing discussion and research on ethical issues that continue to arise in their countries as well as in the Asian region generally.

This book is an end product of this project; and, though coordinated by the Marga Institute, it represents the collective endeavor of the scholars and policymakers who participated in this exercise. In particular we need to acknowledge the continuing involvement of Mr. Robert Bordonaro in the conception and fulfillment of this project. His deep intellectual concern for the issues raised in this book and his unfailing courtesy have been a source of encouragement to the editors. Sakuntala Kadirgamar and Nelun Gunasekera of the Marga Institute devoted long hours to the correction of drafts and meticulous checking of texts and references.

The Marga Institute is a nonprofit, interdisciplinary organization concerned with development alternatives and with restructuring the relationship between developing societies and industrialized countries. The Asia Society is a nonprofit, nonpolitical public education organization dedicated to increasing U.S. understanding of Asian cultures and contemporary affairs.

The program of research and the seminars on which this book is based were made possible by a grant from the United States Agency for International Development (USAID) to The Asia Society under its Asian Development Seminar Program.

The views expressed in the chapters of this book are those of the individual authors and do not necessarily reflect the outlook of the Marga Institute, The Asia Society or USAID.

1 The Ethics of Order and Change: An Analytical Framework

Godfrey Gunatilleke

The chapters of this book deal with the ethical dilemmas that face policymakers and governments of developing societies in their effort to manage the process of development. In a wider sense, however, the dilemmas that are discussed go beyond those of the elites who hold power and manage society. Equally, they are the dilemmas of the people in these societies as a whole, of their intelligentsia, of the political actors, and of other social groups that consciously participate in setting development goals and, in the numerous choices they make, decide the direction in which their societies should move. The dilemmas that arise out of the development options that face these societies concern, on the one hand, the strategies and instruments chosen to bring about the desired changes and, on the other, the quality of the new life that the societies hope to realize through these changes.

This chapter attempts to provide a framework of concepts and values to help us define and analyze the nature of the dilemmas inherent in the processes of development—dilemmas that seem to arise from inescapable choices between alternatives each of which results in some loss of human values, some cost in human suffering. Instability and discontinuity are endemic to development. The management of a crisis in law and order will entail some denial of democratic freedoms; the rediscovery of cultural identity can heighten ethnic antagonisms in the pluralistic society; the effort to discriminate in favor of historically disadvantaged groups may create new problems of intercommunal equity; the emphasis on goals of productivity and efficiency may lead to the neglect of social welfare and equitable distribution.

Choices in these situations, however, should be made with the fullest understanding of the human implications and the values that underlie these choices. The analysis in this chapter explores what is involved in such an approach. It attempts to show that in fact no trade-offs are possible between the different economic, political, and social goals in a genuinely human process of development. Thereafter, it examines the implications of this in terms of a social vision that must guide and dis-

1

cipline the development process. The chapter argues that in the final
analysis development choices become embedded in fundamental conflicts
between different visions of man and society.

Much of our thinking about development continues to rely on the
paradigm of modernization developed by social scientists a few decades
ago. In this paradigm the traditional order was ascriptive, status oriented,
nonrational, hierarchical, and based on kinship and family; the modern
order was achievement oriented, rational and empirical, increasingly based
on formal social structures, and organized on merit and equality of opportunity. Development was conceived essentially as the transition from
the former to the latter. The analytical framework in this chapter challenges some of the basic assumptions in these simplified polarities; it
attempts to examine the interpretations of reality in each of these models
and the patterns of meaning that each gave to the individual and society,
and to indicate their relevance for our understanding of the dilemmas of
development.

The Order-Oriented Ethos

An inquiry into the ethical dilemmas of development starts with several
assumptions that are already implicit in the terms that are used. There is
an initial assumption that the ethical problems societies face in the development process are somewhat different from the moral issues relating
to good government, the exercise of political power, and the management
of social affairs that have always confronted civilized societies. The
ethical dimension of development would therefore have to be conceptualized differently. It follows from this that such an inquiry should yield
special insights—insights that are different from, and additional to, those
already provided by the major religious and intellectual traditions in their
wide-ranging and profound exploration of the problems in this field. A
second assumption is that development dilemmas have an intrinsic ethical
content—a component of human values that demand specific responses
in the management of the development process—and that no major choices
in development are value neutral or based exclusively on technoeconomic
criteria.

Both assumptions require some elaboration before going on to a
discussion of issues that are more central to the inquiry. When we examine the first assumption, we need to concede initially that the ethical
problems in development originate in a concern for primary human values
that is not intrinsically different from the nature of the ethical concern
in all societies. This concern stems from the inescapable contradiction
between the actual and the ideal—between the social imperfections that

are an organic part of the living reality and the social ideal that has evolved from a vision of the good life as conceived by a given society. Different phases of human history and different societies have grappled with this contradiction in different ways. During relatively stable periods, when the process of change is slow, incremental, and continuous, the concept of *order* acts as the unifying element in the social ethos. Most traditional cultures developed a richly variegated ethical framework that supported and gave meaning to an elaborate hierarchy of social roles. Each role had its ethical ideal, its code of conduct, its *dharma* or moral being—whether it be the role of the priest, the warrior, the state official, or the trader.[1] The goal of society then became the regulation of human behavior to achieve this ethical ideal. The exercise of political power and the relationships of the ruler and the ruled were themselves subject to the overriding sanctions of this order and had to be measured against the norms of righteous authority and just rule. Kingship itself was subordinate to dhamma.[2] The personal order, the social order, and the universal moral order were perceived as a unified organic whole. Within such a framework, the great social evil was the breach of the order, the disturbance of the harmonious balance.

One of the most powerful imaginative expressions of this traditional ideology of order is found in the often quoted speech of Ulysses in Shakespeare's Troilus and Cressida:

> The heavens themselves, the planets, and this centre,
> Observe degree, priority, and place,
> Insisture, course, proportion, season, form,
> Office, and custom, in all line of order:
> . . . How could communities,
> Degrees in schools, and brotherhoods in cities,
> Peaceful commerce from dividable shores,
> The primogenitive and due of birth,
> Prerogative of age, crowns, sceptres, laurels,
> But by degree, stand in authentic place?
> Take but degree away, untune that string,
> And hark! what discord follows; . . .
> Strength should be lord of imbecility,
> And the rude son should strike his father dead:
> Force should be right; or rather, right and wrong—
> Between whose endless jar justice resides—
> Should lose their names, and so should justice too.
> Then everything includes itself in power,
> Power into will, will into appetite;
> And appetite, a universal wolf,
> Must make perforce a universal prey,
> And last eat up himself.[3]

The imagery in the passage is derived from a vision of order in which the individual, society, and nature are part of a universal design. Personal, social, and political relationships acquire meaning as part of this design. Even while the poetry communicates the symmetry and harmony of this structure, however, it also expresses a profound dread of chaos and disorder, a primal terror of the dark forces of predatory nature and brute violence that lie beneath the surface of the fragile human order that has been achieved. The poetry holds together the harmony of the universal order with the Hobbesian awareness of the "nasty, brutish" potentiality of nature. Power, broken loose from order, must prey upon itself.[4]

The order-oriented ethos was naturally biased strongly in favor of the stabilization of existing structures; it concentrated on the humanization and moral ordering of relationships within these structures. It was derived from a particular vision of humanity and human destiny. It perceived human and social imperfection as an inherent and necessary attribute of the natural order—as setting the inescapable boundaries of the human condition. The realization of the ideal itself therefore lay outside the bounds of the temporal and became part of the transcendental reality. An ethos of this nature placed the emphasis on personal perfection and the spiritual liberation of the individual within a given system. To that extent, it deflected attention from the imperfection of the system and the social structures themselves. Such an approach could easily lead to a moral complacency that acquiesced in social evils and readily accepted the imperfections of the system. It could become an ideology for the legitimation and rationalization of inequality and social oppression. At each stage of human history, the order-oriented ethos accepted and legitimized the imperfections and deformities of that time—slavery, serfdom, or any other exploitative socioeconomic system and structure of power. It enabled a minority of human beings to appropriate an inequitably large share of the material output of a society. It also often became the basis of an ethical authoritarianism that purported to discipline people who are prone to imperfection and evil for their own spiritual betterment and the collective good. These propensities in the order-oriented ethos have all been demonstrated at different times in different societies, and the critique of religious ideology has dealt adequately with these aspects.[5]

It would be an oversimplification, however, to conclude that these were the essential attributes and main outcomes of the order-oriented ethos. The moral dilemmas it contained for both the individual and society were infinitely more complex and more contradictory. The inner core of the ideology was the profound antithesis of spiritual complacency. The ideal was never to be fully realized in the human condition, but human spirituality lay in a restless striving for the ideal within this awareness, an inability to rest until one rested in the perfect. The transcendental image of perfection was a powerful compulsion for the improvement of the terrestrial scheme of things. This ceaseless striving for the ideal, coupled with anguish of knowing that it was never to be realized in the temporal order, was humanity's tragic destiny. This striving had to be the sustaining spiritual force in both the personal and the social order. Even the imperfection that accepted and sustained inequality in the temporal order was held in balance with the universal equality of man in God. Almost all societies provided the still center—the church, the temple, the holy place—where equality was manifest before the transcendental presence. The symbols that exalted earthly power and material wealth were opposed by those that renounced them and proclaimed their vanity and nothingness. The holy mendicant, the *sanyasi,* the *bhikku* dedicated to a life of poverty, were accorded the most revered places in society. The social ethos therefore encompassed duality and paradox.

Redefined in this form, the order-oriented ideology contains a profound inner tension. The ethical quality of a society is reflected to the extent that it is disciplined by this striving toward its own ideal and is capable of giving concrete expression to this inner tension. The social and the personal were inextricably intertwined as part of a unified moral order. The dilemma of the king in the tasks of government was also his personal moral dilemma; his striving for a righteous external order was also part of the striving for his own inner perfection. The moral being of a society was therefore the product of the internalized discipline of its members in all their relationships—within the household, in society, and with the transcendental. Within this ethos we find numerous cases in which the moral dilemmas in the governance of men and the ordering of society find expression in their full complexity.

Within the same structure of social relations, historically conditioned by the level of technology and the modes of production, there were innumerable variations in the quality of life, the humanity of the political institutions, and the degree of civilization that characterized various societies and sociopolitical systems. These variations in the human response are in fact the substance of the ethical issues relating to the management of a society. To cite two examples, the statecraft of Justinian and that of Dharmasoka reflect the manner in which the ethos of two different civilizations grappled with the dilemmas of secular law and spiritual order. The strict drive toward a conformist orthodoxy in the one case, and a regime of *ahimsa* (nonviolence) and tolerance in the other, illustrate different approaches to the exercise of state power and its relationship to the norms of justice and to the social and spiritual well-being of the subjects.[6] It is important to recognize here that the conflict between the core value system and the historical evolution of a society has always brought out fundamental ethical issues that have contributed to the re-

newal and refinement of human values relevant to our inquiry, to which
we need to return later on.

The Ethics of Structural Change

For the present, however, we need to go beyond the generic elements
common to the ethical concern of all societies and ask the question with
which we began this discussion: How are the ethical dilemmas of managing a society within an order-oriented ethos different from those of
managing the rapid process of socioeconomic change that is the primary
characteristic of development? Can rapid change be singled out as a
distinguishing attribute of the current phase of human history in that part
of the world we describe as *developing*? A simple affirmative answer
represents a sweeping generalization that ignores the complexity of historical reality.

First, fundamental ideological changes have taken place in different
phases of human history, even during the preindustrial era. These—like
Christianity, Islam, and to a lesser extent Buddhism—often went together with far-reaching changes in the entire structure of social relations,
replacing existing value systems with radically new ones. Christianity,
for example, provided the ethical framework for the major social transitions from a tribal slave society to a feudal system and, in the period
of the Reformation, from feudalism to capitalism. Without debating the
relative roles of ideology and the productive forces in these major social
transformations, we can safely conclude that the goals of structural change
were an essential part of these ideological movements. After these changes
were accomplished, however, the ideology moved away from its reform-
ing role and became the major stabilizing agent for the new order. Its
main task then became the achievement of a new stasis. We know too
little of the inner processes that governed these transitions, how they
were managed, how the dilemmas of conflicting value systems were
resolved, and how the old and the new were reconciled to make any
valid generalizations. We do know that the transitions were periods of
great conflict, violence, and discontinuity, and that the human cost in
the form of liquidation of social groups, religious persecution, and destruction of past achievements was enormous indeed.

Second, the social ethos of traditional societies was not necessarily
order oriented. They were not exclusively devoted to the stabilization of
existing social structures, totally bypassing the need for structural change.
Within these traditions there were elements that struggled for systemic
changes that would result in a spiritual transformation of the terrestrial
order. Many traditions fostered the messianic hope, the search for the

kingdom of heaven on earth, the longing for the rule of the *dharma-chakravarti*. These religious and social impulses moved toward the ideal of a fundamental reordering of the life of the individual and society. It is true that these aspirations did not take the form of a social agenda that the adherents would systematically strive to implement. The historical materialist would argue that the objective historical conditions were not yet ripe for the realization of such near-perfect, classless societies. Mainstream religious thinking, on the other hand, considers it misguided to aspire to the condition of a perfect or timeless *being* in the historical or temporal state of *becoming* something never to be realized in time. In many traditions these ideal transformations assumed the form of an apocalyptic intervention, but minority movements within the main tradition directed themselves toward less ambitious goals and strove to bring about major structural reforms, with occasional success.

The growth of capitalism and the breakdown of the feudal order, however, has witnessed a continuous process of far-reaching change that differs significantly from that in any previous period in human history. Past societies experienced a long period of relative stasis within a stable value system after the initial period of convulsion and change, but the industrial societies ushered in a period in which dynamic processes of change became the principal attribute and sustaining rationale of the system. This made the processes of change that came with the scientific and industrial transformation fundamentally different from the changes and discontinuities within the order-oriented ethos discussed earlier. It was this period that saw the evolution of the value system and the institutional framework that pose the major ethical dilemmas for the developing societies. Each value and institution had to be formed, molded, and established through sustained struggle and effort—the secular state, the abolition of serfdom and slavery, universal franchise and elected and democratic forms of government, religious tolerance, public welfare and state responsibility for the poor, a free press, civil rights, the independence of the judiciary. Free-enterprise systems provided their own strategies for achieving these goals through a mixed economy in which market forces were allowed to play a predominant role. Here structural changes were the result of a long incremental process that took place within structures of power that allowed for conflict resolution. The socialist system provided its own path to some of the goals through a socially owned, centrally planned system, often emerging out of a deepening of social cleavages and conflicts.

It is in this historical context that developing countries must manage processes of change that have their own special character and attributes, if only because change is much more rapid and intense than what societies faced in the past. Politically, the pressures for new forms of social decision making and the pace at which progressively larger sections of the population enter the political processes are of an unprecedented order. Demographically, the increases in population that have occurred in these societies over a few decades surpass what has occurred in centuries in any part of the world, including the developed societies during their period of development. Economically, growth has occurred at rates much higher than those that prevailed when developed societies were undergoing their socioeconomic transformation—5–6 percent on the average compared with 1–2 percent for most developed countries.[7] Technologically, societies are propelled from systems largely dependent on human and animal energy to the use of increasingly complex forms of inanimate mechanical energy; they are able to acquire, albeit only piecemeal, the advanced technology of the developed countries—even while large parts of their societies function at a preindustrial level.

Second, a new international value system has emerged that seeks to define the parameters within which change should occur. Growth and change of the order described would place an immense strain on the inner coherence of social systems and structures, on their capacity for constant adaptation, and on the sensitive living tissue of human relations within these structures. Transitions in the industrial societies, even proceeding much more slowly over longer periods, often burst the bounds of rationality and humanitarian constraints. These societies achieved their new equilibria through open conflicts, violent displacements, and a long record of social oppression and inhumanity. Through these processes, new value systems emerged. The developing countries, however, are in a different historical situation. The lessons and experience of the transition and the value systems that accompany it are already available. The value systems themselves act as a powerful conscientizing force within the developing countries. They have altered the fundamental structures of knowledge and perceptions among crucial elites and social groups in these societies and have transformed the rules of the game for the transition, setting the limits within which change should take place.

Therefore, an evaluation of how developing countries manage their transition is itself an exacting moral task. On the one hand, there must be a profound understanding of the historical processes in these societies, a capacity to see the ethical issue in relation to these processes, and a sensitivity to the inner struggle of a society in the midst of an unprecedented transition. The moral excesses and social deformities themselves must be understood in terms of this struggle before they are judged in terms of ethical norms. On the other hand, such an analysis should not imply either a tolerance for the violation of human values or a lowering of ethical norms and goals. It is important to recognize that only through sensitivity to the historical processes that underlie the present dilemmas is it possible for us to perceive the modes of action that enable these societies to mitigate and contain the excesses and create the right ethical framework to guide the development process.

Finally, another issue lies at the heart of our inquiry into the ethical dilemmas of development. We can state this in terms of the conflict between the order-centered ethos, which is the historical heritage of the developing societies, and the change-oriented ethos that came out of the industrial revolution and that they must adopt for their transition. The opposition, however, goes much deeper than the dualities of order and change, of traditional stability and future shock. Acceptance of discontinuity and change as essential attributes of social and personal life seems to alter the perception of values themselves. No longer do values function as the stable centers of meaning they had been in the past. Rather, they are subject to continuous displacement. They are pushed into a realm of relativity in which every value is time bound, is specific to a historical context, and has validity only in a relative sense. These contemporary processes of change break loose from the transcendental value centers around which all discontinuity and changes in the past had revolved. In doing so they disturb the unity that those value centers had strived to impose on both the personal and the social morality. Developing societies must grapple in the course of development with confrontation between different visions of life, different modes of knowing reality. The development process brings the transcendental model of man and society that has organized human experience in the traditional societies into a sharp encounter with the secular humanist model centered on the present life span and the satisfaction of material wants.[8] The empirical positivist structures of knowledge and reasoning that usually underpin the development process become the unrelenting adversary of the holistic, existential mode of knowing, the inner experiencing of reality that is part of the religious vision of life.

This fundamental clash of value systems and structures of knowledge has a pervasive impact on development goals and choices. It impinges on all major development goals, as well as on the strategies selected to achieve these goals. On the one hand, there is the need to preserve, renew, and redefine the holistic vision to enable these societies to respond critically and selectively to the processes of modernization and the massive intrusion of new values and life goals that destroy that vision. On the other hand, it is necessary that these societies remove the historical outgrowths of the traditional value systems that perpetuate structures of oppression and ignorance and, in doing so, make room for new processes of humanization and new sources of spirituality. Many elements in the system of production and the framework of social and political institutions that we associate with modernization will unquestionably form part of the inevitable changes in developing countries. For each of these elements, however, the question arises: How should developing countries absorb the new into their own indigenous experience and culture? For example, is the technology of the industrial societies separable from the entire value system, organization of human life, and vision of reality that seem to go with it?[9] Can developing societies acquire the former selectively while rejecting the entire value system in which it is embedded? How can these societies assimilate elements of the new humanism, with its emphasis on social equality and individual creativity, into their own concept of the intrinsic transcendental worth of the individual being? These tensions between past and future are particularly significant for Asian societies, where the presence of history is felt more profoundly than perhaps anywhere else. They are the societies with the longest human memory, together representing almost all the major civilizing traditions of humanity—the Hindu, the Islamic, the Buddhist, the Confucian, and the Christian.

Ethics and Technoeconomic Rationality

Let us now consider the second assumption implicit in the title of the project—that there is an intrinsic ethical component in the dilemmas of development that needs to be conceptualized clearly in any development strategy. The discussions held over the course of the project often reverted to this basic question. A variety of positions were taken during the initial defining of terms. They oscillated between two extremes— one that held that developmental dilemmas should be defined exclusively in technoeconomic, nonethical terms and that there was little purpose in introducing an ethical component, and the other arguing that all developmental dilemmas were ethical in character because all development outcomes were human outcomes about which we must eventually make value judgments involving ethical criteria. As the discussion unfolded, it became clear that these positions were themselves based on underlying concepts of development that in turn were derived from fundamental assumptions about people and society.

The first position is based on the premise that development is essentially a technoeconomic process involving the growth and expansion of productive capacity. This supposition implies that all noneconomic outcomes of development have their source in the technoeconomic component. If this were so, then the primary criterion governing development choices should be technoeconomic criteria and the basic principle guiding the development process should be technoeconomic rationality. In this framework technoeconomic rationality is not merely one among several important principles; it is the key principle, superseding others and directing and managing the development process as a whole. The increase in human welfare in this framework is measured in terms of the increase in material output, which in turn leads to the improvement in material well-being, all of which is derived from the way in which the productive system is organized, developed, and utilized. This would imply that the best technoeconomic solutions to development dilemmas are also the best decisions in terms of human welfare. The introduction of independent ethical criteria would thus become unnecessary.

Development ideologies that make material well-being the primary goal of development adopt a conceptual frame in which technoeconomic rationality emerges as the organizing center. This applies to ideologies based on the market system as well as to those based on socialist principles. In the former case social welfare can be best achieved through an efficient market system that gives full play to individual and collective preferences. No conscious ethical choices are necessary apart from technoeconomic ones. The basic presuppositions of this approach rely heavily on the model of people and society derived from the discipline of economics, particularly the neoclassical model.[10] In this model the political processes themselves recede into the background. Conflicts are moderated through the competitive system that provides for their resolution. The main role of the political process is to create the conditions for the full interplay of the market forces that enable the correct technoeconomic choices to be made.

In contrast to this model, the various approaches derived from socialism, especially those based on the Marxist interpretation of social change, move the political processes to the center. In the first instance, the framework conducive for development is set through conscious social action directed at structural changes that can release the productive forces that are being obstructed by the prevailing structure. These relate primarily to the structures that determine the ownership of the productive resources in a society and the relations among those engaged in production. When this agenda is completed, the solutions to development problems that arise thereafter would be essentially technoeconomic solutions, which are obtained mainly through centralized planning. In this conceptual framework, the rationale for the structural changes that are sought is perceived as historical rationality. What is ethical is ultimately what is necessary and inevitable in terms of historical forces and objective historical conditions. Therefore, the solutions and choices that are available are characterized as scientific even while they encompass political choices and modes of social action. In the final analysis, the ethical is subsumed in historical rationality.[11]

Although these ideologies confine the concept of development within the framework of material output and material well-being, however, they cannot avoid addressing themselves to the issue of distribution, as even within this framework well-being implies not only increases in output but also their distribution. One would expect, therefore, that with the distributive issue we move into the ethics of structural change; for here we are involved in political and social choices that lead to the right and equitable structure of production and distribution. Even these issues, however, ultimately tend to be reduced to technoeconomic and historical rationality. The choices and modes of action that move humanity along this path of structural change could be either the entrepreneurial neo-capitalist transformation offered by the market system or the revolution-ary strategies offered by the socialist approach. Two aspects of both ideological types are relevant to this discussion. First, in both, structural change will inevitably bring about the liquidation of social groups, often necessitate violence and destruction, and result in political systems that are authoritarian and oppressive. These tend to be perceived as the nec-essary human costs of achieving the collective good. Second, in both, the main goal of structural change is the transformation of the productive and distributive system, which is seen as the basic determinant of the nature of people and society. The central societal problem is the sharing of material output.

In each case, therefore, technoeconomic efficiency, productivity, and growth emerge as the dominant values. In the analysis of what is con-ducive to human welfare, the ethical component is progressively dis-solved. For example, it is interesting to see how within the Western discipline of economics, attempts to correct market imperfections through interventionist measures such as public welfare remain controversial. The proponents of productivity and growth would contend that the effort to reach a better distribution of well-being through public welfare is self-defeating, as it constantly interferes with the incentive system that promotes productivity and growth. Distribution is better achieved on a sustained basis by permitting market forces to operate in terms of pro-ductivity and growth. A system that is excessively distributive slows growth and will eventually reduce the well-being of all, whereas an efficient growth-centered system will eventually lead to better distribu-tion and greater well-being for all. The choice of instruments would then revert back to criteria that are exclusively technoeconomic.

Within the socialist framework the political processes are primarily concerned with the sharing of material output and the conflicts that con-sequently arise. It is significant that the measurement of growth in the socialist system is much more rigorously confined to the material product and excludes much of the output in the service sectors. The bias in this form of measurement and valuation leans much more heavily toward quantifiable material output. The rationale for the equitable structure is ultimately historical; that is, only this structure is capable of solving the contradictions that have arisen in the production system. Therefore, the ultimate criterion for choices relating to structural change is whether they accelerate the processes that are historically necessary. This criterion of historical rationality leads certain neo-Marxist schools to argue that, historically, capitalist relations of production have not outlived their capacity to carry through a major program of industrialization and structural change in certain parts of the developing world,[12] or to present a scenario wherein the next phase of capitalist expansion is transnationalization, which will solve some of the internal contradictions that have arisen and may thereby enable capitalism to survive for a long period in world history.[13] Whether these developments are good or bad, ethically desirable or undesirable, is irrelevant in the face of what appears to be the inescapable historical outcome. Any other approach that attempts to push toward an egalitarian society primarily on the ground that it is ethically desirable becomes unhistorical, unscientific, and utopian.[14]

In both the market and the socialist approaches, there is a fundamental assumption that the historical evolution of humanity leads to progressively higher stages. These higher stages, however, are measured primarily in terms of human technological capability, man's capacity to dominate nature and to transform natural resources for his own material uses. Both approaches are basically deterministic, severely restricting individual human choice and reducing it to insignificance in the context of external environmental and historical forces, on the one hand, and internal psychophysical determinants on the other. Both tend to produce their own forms of inhumanity, in which the means are justified by the end, whether it be technocratic efficiency, totalitarian rule, or larger concepts of military deterrence or restricted nuclear warfare. The human suffering involved is seen as irrelevant within a scientifically well designed and efficient program; human beings are simply another disposable input in a larger calculus directed toward goals of growth, power, and aggrandizement of the system.

The line of argument followed here is open to the criticism that it is an oversimplification of both the neoclassical and Marxist models. Proponents of both schools of thought deny vehemently that they reduce complex historical and social processes to the technoeconomic base. Marxists point to the writings that analyze the complex interrelationships between the superstructure of culture, ideology, and social institutions, on the one hand, and the base of production relations on the other. Members of the neoclassical school assert that their model is a partial model of reality, as is any scientific model, and that, in their concern with economic phenomena and the laws governing them, they do not deny the importance of other phenomena.

The main issues raised in such a refutation cannot be discussed fully in this brief chapter. The question posed here relates to the way in which the foundations of an intellectual system, the organizing centers of an ideology, determine the interpretation of reality as a whole. The belief that the "economic structure of society always furnishes the real basis starting from which alone we can work out the ultimate explanation of the whole superstructure and political institutions as well as of religious philosophical and other ideas of a given period," will necessarily lead to certain values and norms regarding the management of human affairs as a whole, if the ideology operates in an internally consistent manner.[15] Similarly, a system of thought that is postulated on the belief that the larger part of human behavior is governed by economic motives will produce a hierarchy of values in which the noneconomic values are assigned a low or indeterminate ranking. The discussion in this section has attempted to indicate only how in the development models that have come from industrialized societies, the principles of technoeconomic and historical rationality are paramount and tend to give the main directions to the development process.

This, however, does not mean that these models or the ideologies that support them refuse to recognize the importance of factors other than the technoeconomic ones, or that they ignore the ethical dimension when they apply themselves to the real world. Marshall, in the introductory chapter to *Principles of Economics,* states that "the two great forming agencies of the world's history have been the religious and the economic."[16] The Marxist model, on the other hand, is inspired by a vision of human freedom and fulfillment that is realized after the contradictions of the class struggle have been finally resolved. Revolutionary action toward this end is animated by a profound moral and ethical concern. This, in effect, seems to demonstrate that human reality in its total material and spiritual essence ultimately breaks through the bounds set by these ideologies and frames of thought. The ideologies themselves must come to terms with the reality, making the necessary accommodation to admit the part of that reality that they tend to exclude by virtue of their fundamental beliefs. Human nature must go to spiritual sources beyond these ideologies to draw moral sustenance for its actions.

The Indivisibility of Development

In a reductionist approach to development, one that ultimately perceives development as essentially a unidimensional technoeconomic phenomenon, there are no fundamental dilemmas. The dilemmas arise when we define development as a process that goes far beyond technoeconomic change, when we perceive it as a process in which technoeconomic changes are the means and accompaniment to other far-reaching societal changes in the political, social, and cultural dimensions that enhance the quality of life. In such a framework, dilemmas are ever present. They are irreducible to simple choices, whether we think within social-democratic limits or a revolutionary framework of fundamental structural change. These dilemmas become those of all political actors, whether they be the elites or the poor and disadvantaged. They will all have to grapple with the problem of choosing the development path and the strategies of change that lead to a fully human society.

Here it is useful to consider how the meaning of *development* has changed and been enlarged over the last three decades. We began by perceiving development in its technoeconomic dimension largely as the growth of productive capacity and output, the increase in national goods and services.[17] At the end of the 1960s we were already asking for a great deal more from development than a rapid increase in material output. Development had to manifest itself in social advances that improved standards of health and nutrition, gave people a longer life span, and raised the levels of education and knowledge. The strategy of development had to be such that the pattern of growth itself would yield these positive social outcomes.[18]

In the 1970s we moved further beyond the socioeconomic boundaries to redefine development in terms of other structural characteristics. Development also had to liberate developing countries from a system that reinforced and perpetuated their dependence on developed countries, and provide them with a capacity for self-reliance, both technologically and economically.[19] We began to emphasize the changes in the structure of society and in the distribution of wealth, income, and power that had to accompany changes in the structure of the economy, the size and composition of its product and work force. The elimination of poverty and the satisfaction of the basic needs of society as a whole became a major objective of development.[20] The international debate on development has added yet other dimensions. There is a need for development to take place within the harmonious balance between man-made structures and the total ecosystem that makes possible the management of resources on a long-term self-sustaining basis.[21] The desirable development process is also seen as one in which the structures of national decision making are established on the basis of civic freedoms and rights, in which dissent can be freely voiced, in which governments can be changed by popular choice, and in which there is increasing participation of the community in both defining development goals and acting on them.[22]

Genuine development therefore must succeed in all these areas. It must aim simultaneously to achieve the entire plurality of goals. This is what gives rise to the dilemmas of development. These goals cannot be arranged in a simple order of priority. The effort to order human needs and development priorities in relation to these needs within a well-defined preordained hierarchy oversimplifies and often falsifies the problem of development choices.[23] Development is a totality that is ultimately indivisible. In the development goals we enumerated, however, it is possible to identify three broad clusters. One is organized around growth and the structures that accelerate and sustain it. These include productive capacity, the technological capability for self-reliance, and ecologically sound management of resources. The second cluster focuses on equity: the distribution of growth, wealth, and income; the sharing of physical well-being, the eradication of poverty and ignorance. The third is organized around participation and freedom—the political processes that ensure human rights and provide for a wide sharing of power. Development, a total process of human growth for the individual and society, encompasses all three clusters.

The experience of development seems to demonstrate that these clusters are closely interrelated, that they are part of an interdependent structure. This requires us to strive toward all goals simultaneously if we are to achieve any significant fulfillment of any one cluster of goals. The equity goals cannot be achieved and sustained without adequate effort to achieve the growth cluster. The growth cluster requires rapid expansion of markets, broad-based purchasing power, and sustained growth of effective demand in progressively larger sections of the population. Both equity and growth require viable political systems that in turn can be sustained only through some degree of participation and sharing of power. The historical constraints may always result in lags and shortfalls in one cluster or another; in the short term, inevitable choices may place emphasis on one more than the other. These, however, will still have inevitable developmental costs in terms of the specific cluster that is neglected; they will have to be corrected and made good eventually in terms of that specific cluster. The interdependence of the development goals implies that no permanent trade-off is possible between any two of these clusters. This does not mean, however, that any one cluster can be conceived as a means for achieving another. In the reductionist technoeconomic approach, all nontechnoeconomic elements are means to the technoeconomic end. Redistribution is rational because it leads to growth; equity is a precondition for increasing effective demand. In contrast, what is suggested here is that each cluster must be recognized for its own intrinsic and autonomous value as an indispensable component in the total well-being.

The Simultaneous Pursuit of Multiple Goals

The analogy of the inorganic hierarchical column in which the fulfillment of development needs can follow in sequence does not represent or explain this process adequately. Development seen as an interdependent organic process is not a sequence but a simultaneity. For example, the approach that suggests growth first, equity later, and freedom to follow is not valid in either political, economic, or human terms. If the relationship between the various components of development is organic, then any part that is lost or neglected results in a process of mutilation. A cost must be borne for which there is no real compensation. The correct analogy is an organic structure in which every part has a living relation to the whole and removal or loss of any, although it may not endanger survival, yet results in an intrinsic loss, an impairment of a faculty or function of that part that is needed by the whole. The need for food, clothing, and shelter will always exist, together with the need for the nourishment of the inner person; for fulfillment in interpersonal relationships; for the possibility of spiritual inquiry.

Thus one cannot regard the choices between development goals as capable of trade-offs. The normal condition is the healthy functioning of the whole. Equity cannot be traded off for growth or stability and order for participation. The choices must always be perceived as part of an effort to sustain an organic process, to promote simultaneous movement toward the plurality of development goals. Development must be a process of harmonious growth. Approached in this manner, the choices must create and preserve a system that enables societies to return constantly to the simultaneity of effort, to the total configuration of development values and goals, even when inevitable choices result in the sacrifice of any one component. Such choices, which result in short-term costs in terms of one or another of the development clusters, are likely to be inevitable in the development process. The total framework guiding development choices, however, would need to make sure that they are indeed short term, that the loss of plurality, the excision of any component is transitional, and that the time span during which the loss must be borne is reduced to a minimum. There have to be social, economic, and political mechanisms built into the development process that will

automatically steer it back to the right path and restore it to the plurality
of development goals.

This approach to development goals implies that each cluster has an
intrinsic value and that they are not substitutable for each other. They
cannot be reduced to a common unit of value in which one cluster can
be valued in terms of another and hence traded off for another, and by
which, given a certain volume of resources, the various alternative pro-
portions of the development goods from each cluster can be easily determined for alternative demand schedules that are equally desirable.
There are no elasticities of substitution between the different development
components.

The fact that development values are not substitutable for each other
also requires a different approach to the ordering of priorities and the
time frame for that ordering. Any given historical situation will demand
an ordering of priorities, and the ordering of priorities itself will change
in response to the urgency of the needs. All the time, however, the
ordering itself will be subordinate to the overriding indivisibility of the
development goal. It will have to discipline the choices and actions and
set the time frame for them so that the living generations have the opportunity to participate in a process in which the full range of development goals is kept in sight.

The time frame for development goals raises an entire set of issues
that have far-reaching human implications. Most of the global scenarios
for development that project the future of mankind at the beginning of
the twenty-first century shows a large part of the human race living in
conditions that could still be described as poverty.[24] In the most recent
projections made by the World Bank, the low-income countries, with
more than 35 percent of the world population (excluding China), will
probably still have annual levels of income below U.S. $275 per capita
in 1990 even on the basis of relatively optimistic projections.[25] These
projections signify the inescapable limits of the expectations of most
developing societies. Within these limits they need to organize their
development effort without illusions. Their development goals must be
disciplined by a clear perception of the material limitations imposed on
them by the condition of poverty. They have to recognize that within a
time horizon that is meaningful for the present generation, the level of
living they could reach is circumscribed by these limitations. This still
does not mean, however, that within the limits of their poverty and the
development path they choose, developing societies cannot organize their
life and their upward movement in a manner that is qualitatively satisfying.

In the imagery that is latent in the development terminology used
here, terms like ''reaching a level of living,'' or ''rates of growth'' suggest that the process of growth is all important and that everything should

be subordinated to the climb to affluence, which itself extends over several generations. In this imagery the imbalances that are inherent in the ascent and the human suffering they cause in the present receive little attention. A balanced social well-being, it seems, must be achieved in the distant future—after the ascent. Each generation, however, seeks a plateau, a point of rest in the movement where it tries to achieve a fullness of living in its own life span. All communities, at every stage of development, are as much concerned with material and spiritual fulfillment in their own lifetimes as with the effort to change their lives in order to enjoy a better life in the future. They are as much concerned with *being* in the sense of experiencing of life fully in the present, as with *becoming*, in the sense of growing into something better in the future.[26]

Although there is no question that the agenda of development requires speedy structural changes that can eradicate poverty and satisfy the basic needs of the population as a whole, it seems equally clear that developing societies are capable of reaching this condition long before they approach the state of material well-being enjoyed by developed countries. Further, the social and political framework, the human organization that promotes equity, participation, self-reliance, and a harmonious balance with the nonhuman environment, need not themselves be specific to any particular level of material and technological development. This framework can be achieved early in the process of technoeconomic change and should be sustained and adapted in that process if technoeconomic change itself is to become the means to full human development.

The human quality of the development that takes place would depend very much on the right dynamic balance between present social need and the drive for economic expansion and improvement—the correct tension between the present and the future. It is in the search for this balance that a society's social and political goals, its ideologies for development are defined. It will, for example, decide whether a country will pursue strategies of forced industrialization, uprooting of communities, suppression of human rights, and destruction of the environment—all in order to accelerate the pace of growth—or will seek a more humane course of development, with more equitable sharing of resources and growth. Here, too, the dilemma lies in the fact that the concept of such a balance could become a recipe for stagnation and backwardness if it were merely employed to make people content with their present poverty and the social system that perpetuates it. Also, like the growth-first strategy, it could become ecologically destructive and neglectful of the resource base that has to support future generations. The optimal balance between present and future is a balance between fulfillment and growth. In the normative framework of development that is defined here, the conflicts inherent in present consumption and future growth are resolved as far as possible within the limits of the temporal; for if development is harmonious growth—if technoeconomic change is disciplined within a fully human, social, and political organization—then the very striving for a better future and the austerities it may impose are also part of present fulfillment. This reiterates the previous statement that genuine development is an organic process arising out of the simultaneous pursuit of the full range of development goals. One essential element of this process is the way in which the time frame is set for the pursuit and achievement of development goals in order to achieve that most humane equilibrium for the present generation.[27]

The Centers of Value and the Societal Vision

The full range of development goals cannot be kept in sight if development is treated as a large aggregate of various elements that must somehow be contained together in the process of change. The intensity and pace of change in developing societies will necessarily generate the corresponding intensity and recurrence of conflicts between the different components of development. What we might describe as the human entitlement to development encompasses all the goals of development. Orchestrating the different goals in response to the conflicts, however, and achieving the necessary balance in the numerous choices that developing societies have to make between competing alternatives, is a task that demands a capacity to envision development as a whole. It requires a framework of developmental values and criteria, an ideology relating to development, that can guide the choices and discipline the development process. It calls for a societal vision of the good life, which is the goal of development. Within such a vision, the entire planning of development goals discussed here is subject to organizing principles and value centers that are ultimately independent of the development process itself. They are independent because they are derived from a vision of people and society that in almost all ideologies goes beyond development goals themselves.

It is the continuing search for and the affirmation of these organizing principles and value centers that produce some of the most profound conflicts in the development process. Here the dichotomies of past and present, the struggle between value systems evolved by traditional cultures and those transmitted through development emerge most acutely. We return then to the theme discussed earlier—the conflicts between the secular model of man and society and the transcendental model, which are manifested in the changes that occur as development proceeds. At this level we witness a conflict between different visions of life, different modes of knowing reality, and different paradigms for organizing human experience.

The conflicts considered here relate to the relatively stable core of human values and life goals that are part of any human society and thus lie beyond development itself. The priorities of development ultimately arrange themselves around this human core. Their arrangement will depend on the questions we ask about the outcome of development as it relates to the core. The questions center on such issues as the way in which the new society or the condition of development for which we are striving provides a pattern of meaning for the individual's life. How does it organize human experience in its totality, teaching the individual how to live through his life cycle and preparing him for death? What does the pattern of development do to structures that promote community or to forms of social organization that protect the interpersonal world of voluntary relationships based on love, kinship, and the interior moral life? What is the equilibrium between material and spiritual well-being that development expects to produce? These are questions to which current development thinking rarely addresses itself. They are regarded as part of a subjective world that cannot be brought into the framework of such thinking and analysis. The reluctance to confront these questions is itself related to the underlying ideology of man and society on which such development thinking is based.

It is not possible here to examine in detail the nature of these conflicts or inquire into their validity. Such a task requires an extensive philosophical inquiry. We can, however, present the conflicts in terms of broad dichotomies between the two models. First, the ideology of development that comes to the developing countries out of the experience of developed countries—the ideology of the secular model—gives primacy to technoeconomic rationality, which becomes the organizing principle for individual and social action. Second, this ideology places the pursuit of material well-being at the center of human life goals. Third, it is based on a methodology and a structure of knowledge that is positivistic and empirical. The reality that is not capable of empirical verification, not capable of being identified and treated as an object of knowledge through the methodology of the empirical sciences, is not reality; it is a linguistic creation produced by the structures of language themselves. Fourth, the frame of reference in this ideology is anthropocentric; it is confined to man and his experience, and this experience itself has a limited life span, with no before or after. This centrality of man has perhaps been the driving force in the liberal humanist movements that redefined individual freedoms and human rights, that liberated man from many forms of social oppression and moved the social order toward equality. At the same time, by making man the ultimate source of meaning, it limited all meaning to man. The larger configuration that contained the human scheme became devoid of meaning, and man himself became a meaningless entity within a materialist, spiritless universe.

Fifth, all these elements combine to promote a way of life that is hedonistic and consumerist. The driving force in this system is the continuous expansion of demand, the ceaseless multiplication of new material wants and the flow of goods and services to satisfy them. Sixth, in the secular model the emphasis is on human rights and the institutionalization of these rights through juridical systems, contractual relationships, and systems of reward and punishment that are administered by bureaucracies and formal organizations. It has the virtue that these rights depend more on the rightness of the system than on individual power and the personal morality of individuals. Finally, implicit in this ideology is an underlying presupposition that leans it toward forms of determinism, whether we characterize it as economic or historical determinism. Historical economic and social forces become reified and assume specific identities as major actors in human affairs, whether they be "the market" or "history." They acquire an independent existence in our conceptual framework in relation to human choice. It is true that human will has a place in all these ideologies and that the dialectics of interaction between the individual and society attempt to allow for the freedom of human action. Even so, however, human volition and the capacity to choose between alternatives, the essence of ethical action by an individual or by society, are progressively diminished to the point of becoming immaterial as variables in the process of change. The individual exists only in society and in the vast collective reality of which he or she is a single psychophysical unit. Each person is subsumed within the material forces and the impersonal laws governing them. In the process, the concept of *the person* tends to get removed from our field of vision.

In contrast, the transcendental paradigm is posited on a different concept of rationality. Rationality is derived from life goals that link man to a transcendental reality, whatever conceptual form it assumes—Brahman, Nirvana, Tao, the Christian God, the Islamic Allah. Rationality in the transcendental model is therefore irreducible to any single principle that can be grasped through logical reasoning. The rationality of individual and social action in this condition is rooted in the perception of the contradictions and paradoxes of human existence. If we take one major transcendental tradition, rational action is related to the different stages in the life cycle of the individual as he moves through the many *asramas* or dwelling places in life—childhood and adolescence (the stage of the *sisya*), adulthood and the householder's life (the stage of the *grhasti*), contemplation and the spiritual search (the stage of the *vana-prasti*), and the journey on the path to deliverance (the stage of the *sanyasin*). The states of well-being are also numerous and are related to these stages. They include economic well-being (*artha*), sensual enjoyment (*kama*), responsibility in action in everyday life (*dharma*), and the final release or liberation from desire (*moksha*). Each has its rationality that might be contradicted by the other—*kama* by *dharma*, *artha* by *moksha*. The social and moral order provide for their coexistence, however, as at a given time some part of humanity is at each of these *asramas*.[28]

In opposition to the second attribute of the secular model, the transcendental model gives material well-being a limited value in the total well-being of the body and the spirit. *Artha* is constantly in tension with *moksha*. In the transcendental model the metaphysical is real; and the modes of cognition that go with it are intuitive, holistic, existential modes that illuminate reality in ways different from the analytical, empirical modes. Again, in this transcendental order man, despite his central place, exists within a reality that is more than human, to which the human order is subordinate and is related in a pattern of meaning that goes beyond the dimension of time. The concept of the *person* in the religious paradigm is different from the concept of the *individual* and the values of freedom and equality derived from it in the secular ideology. The person is nevertheless at the center; meaning is ultimately related to the person and his personal relationship with the transcendental reality. The consumerism and immoderate pursuit of well-being that characterize the secular model are incompatible with the equilibrium and moderation cultivated in the transcendental model, where the value clusters in each stage of life must be in harmony with the other clusters and the individual must move harmoniously, liberating himself from one stage as he enters the next, and must respond to the world of material well-being with the inner detachment provided by a spiritual center of gravity.

In the transcendental model human rights are inseparable from social and moral obligations that are part of a total order. The way they are upheld in society depends greatly on the voluntary human relationships and the internal moral discipline of the interpersonal world. By this process of internalizing moral codes, the transcendental model develops the capacity to regulate those components of human interaction—whether in communities, families, or organizations—that cannot be brought within formal structures of law and order and that depend on voluntary relationships based on love and compassion. On the other hand, by emphasizing individual moral conduct, it tends to make the protection of human rights a matter of personal choice and ethical behavior rather than an automatic outcome of the system.

Finally, in both the materialistic and the religious paradigm, there is a basically deterministic character in the relationship between human action and total reality. In both the individual is reduced to insignificance within the larger order; the personal act is altered beyond its original purpose; almost all religious ideologies are themselves rooted in the paradox between human freedom and divine will that finds expression in various forms of determinism. Here, however, the similarity ends. The religious approach to the insignificance of the person comes from a direction opposite to that of the materialistic ideologies. In the latter the deterministic pattern and the individual insignificance are part of a larger physical or material reality that eventually effaces the individual and in which the individual encounters the finality of nothingness. In the religious paradigm both what is preordained and the insignificance of the person within it are restored to a transcendental meaning that wholly transforms them. The different values and meanings assigned to the person and the individual within an ideology will have a profound influence on the way a society organizes itself for the alleviation of human suffering, on its balance of concern for present and future welfare, and on its perception of human rights and values as a whole. It will influence its social ethos, moving toward either a totalitarian value system or a more humane ideology.

Development implies choices that take a society toward or away from one or the other of these paradigms. Development requires a conscious, sensitive resolution of the conflicts between these value systems and world visions. A society that is in the process of development must have the capability to adapt to change while preserving the identity and integrity of its own collective historical experience. While renewing the life-giving sources of its own past, it has to create the freedom to move toward its future. In order to do this, it must develop a center of values out of the understanding of life that has emerged from its cultural accumulation, from which it can both be receptive to new values and respond critically and selectively to them. On this depends the capacity of a society to evolve the moral order within which it can guide and discipline the development process.

The Nature of Choice in the Dilemma

We will now examine briefly some of the concepts implicit in the term *dilemma* and the reasons for defining the choices in the development process as dilemmas. The conceptual framework developed for the studies attempts to restore human choice to the center of the development process and human fullness to the center of the development goal. First, the approach of the study as a whole is essentially nondeterministic, although individual researchers have been free to adopt the emphasis of their choice. The study is concerned not so much with the broad direction of human well-being, as demonstrated by long-term trends in human history, as with the particular paths societies choose in this wide terrain, how they make these choices, and what their total human benefit and cost has been and is likely to be. In each historical situation the space for maneuverability and choice is always present, and the choice that is made will reflect a concern or a disregard for the central human values. In modes of social action directed at far-reaching structural changes, the available choices can take different paths, ranging from those that are highly conflict-ridden and entail heavy human costs to those that have a capacity for conflict resolution and for minimizing the short-term human costs. They can lead to sociopolitical systems that vary greatly in their framework for participation and dissent or their protection of human rights. For example, within the framework of a socialist revolution itself, there will be options for a strategy of forced industrialization, rapid structural change in the rural sector with enormous human cost, or a more humane participatory process of rural change. The collectivization process in the USSR and the development of communes in the People's Republic of China offer contrasting strategies, with a different balance sheet of gains and losses in human terms. Second, the study's approach attempted to place development processes within their cultural context and relate them to value centers that are derived from the historical experience of these societies and the visions of life that informed it.

The term *dilemma* implies a particular kind of choice, a situation in which the best alternative cannot be readily and definitely identified. Rather, the choice is between alternatives each of which is valid and important in its own right and none of which can be sacrificed indefinitely. The indivisibility of development and the need for simultaneity in its pursuit constantly confront developing societies with situations that can be called dilemmas. A dilemma offers no easy choice, no single alternative that is conclusively right. The thought frame in which the choice is always clear and the methodology for finding the right solution for every choice is always available is essentially totalitarian in its outlook; it imposes the inorganic certainty of the natural sciences on the infinitely variable living human reality. It then acquires an orthodoxy, whether religious or secular, that tries to fit this reality into its procrustean frame. It provides no outlets for communication with approaches and choices other than its own. In its inflexible search for the good it thus becomes inhumanly oppressive, transforming itself into the opposite of what it desires to be and becoming a source of evil. Both religious and secular ideologies amply illustrate this transformation throughout human history—the Inquisition and religious persecutions in feudal Europe, the revolutionary terror in France, the worst phases of the Stalinist era after the Bolshevik revolution, the holocaust in Kampuchea.

Dilemma, in contrast, implies humility in the presence of life's complexity, an acceptance of the limitations of human knowledge, an anguish at the possibility of losing one value when choosing another value. The unfolding of reality confounds the simple principles of logical order and sequence where every object, condition, and value has a separate identity and is not to be confused with another. In the *logical* order the good and the bad can be perceived unerringly in distinct antagonistic manifestations. The dialectical approach, on the other hand, perceives that reality cannot be contained entirely within these logical relationships; it accepts and seeks to understand the contradictory nature of reality; it recognizes that any particular condition or state of being *can,* and in the historical process *will,* become its opposite until all contradictions are resolved. The dialectical approach in its materialistic form, however, still works within the historical process; it moves from one antagonistic form to another. In this progression the contradictions in reality are successively resolved. This must be contrasted with the religious approach, which reaches further than the categories of the dialectic; in this approach the opposites are always immanent in reality; it uses the language of *paradox* and communicates through symbols to express the aspects of reality that are irreducible to a logical system. The opposites then become aspects of one overarching identity. Thus the Preserver and the Destroyer are different faces of the Infinite Being. Evil resides within good; and, as in the vision that was vouchsafed to Dame Julian, "Sin is behovely and all manner of things shall be well."[29] The diversity of the historical is contained within the unity of the transcendental.

In the religious paradigm, therefore, these fundamental paradoxes define the human condition. In Time, man has no choice but to distinguish the opposites and deal with reality through logical categories, but he needs to do so in constant awareness of the limitations of these categories, their interchangeability, and their existence in the ultimate unity. In the last frontiers of human knowledge, language folds in on itself in silence, and reality can be sought only through "the cloud of unknowing".[30] In the materialistic dialectic, on the other hand, the bourgeois relations of production are the last antagonistic forms of social production, and the communist synthesis brings "the prehistory of human society to a close;"[31] but in the latter there is no historical solution, the paradoxes are immanent in the whole of history and existence. There is no simple historical progression that fundamentally alters the paradoxical character of human existence. The synthesis always remains beyond time. The dilemmas of choice in the religious framework are best illustrated in the predicament of Arjuna in the field of battle in the Bhagavadgita.[32] What is of supreme importance is personal action and the purification of the motive in personal action. Although the correct outcome is kept in sight and the effort is directed toward that outcome, what is fundamental is the right effort, which enters the universal order—an order that may produce its own outcome, different from the original personal goal. Secular power and progress therefore must humble themselves before this knowledge. The major human choices need to be sensitive to all three categories—the logical order, the dialectical process, and the condition of paradox. To the extent that the values pertaining to all three categories are present in the ideology of a society, it is likely to have greater or lesser capacity for openness, tolerance, and humanity in the task of social engineering that it undertakes.

The intrinsic character of the dilemma also lies in the fact that the true nature of the choice itself and its outcome are never perceived in their entirety at the time the choice has to be made; neither is the full knowledge of the solution to the problems posed by the dilemma available.[33] This awareness informs the ideological approaches that perceive true knowledge as knowledge gained only through praxis or existence. *Praxis* yields the understanding of reality and the knowledge to cope with it through immersion in social action and struggle. In this sense it is essentially a methodology that belongs to the materialistic dialectic.[34] Existential knowledge, although it includes praxis, reaches out to the totality of human experience, both material and spiritual needs.[35] In a dilemma it could be said that the true choice is existential. The solution or outcome can never be anticipated in full but has to be borne out of lived experience; it has to grow, change, and mature in existential reality out of the unremitting search for genuine values. This means a continuing process of self-appraisal and renewal, and it has important implications for the ethos of a society.

The Main Elements of the Normative Framework

Figure 1–1 is an effort to represent the main elements of the analysis so far made and to depict some of the broad interrelations between them as they act on the processes of development and the choices that have to be made. Development itself lies between the two encompassing models of man and society—the secular and the transcendental. These in turn are in conflict for the societal vision and the life goals that should govern the development process. Within the development category itself, the values and attributes that are indicated on the right are presented as what would be desirable for the development process.

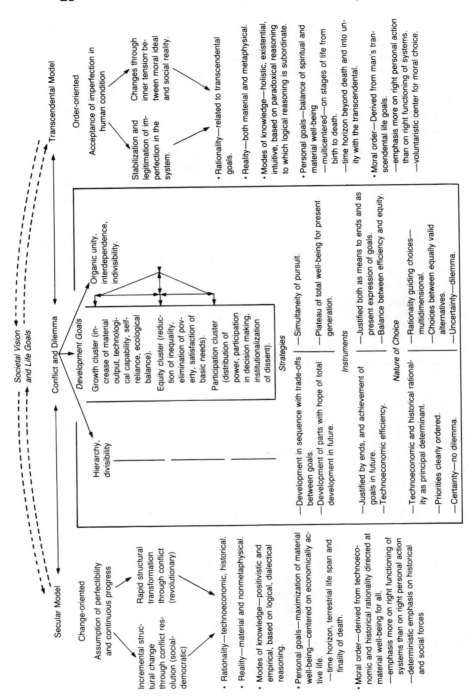

Figure 1-1. Societal Vision and Life Goals

1. In this normative value framework, development goals have to be perceived as an organic unity.

2. The strategies must commit themselves to a simultaneity in the pursuit of the goals. Whether they be strategies of export-oriented growth and greater integration with the world economy, or of delinking and self-centered growth, they need to be measured in terms of these criteria. Methodologies of change, whether they be based on conflict and discontinuity or on incremental transformation, should then be evaluated in relation to this framework.

3. There should be minimal concession to substitutability of goals. The effort must be to create a plateau of total well-being for the present generation while sustaining a continuous process of renewal and growth.

4. The instruments that are chosen must manifest the development goals in their very operation. They should not be justified as the inescapable means that deny the goals in the present to be able to achieve them better in the future. This calls for a correct balance between efficiency and equity. The institutional forms such as central planning or the market system, as well as specific instruments such as foreign investment, emergency rule, or public-welfare programs, should be assessed by their capacity to realize these values in their operation itself.

5. Within such a process choices are rooted in dilemma. The awareness that there are never easy or completely correct solutions and that the choice lies between equally desirable components of development must inform the whole process of social action with a profound humanity and tolerance.

As stated earlier, the development inset in figure 1–1 is enfolded by the societal vision and the life goals that are implicit in it. There is no intention in the presentation, however, to claim that the more desirable part of the development inset comes exclusively out of the transcendental model. The basic problem derives from the fact that both the components of the transcendental model and those of the secular model could lead to the sequence to the left of the development inset. Technoeconomic rationality and the emphasis on systems, together with the approach to human beings as factors of production or inputs into a larger entity, could lead the secular model toward totalitarianism, the denial of human freedoms, and the restriction of personal fulfillment. This direction has both a capitalist and a socialist variant. Also, the transcendental model can lead to the revival of orthodoxy and fundamentalist approaches that can have similar political, social, and human outcomes, as occurred in the Iranian revolution. Again, although the technology and institutional forms for the three development clusters have evolved primarily within the secular model, the processes and value clusters to the right of the inset appear to be more closely associated with the moral order of the transcendental model. Nevertheless, the choice between the secular model and the transcendental one should not be seen only in terms of their capacity to engender the desirable development process. The is in relation to their intrinsic validity and capacity to give meaning to life goals.

It might be asked whether in this presentation there is a basic assumption that the developed industrial societies are organized exclusively in terms of the secular model. Perhaps these societies, while pursuing the goals of technological change and material well-being, have not broken loose fundamentally from the transcendental value centers that molded their cultures over a long period. In fact, the capitalist transformation itself found a vehicle of religious beliefs and values in the Reformation. The movement toward human equality and freedom that emerged with the breakdown of feudalism in these societies drew its energy from the spiritual core of their transcendental traditions. The analysis so far has attempted to show, however, that the dominant value system that has emerged in these societies has moved away from this core and is derived essentially from the secular model; that it is the societal vision and the set of life goals that are part of this model that are being transmitted to the developing societies. The dilemmas examined in this study, therefore, are those that arise out of the effort to adapt the transcendental model to those elements of the secular model that are indispensable for achieving the development goals and generating the development processes as set out to the right of the inset.

The normative framework that has been delineated in this chapter is elicited partly from the empirical studies of development dilemmas in selected national situations that are analyzed in the chapters that follow. It is derived partly from the inquiries and discussions on the conceptual issues undertaken independently of these individual studies. The methodology adopted was, therefore, an attempt to combine the normative with the empirical approaches in order to gain insights into the ethical dimensions of development. The normative framework that was initially formulated to guide the country studies was itself expected to go through the continuous process of revision and reformulation in the light of the knowledge gained through the country studies. This book, however, should be regarded as the first phase of the more comprehensive and representative inquiry that must follow. Within the limits of this first phase, it has not been possible to select the full range of themes that could adequately illustrate the main issues discussed and elaborated in the normative framework. Nevertheless, the studies that have been in-cluded cover the main categories under which we have grouped the eth-ical concerns of development.

Main Themes of the Empirical Studies

As noted earlier, there are, first, dilemmas that relate to the conflicts between the societal visions that animate the developmental process, provide it with a measure of coherence, and guide the choice of devel-opmental goals. Second, there are problems relating to the ordering of the development goals themselves—the dilemma of maintaining correct equilibrium between the different clusters of development goals. Third, there are concerns that relate to the strategies of development that are adopted in order to achieve the goals. These would include, for instance, choices between a free-enterprise-oriented social-democratic path of de-velopment; the centrally planned socialist direction; and an authoritarian, growth-oriented model. Finally, there are dilemmas relating to the choice of instruments employed to implement such developmental strategies. These would include the legislative, administrative, and policy means employed to achieve specific developmental goals—for example, emer-gency rule for the management of crises of law and order, legislation providing special opportunities for disadvantaged groups, social-security programs to compensate for unequal distribution of benefits from growth.

We may now turn to each of the case studies included in this book. Each of these studies focuses on a set of developmental problems that illustrate selected components of the ethical dimension of development as set out in this introduction. The identification of the themes of the case studies has grown out of the research process involving represen-tatives of different disciplines as well as ideological trends within each of the countries concerned. We may now briefly outline some of these studies.

Islam, the State, and Development in Indonesia

This study examines the conflicts between the goals of the transcendental societal vision and the secular vision in the Indonesian context, through an institutional analysis of the Department of Religious Affairs and its management of the conflicts in a pluralistic religious environment. The study also outlines the emergence of several Islamic revivalist movements that sought to reconcile the scriptural and mystical traditions of Islam with development goals such as those relating to the elements of poverty and inequity. The study introduces us to the dilemmas of balancing material well-being and the fulfillment of spiritual and religiocultural needs in contemporary Indonesian society.

Intercommunal Relations and Problems of Socioeconomic Development: The Malaysian Dilemma

This study examines the social and economic factors that shaped the evolution of a plural society in Malaysia. The analysis takes into account the political compact that was forged between indigenous groups and those that were perceived as immigrants and late entrants to the Malaysian polity. It focuses on the challenge posed to the political processes by the implementation of policies conforming to the preferential treatment of the Malay majority on the one hand and the demand of the non-Malay minorities for equality of opportunity on the other. The study is thus illustrative of the dilemmas of affirming equality and equity in the distribution of resources in a plural society where the majority group has been historically disadvantaged. It focuses on the complexities of reconciling developmental goals in such a context and the need for an ultimate societal vision to discipline the implementation of the policy of protective discrimination in favor of a politically dominant group.

Violence and Development in Sri Lanka

This is a case study of the political and socioeconomic processes underlying the propensity for violence in a society undergoing rapid change. The case study examines how the pattern of development on the one hand reduced the propensity to violence inherent in such socioeconomic conflicts, and on the other still continued to produce various manifestations of violence. It deals with the problems of violence arising out of trade-union agitation, revolutionary protest, ethnic conflict, and antagonisms of political parties. It goes on to examine the way in which extraordinary instruments of state power were designed to cope with these manifestations of violence while retaining the continuity of the democratic process. It also analyzes the implications of these instruments for the development of political institutions aimed at facilitating participation and ensuring individual freedoms.

Technocratic Authoritarianism and the Dilemmas
of Dependent Development

This study deals with the strategy of development described as developmental authoritarianism that grew out of the declaration of martial law in the Philippines. The study addresses itself to some of the presuppositions of this development ideology in which developmental goals relating to participation are sacrificed or deferred in order to achieve growth and technological capability. The study also critically assesses the self-justification of the regime—that martial law was a means of promoting social equity and redistribution.

The Quest for Equality: Protective Discrimination
or Compensatory Justice?

This study examines the struggle to extend equality of opportunity and an equitable share in the benefits of development to historically disadvantaged and virtually excluded groups and communities in India. Two alternative approaches to the quest for equality of these groups are examined: (1) the articulation of new egalitarian norms and the implementation of programs of preferential treatment by the state to provide opportunity for upward social mobility to a minority in these groups; and (2) modes of self-help and self-reliance that enable the disadvantaged groups to act collectively to overcome historical forms of exploitation and discrimination.

In evaluating these two approaches, the study directs attention to the interdependence and indivisibility of the development goals relating to equitable distribution of resources on the one hand and to participation in decision making on the other. The analysis also addresses the conflicts that arise between the values of the traditional order and the norms emerging out of the forces of secularization and modernity.

Dilemmas in Developing Social-Security Programs:
Korea

This study looks at the attempts of a newly industrializing society to mitigate the imbalances of a growth-oriented developmental ideology with social-security and social-welfare policies. The study examines some of the instruments that are capable of implementing such policies and presents the dilemmas inherent in reconciling such policies with the goals of efficiency and productivity. The study also alludes to some of the implications of these policies for traditional social and extended familial relationships, which had their own structure of obligations for the support of the disabled.

Ethical Dilemmas Arising from Urban Development and Environmental Change

This study deals with the problems of urban development and the management of physical environment in Singapore. It identifies some of the important human dilemmas in the strategies that Singapore has developed to cope with its problems. It shows how a growth-oriented and efficiency-centered development strategy might apply policy instruments in specific areas with a constant concern for the human issues that are involved and thereby enhance the quality of life that results from development.

The concluding chapter of this book examines in greater detail the main issues of each case study in relation to the analytical framework that has been delineated in this chapter. In doing so it attempts to elicit the policy relevance of these experiences for goal setting, for formulating strategies, and for designing instruments for the management of the development process.

Notes

1. The most elaborate expression of this ethos is in the Hindu tradition and its scriptures—the Vedic literature, the Dharmasastras, the Upanishads, and the imaginative literature such as the Mahabharata and the Ramayana. A selective list of modern writings which provide an introduction to this tradition would include: Kewal Motwani, *Manu Dharmasastra* (Madras: Ganesh & Company, 1958); S. Radhakrishnan, *Eastern Religions to Western Thought* (London: Oxford University Press, 1939); H. Zimmer, *The Philosophies of India* (New York: Meridian Books, 1956); Max Weber, *The Religion of India*, trans. (New York: Free Press, 1958); and Ananda Coomaraswamy, *Selected Papers: Metaphysics,* ed. Roger Lipsey (Princeton, N.J.: Princeton University Press, 1977).

2. Ananda Coomaraswamy, *Spiritual Authority and Temporal Power in the Indian Theory of Government* (New Haven: Yale University Press, 1942):

"The King should consider himself subject to the rule of Law or Dharma, which no earthly monarch dare ignore. Dharma rules monarchs and men alike.'' Motwani, *Manu Dharmasastra,* p. 138, commenting on chapter 7 of the Manu Dharmasastra: ''Manu says that a King should be fined a thousand times as much as a common Man for the same Offence'' (ch. viii. 336). Radhakrishnan, *Eastern Religions,* p. 374n.

3. William Shakespeare, *Troilus and Cressida,* Act 1, sc. iii.

4. For a sensitive analysis of the complex interaction between the personal disorder in the main characters and the political disorder within the Trojan-Greek conflict, see D.A. Traversi, *An Approach to Shakespeare* (London, Cambridge, 1950). pp. 63–80.

5. Karl Marx, *On Religion* (London: Lawrence and Wishart, 1960), pp. 83–89; Bruno Bauer, ''Die Judenfrange,'' in *Early Writings,* trans. and ed. Tom Bottomore (London: C.A. Watts & Company, 1963).

6. ''Theological speculation became a servant of the tradition of Justinian, who closed the schools at Athens, codified the law and restored the Byzantine Church. Learning was lost and with it the capacity in speculation. . . .'' Radhakrishnan, *Eastern Religions,* p. 275.

''His Sacred and Gracious Majesty (Asoka) does reverence to men of all sects . . . there should be a growth of the essence of the matter in all sects . . . a man must not do reverence to his own sect by disparaging that of another man without reason. . . . The sects of other people deserve reverence for one reason or another. Concord therefore is meritorious, to wit, hearkening willingly to the law of piety as accepted by other people. For it is the desire of His Sacred Majesty that adherents of all sects should hear much teaching and hold sound doctrine.'' Asoka rock, edit. XIII, quoted in Zimmer, *Philosophies of India,* p. 497.

7. Simon Kuznets, *Modern Economic Growth-Rate, Structure and Spread* (New Haven: Yale University Press, 1966), pp. 34–85; U.N. Statistical Yearbooks; World Bank Atlases. ''Between 1950 and 1980, GDP of developing countries increased at an annual rate of 5.4 per cent which represents a remarkable performance. . . .'' *Trade and Development Report 1981,* U.N. Conference on Trade and Development, p. 33.

8. The discussion in this section draws on Godfrey Gunatilleke, ''Re-thinking Modernisation: Asia 2000 A.D.,'' paper presented at the seminar on Asia 2000 A.D., organized by the Asia Society in New York, 17 July 1981, and idem, ''Pluralistic Strategy of Development,'' *Marga Quarterly Journal* 6, no.1 (1981).

9. Ibid.

10. ''Neo-classical economists like to consider themselves 'scientific,' able to emulate in their own field the accelerating progress in the physical sciences. . . . Such an approach has stimulated the systematic elaboration of models which reduce complex social phenomena to simple causal relationships, linking a few variables in a priori models, for which

confirmatory material is then obtained.'' Dudley Seers, ''The Congru-
ence of Marxism and other Neo-classical Doctrines,'' in *Toward a New
Strategy of Development,* A Rothko Chapel Colloquium (New York:
Pergamon Press, 1979).

11. ''The danger of constructing a morality within a historiosophical
vision . . . does not lie in the attempt to interpret one's life as a fragment
of history. . . . The danger consists in the total replacement of moral
criteria by the criteria of the profit which the demiurge of history derives
from our actions. . . .'' Leslek Kolakowski, *Marxism and Beyond* (London: Paladin, 1971), pp. 157–158.

12. Bill Warren, ''Imperialism and Capitalist Industrialisation,'' *New
Left Review,* no. 81 (London, September–October 1973). See also ''The
Postwar Economic Experience of the Third World,'' in Seers, *Toward
a New Strategy of Development.*

13. Seers, ''Congruence of Marxism''; F. Froebel, J. Heinrichs, and
O. Kreye, *The New International Division of Labour,* trans. of *Die Neue
Internationale Arbitsteilung* Reinbek bei Hamburg: Rowohlt Taschen-
buch Verlag, September 1977. English translation of introduction published in *Social Science Information,* 17, no. 1 (1978): 123–142.

14. This is a recurrent theme in all standard texts on historical materialism; for example, see Friedrich Engels, *Socialism, Utopian and
Scientific* (London: Allen & Unwin, 1892), Social Science Series.

15. Ibid., p. 41.

16. A. Marshall, *Principles of Economics,* 8th ed. (London: English
Language Book Society and Macmillan, 1972).

17. The writings on development in the 1950s treated development
essentially as an economic phenomenon. For example, see W.A. Lewis,
Theory of Economic Growth; W.W. Rostow, *The Take Off into Self-
Sustained Growth* (New York: MacMillan, 1963); P.T. Baur, *Economic
Analysis and Policies in Underdeveloped Countries* (London: Routeledge,
Kegan and Paul, 1965); *The Second Five-Year Plan of the Indian Government, The U.N. Strategy for the First Development Decade,* U.N.
Resolution 1710 (xvi), 1961, reflected this emphasis, although a cau-
tionary note was already present in the discussion on development in the
early 1960s. ''One of the greatest dangers in the development policy lies
in the tendency to give the more material aspects of growth an overriding
and disproportional emphasis. . . . Human rights may be submerged
and human beings seen only as instruments of production rather than as
free entities for whose welfare and cultural advance, the increased production is intended.'' *Five Year Perspective, 1960–1964,* U.N. Publication, 1962.

18. *International Development in the Second U.N. Development Decade*, U.N. Resolution 2626 (xxv), 24 October 1970, para. 18: "Qualitative and structural changes must go hand in hand with rapid economic growth and existing disparities should be substantially reduced"; Gunnar Myrdal, *The Challenge of World Poverty* (London: Allen Lane, 1970).

19. *The Declaration of the New International Economic Order*, U.N. Resolution, April 1974. The ideological framework of the new international economic order (NIEO) owed a great deal to the work of Third World intellectuals and scholars, such as R. Prebisch, *The Economic Development of Latin America and Its Principal Problems*, U.N. 1950; Celso Furtado, *Development and Stagnation in Latin America—a Structural Approach*, Studies in Comparative International Development, vol. 11 (1965); Oswaldo Sunkel, *National Development Policy and External Dependence in Latin America* (1967); Samir Amin, *The Development of Capitalism in Black Africa;* Norman Girvan, ed., *Social and Economic Studies*, special issue; and *Dependence and Underdevelopment in the New World and the Old* which appear in 22, no.1, special issue, (Kingston: Institute of Social and Economic Research, March 1973).

20. International Labor Office, *Employment Growth and Basic Needs*, Report of the Director-General, ILO, to the Tripartite World Conference on Employment, Income Distribution, and Social Progress, and the International Division of Labour (Geneva: ILO, 1976); Robert S. McNamara, *One Hundred Countries, Two Billion People—the Dimensions of Development* (New York: Praeger, 1973).

21. *Report of the United Nations Conference on Human Environment*, June 1972 (New York: United Nations, 1973).

22. Andrew Pearse and Matthias Stiefel, *Inquiry into Participation—a Research Approach*, and the related series of documents (Geneva: U.N. Research Institute for Social Development, 1979 and thereafter).

23. This discussion draws on sections of Godfrey Gunatilleke, "Pluralistic Strategies of Development," *Marga Quarterly Journal* 6, no. 1 (1981). The concept of *total development* has been defined from different points of view in Dag Hammerskjold Foundation, *What Now—Another Development*, 1975; Johan Galtung, Roy Preiswek, and Monica Wemeigah, "A Concept of Development Centred on the Human Being—Some Western European Perspectives," in *Canadian Journal of Development Studies* 11 (1981); and Denis Goulet, "An Ethical Model for the Study of Values," *Harvard Educational Review* 41, no. 2 (May 1971).

24. Organization for Economic Cooperation and Development, *Facing the Future—Mastering the Probable and Managing the Unpredictable*, 1976; M. Messaric, and E. Pestel, *Mankind at the Turning Point*

(London: Hutchinson, 1975); W. Leontief et al., *The Future of the World Economy* (London: Oxford University Press, 1977); Amilcar O. Herera et al., *Catastrophe or New Society* (Ottawa: International Development Research Centre, 1976); and Gerald O. Barney et al., *The Global 2000 Report to the President of the U.S.* (New York: Pergamon Press, 1980).

25. *World Development Report 1981* (Washington, D.C.: World Bank, 1981).

26. The critique of development that might be described as existentialist has drawn the distinction between *being* and *having*. See Denis Goulet, "Development Experts—the One-Eyed Giants," in *World Development* 8, no. 7–8 (July–August 1980); and Erich Fromm, *To Have or to Be* (New York: Jonathan Cape, 1978). This distinction is between the mode of life in which satisfaction is gained primarily through acquiring and having (characteristic of a technologically oriented society) and a mode in which the satisfaction is in the inner equilibrium achieved in relation to the world of things and the enjoyment of possessions. In the distinction between *becoming* and *being* made in this chapter, the emphasis is on the dimension of time and the equilibrium achieved in relation to wanting in the future and finding fulfillment in the present. The concepts are interlinked, as they are both concerned on the one hand with dynamic and static conditions, and on the other with moderation and excess.

27. This discussion reiterates some of the points made in Godfrey Gunatilleke, "Commitments to Development," in *Marga Quarterly Journal* 1, no. 1 (1971).

28. Radhakrishnan, *Eastern Religions;* Zimmer, *Philosophies of India*.

29. Julian of Norwich, *Revelations of Divine Love* (London: Penguin, 1966), chap. 27. The methodology of the paradox is probably best illustrated in the philosophical and mystical writings of the Hindu, Buddhist, and Taoist traditions. The inadequacy of the logical category to explain reality is progressively unfolded, and the mind is finally confronted with the irreducible paradox—for example, the concept of Nirguna Brahman: "It is not this, it is not that." The Mahayana text Prajna Paramita is a magnificient example of this method. "The Mahayana Way," states Zimmer, "is to reassert the essence by means of a bold and stunning paradox." *Philosophies of India*, p. 485.

30. *The Cloud of Unknowing*, trans. Clifton Wolters (London: Penguin, 1961).

31. Karl Marx, "Preface to a Contribution to the Critique of Political Economy," in K. Marx and F. Engels *Selected Works*, vol. 1 (London: Lawrence & Wishart, 1960), p. 369.

32. Arjuna, having to do battle with his close kin, is "stricken by

compassion and despair." "Before us," he says, "stand Dhritarashtra's folk, whom if we slay we shall have no wish for life." Krishna's reply in the second lesson of the Bhagavadgita expounds the metaphysic of action within the Hindu version: "Holding in indifference alike pleasure and pain, gain and loss, conquest and defeat, so make thyself ready for the fight." *Bhagavadgita* 2.38.

33. For an economist's view of uncertainty see Kenneth Boulding, *The Image—Knowledge in Life and Society* (Ann Arbor: University of Michigan Press, 1956). "By all means let us be manifest as we can. Let us probe the secrets both of nature and her history, but let us also cultivate a sense of mystery as well as a sense of history. . . . The searchlight of the manifest makes more apparent the darkness of the latent beyond it. What this means in practice is that our response should be always to an uncertain image," pp. 130–131.

34. Karl Marx, "Theses on Feuerbach," in *On Historical Materialism: A Collection*. (Moscow: Progress Publishers, 1976), p. 11. Thesis II: "The question whether objective truth can be attributed to human thinking is not a question of theory but is a practical question. In practice man must prove the truth." Adolph Sancha Vasques, *The Philosophy of Praxis* (London: Merlin Press, 1977).

35. To both the nonreligious existentialists (Heidegger, Jean-Paul Sartre, Merleau-Ponty) and the religious thinkers of this tradition (Kierkegaard, Jaspers, Marcel), human reality is free and responsible. Present choice and action *create* the future field for choice and action.

2 Islam, the State, and Development in Indonesia

Abdurrahman Wahid

The development of Islam in Indonesia provides an interesting picture of a unique experience, one no less dramatic than the recent events in the Middle East—from Libya's tinkering with government by militant People's Associations to Saudi Arabia's petroleum-supported state welfarism to Iran's *wilayat-e-fageeh* (government by religious scholars). The Indonesian development is no less dramatic in its long-term impact on the future of Islam itself, although its silent dynamics have almost eluded the media so far. Less well covered by the media than those other developments—indeed, almost entirely ignored—events in Indonesia give us deeper insights into a world religion's continuous dialogue with the process of modernization and, by extension, offer some universal elements of the responses of world religions to the disturbing effects of modernization.

This chapter does not attempt to deal with the substantive problems arising from the interaction between religion and the processes of development. It does not, for example, seek to examine the nature of the conflict between Islam and the structures of modern knowledge or value systems transmitted through development. The analysis initially assumes the validity of the religious experience and its overriding importance for societal changes in Indonesia; it proceeds on the premise that the religious vision of life and the goals of development will need to readjust to each other at a more meaningful level than at present. On these assumptions the chapter focuses on the institutional framework currently available for managing the relationship between religion and political authority and directing the religious responses to the processes of secularization that are taking place through development. The challenge to national policy is one of containing a vast heterogeneity of religious responses, ranging from inflexibly conservative positions to innovative and creative adaptations. Indonesia's government must provide a framework of commu-

This chapter represents the efforts of different individuals involved in various national dialogues on this topic in 1980–1981. These dialogues were conducted under the direction of Dr. Mochtar Buchori, deputy chairman for social sciences and humanities of the Indonesian Academy of Science. Although the author is indebted to many others for the ideas expressed here, he is solely responsible for any inaccuracies in the entire chapter.

nication and tolerance among them that avoids explosive and irrational conflict and sets in motion a process of collective selection and discrimination that enables the creative forces to assume leadership and guide the transition. In this context, the Indonesian experience offers many significant lessons.

A striking phenomenon that differentiates Indonesia from other Muslim countries is that, although the other countries have religious offices at the ministerial and subministerial levels, the Ministry of Religious Affairs (Departemen Agama) in Indonesia becomes the crucial battleground for the diverse (and often mutually conflicting) politicoreligious aspirations of the governing circles and the opposition alike. Except in Egypt, religious offices in Muslim countries tend to assume the exclusive right to formulate and then implement religious policies, and thereby become instruments of state control over religious affairs. No genuine participation of nongovernmental organizations is sought; neither are these offices accountable to anyone outside the government. Even the exception to that situation, namely Egypt, does not provide any means of articulating the needs and aspirations of those outside the governing circles. Although Al-Azhar, the universally venerated body of Muslim religious scholars (*ulamas*), is headed by a grand scholar (with the title of Shaikh Al-Azhar) with an office outside the governmental structure, the administrative jurisdiction over him and Al-Azhar itself comes under the authority of a state minister. Budget allocations and administrative appointments are made by him, not by the grand scholar. Consequently, only those scholars with the "right" understanding of the government's intentions have the opportunity to be appointed to that post.

Dilemmas of the Mediating Role

The Indonesian Ministry of Religious Affairs has changed greatly in its relationship to the political structure of power and in its role in society. During the first phase after its establishment in 1945, it developed into the forum in which members of the opposition could express their politicoreligious aspirations. Although the president's appointed the minister of religious affairs, the person selected was not necessarily a spokesman for the government or an executor of governmental or presidential policies. The president had to be someone who was acceptable to the different Islamic movements in the country. Furthermore, because of the active participation of various mass-based religious organizations, the ministry could not afford to be a mere mouthpiece of the government. It had to be able to interact positively with these different groups and to be sufficiently independent of government to be credible in its role.

In this complex situation the ministry is called on to play different and even conflicting roles in a wide range of activities. The ministry promotes religious education through an extensive network of nongovernmental educational institutions, a network about one-fifth as large as the entire national system of education. At the same time, the ministry is required to ensure that the nongovernmental system conforms broadly to the state system of education, with its entirely different aims and objectives. Likewise, although the ministry has to facilitate the integration of existing religious laws into the developing national legal system, it often has to act in a way detrimental to that task by responding sympathetically to the existing religious organizations' desire to preserve the integrity of these religious laws in anticipation of their full implementation in the future.

The ministry therefore must steer its way through the conflicting expectations about its role held by the various actors in the politicoreligious arena. Meanwhile, other developments that take place outside its jurisdiction further compound its problems. Various other ministries and subdepartments, pursuing their own programs and objectives, formulate policies that have implications for religious issues and that are often inconsistent with the main policies followed by the religious ministry. These initiatives invariably lead to hostile reactions from powerful nongovernmental organizations, with the Ministry of Religious Affairs caught in the cross fire of contending groups. In the effort to find a middle ground between opposing forces, the ministry is pushed into a mediating role that renders it ineffective. It tends to avoid initiatives of a creative nature and lacks a sense of constructive purpose. Instead, it devotes itself to formulating and implementing routine programs, thereby losing its capacity to respond to the genuine religious needs of the people.

The present situation poses a serious dilemma to both policymakers and the major organizations concerned with religious life in Indonesian society. The present institutional framework of the Ministry of Religious Affairs provides little scope for evolving dynamic, creative policies that can resolve the conflicts between religion and modernization. There is grave danger that, continued in its present form, it will stifle any genuine creative forces that emerge. On the other hand, the alternatives to the existing institutions raise a different set of problems, which can arise if the mediating role of the Ministry of Religious Affairs is removed from the scene entirely. Such a situation could lead to a heightening of conflicts between opposing factions and a deepening of the cleavage in the country's religious life. Therefore, the effort to create an overarching framework that contains conflicts and provides for constructive interaction that can enrich the spiritual life of Indonesian society presents a crucial challenge.

To understand fully the origins and nature of this dilemma, it is necessary to examine the various efforts made to provide solutions that were fair and equitable to all parties with an active interest in the relevant issues. Within this context we should also examine the role played by a small group of young intellectuals seeking more viable and satisfying alternatives. Such an exercise requires a broad analysis of the main trends in religious thinking among the Muslims in Indonesia throughout its modern history and an identification of the crucial problems faced by Islam in contemporary Indonesian society. Such a survey also needs to define the role of the dynamic indigenous Islamic institutions that lie outside the modernized segment of Indonesian life, and their potential for regenerating and reorienting Indonesian religious consciousness.

The dynamics of interreligious relationships spring from the fact that Islam has not yet clarified its basic objectives in Indonesia—whether to pursue a legal-formalistic attitude toward life with its exclusive and sectarian orientation, or to open itself to a more cosmopolitan world view with tolerance toward other religious experiences and a readiness to gain new insights for developing itself. The approach to religious laws provides a reliable means of identifying the basic objectives pursued by Indonesian Muslims. Should past laws be accepted and implemented literally by being imposed superficially on the population at large, or should new methods of religious interpretation be pursued diligently? Should the religious approach to life be scriptural—implying a strict adherence to scripture—or more accommodating to the real situations of human life?

The legal-formalistic attitude, with its scriptural approach to life, demands a monocultural environment for its religious expression, with rigorous conformity to the prescribed life pattern and no room for any deviation. Such an approach is not consonant with the cultural plurality that is one of the salient historical characteristics of Indonesian life. It leads to a fortress mentality among minority groups—whether Islamic or non-Islamic, whether religious in nature or not—and creates socially disruptive conditions that foment deep mistrust and suspicion between Islamic and other communities.

Efforts to overcome this deplorable situation through the reformulation of Islam's attitude toward life in general—a profoundly agonizing task presenting extremely hard choices from a very limited list of options—provide another perspective of the grave problems facing Islam in Indonesia today. The intensification of these problems itself creates the conditions that stimulate the Islamic intellectual community to new efforts to discover the appropriate answers and make the adequate responses. It is the impetus needed to develop a creative process in which the positive legacy of the past is used to rediscover the essence of religious experience in its totality, which goes beyond the legal-formalistic framework and monocultural approach to life.

The Dialogue between Religion and the Centers of Power: a Historical Overview

The origins of Islam in Indonesia can be traced far back, but the spread of Islam as a major religion of the region took place only from the thirteenth century A.D., according to available historical accounts and archaeological evidence. The interinsular trade that became the means of propagating Islam concealed the profound fact that Islam actually came to Indonesia in the context of Sufi movements. In this first phase the Muslims organized their efforts to proselytize the Indonesian population by establishing, propagating, and maintaining Sufi orders throughout the Archipelago.

Until recently Islamic studies presented Sufism as an institution that stood in diametrical opposition to Islamic law (*Shari'ah*). This distortion of historical reality has contributed to the erroneous view that the Islamic institutions in the Arabian peninsula were the direct source and inspiration of Islam in Indonesia. The existence of Sufi-leaning kingdoms in the northern part of Sumatra since the thirteenth century does not substantiate this view. It is more probable that the early Sufi kingdoms adopted their religious practices from regions such as present-day Bangladesh, rather than from Arabia proper.

The dialogue between coastal Islamic communities and the non-Islamic hinterland kingdoms of Java and Sumatra showed that a long and protracted chain of spiritual warfare took place between the mainly Sufi culture and the indigenous spiritualism deeply rooted in pre-Hindu and the subsequent Hindu-Buddhist religious beliefs of those hinterland kingdoms. That dialogue ended in bloodbaths during different periods, such as when the Kartasura (Central Java) ruler Amangkurat slaughtered more than six thousand of the Muslim religious scholars in his kingdom, as well as the sixteen-year war between adherents of the Shari'ah and the followers of indigenous common laws in West Sumatra during the first half of the nineteenth century.

The dialogue Islam had with centers of power throughout its history in Indonesia reveals three main types of interaction. The first type, developed first by the Acehnese at the northern tip of the island of Sumatra, shows Islam as the polity that established unified kingdoms out of a plurality of smaller communities. In this type of relationship between Islam and the state, reality as defined by religious concepts is accepted formally as the doctrine of the state. With later developments, however, when political authorities and holders of state power became incapable of maintaining the purity of religious doctrine and upholding the religious norms, and failed to resist the penetration of foreign political power and the concomitant expansion of alien culture, the function of defending the teachings of Islam as formalized in the state doctrines was taken over by the religious scholars, both intellectually and institutionally. Subsequent military defeats suffered by the Indonesian rulers could not dislodge the fact that the view of governance held by the scholars had become accepted by the people. The former rulers lost their rights to reestablish their rules, since they were so thoroughly discredited in the eyes of the scholars by their collaboration with the enemy—so much so that it was impossible to bring about a genuine reconciliation between the two groups that could be regarded as the elite and the counterelite.

The second type of relationship between Islam and the state could be found in the case of West Sumatra. The absence of a strong central government in that area in the past created an environment in which the Muslims were able to develop their ideology, adapting and adhering to the existing indigenous beliefs and faith, and unchecked by any formal establishment. The sixteen-year-long Paderi (Priests') War demonstrated the capability of the religious scholars to challenge the authority of the indigenous pre-Islamic common law. The fact that the Dutch colonial government championed the common law and finally defeated these religious scholars militarily did not alter the fact that ultimately these scholars achieved what they had sought: the redefinition of reality in a fundamental manner. That common law is based on religious law, and that the latter is based on the Qur'an is the guiding principle accepted formally for the whole community ever since.

The third type of interaction between Islam and state power is symbolized by the Javanese case. Islam came to the island when the Hindu-Buddhist tradition began to disintegrate. Although Islam contributed greatly to the final demise of the last East Javanese Hindu-Buddhist kingdom of Majapahit, it failed to replace that kingdom with a new central-hinterland power that was Islamic in nature. Instead, Islam contented itself with establishing small coastal kingdoms, whereas the Hindu-Buddhist tradition was left intact to become the nucleus of a future strong central power (*kraton*). With the emergence of a powerful kingdom in Central Java, not yet fully Islamic, which replaced the kingdom of Majapahit, a new interaction developed—a multikratonic relationship between the central power and peripheral kingdoms, analogous to a cluster of kratons in which the strong one had to keep the weaker ones always weak. The religious establishment in the form of those peripheral kingdoms (and later the religious scholars) emerged as the rivals contending for power with the ruling centers. An uneasy interaction developed and has continued between the two ever since.

Along with this type of relationship that grew in seventeenth-century Java, however, there were other developments, particularly in the modern period after independence. Religious scholars of other islands, especially from Minangkabau in West Sumatra and Aceh, who derived their own realities from their respective situations in the past, gave expression to different aspirations. Deriving those aspirations from historical situations in which the religious establishment played a more central role in the state and the structure of power, they found it hard until the last decade to get used to the idea of a peripheral relationship for Islam vis-à-vis the state. With the demise of the widely dispersed Islamic political party Masjumi in the last quarter of the 1950–1960 decade at the hand of the Sukarno government, as expressed by the national orientation of Java-concentrated Islamic movements such as the Nahdatul Ulama (Awakening of the Religious Scholars) and Muhammadiyah, the more centrally functioning relationship between Islam and the state in the past periods of Aceh and West Sumatra became a local pattern, to be tolerated or not according to the wishes of the central government in Jakarta.

A surprising interaction did take place as a result of the dialogue between the peripheral and central variants—for example, the Javanese variant of the heretical branch of Islamic mystical movement, the Wahdaniyah. This "Javanese belief" (*kejawen*), in which full communion of a worshipper with his God is stressed in the most expressive form—the anthropomorphic doctrine of *manunggaling kawula lan Gusti* ("full union between the servant and his lord")—is prevalent in the Javanese elite culture up to modern times and forms the basic aspiration of the formally acknowledged *aliran kepercayaan* ("creed without religious affiliation") now supported heavily by the government and looked on with misgivings and outright anger by the leadership of Islamic movements at large.

One integrative element in what was seemingly a divisive and conflict-ridden process was the adoption of the pre-Islamic institution of *pesantren* by the Sufi leaders for their mystical endeavors. (*Pesantren*, the place of the *santri*—the learned ones in the scripture, derived from the word *shastera*—is a residential educational institution—not necessarily school—where the students try to master religious sciences and the members of the outside community get their basic religious public instruction and personal religious guidance from the master, called *kiyai*. Now there are about 7,000 *pesantren* dispersed among Indonesia's 65,000 villages, ranging from small compounds with only a few santris to those with more than 3,000 students schooled in different types of schools and courses, including nonreligious ones.) They transformed this institution into the place used for their collective religious rituals such as *nyepi* (literally, "isolating oneself"), which differs from the original Javanese concept of self-annihilation, as a temporal rejection of worldly life. Pesantren was transformed into the place for pursuing a more purified life and gaining a deeper understanding of the "secret of the righteous life according to Allah." Individual instructions for attaining that secret (*ma'rifah*) in the form of personal guidance in rituals through different stages under a master (*murshid*), made up the main feature of life in pesantren for centuries, up to the time of the abrupt changes that followed the first onslaughts of the process of modernization.

Responses to the Process of Modernization

During the first half of the nineteenth century, the colonial administration introduced the beginning of a socioeconomic change so profound that it influenced irrevocably the history of Muslims in the Archipelago, then known as the Netherlands Indies by the colonialists and Nusantara by the natives. The abrupt change consisted first in the forced cultivation system (*cultuurstelsel*) to provide the mother country with practically unpaid crops of export commodities, and subsequently the outright exploitation of large tracts of land by the big plantations and sugar mills owned by private capital. This socioeconomic change resulted also in a profound change in the nature of adopted religious institutions such as pesantren. Capitalist exploitation of the economy resulted in the emergence of active rich farmers in Java's rural areas and a cluster of dynamic groups of native entrepreneurs in the towns.

　　With the improvements in communication, the newly emerging well-to-do class of farmers and urban entrepreneurs established links with the Middle East. They began to send their sons to institutions in the Middle Eastern countries to be educated. There was a growing consciousness of the need to reformulate and redefine the functions of the prevailing religious institutions and approaches. The *nouveaux riches* were not satisfied with the ritualistic approach of the Indonesian Sufist institutions. The reformist ideas that were gaining ground in the religious states of the Middle East offered some basis for a reorientation of the religious establishment in Indonesia. The new elite consequently gave a new socioreligious thrust that put the main emphasis on developing a legalistic approach. The central concern became the interpretation, application, and adaptation of religious laws in relation to the needs of contemporary society. *Fiqh,* the discipline of religious law, became the main vehicle for the propagation of Islam. The formulation of religious laws came to be regarded as an important part of the religious scholars' functions, both socially and individually.

The very fact that this kind of legalism proceeded directly to "purify" Sufism of alleged un-Islamic excesses, and thereby made it dependent on the Shari'ah jurists (or juriconsults, according to the late J. Schacht) for legitimacy, proved beyond doubt that a fundamental shift both in ideology and power occurred in the second part of the nineteenth century. Accepted religious disciplines, known as the fourteen religious sciences, as formulated by the renowned sixteenth-century Egyptian Qur'anic exegesist Al-Sayuti in his *Itmam Al-Dirayah,* were adopted as the main curricula for *pesantren* from that time. In this way, Indonesian Muslims relied mainly on a form of adaptive legalism to face the challenge of modernization. One of the main functions of *pesantren* since the end of the last century has been to provide public forums in which religious scholars could instruct the general population in the detailed implementation of adaptive legalism—legalism that, while maintaining Islamic principles, also implied a gradual framework for change through religious laws.

Far from isolating themselves from the changes taking place outside their pesantrens, those religious scholars responded to modernization by formulating a new set of legal decisions reflecting a close interaction between the legacy of the past, as prescribed in the old law books, and the ever changing situation in real life. Legal maxims, legal theories, and legal philosophies of the past were used to discover and formulate answers to questions posed by the community concerning injunctions for or against practices prevalent among the population. The legal maxims (*qawa'id al fiqh*) constitute practical guidance on how to make decisions in particular cases—for example, the popular maxims that whatever is unattainable in full should not be rejected entirely, that local customs should provide a basis for a legal decision, and that prevention of destructive action is given priority over performing good deeds. Legal theories (*usul al-fiqh*) as formulated since the ninth century A.D. provide the complete set of rules on how to treat Qur'anic sayings and the Prophet's traditions (*hadiths*) and apply them to real cases found in everyday life. Although not entirely accommodating to human needs, those theories do provide a good balance between literal adherence to the scripture and human reasoning. The legal philosophy (*hikmah al-tashri'*) of the last two centuries examines ways of relating religious laws to the development of sciences in various fields. Thus ablution, as the ritual required for praying, is explained in the context of health practices; fasting (*sawm*) is explained in a dietary context. Often shallow in spiritual content and meaningless scientifically, those explanations nevertheless provide a viable framework relating religious laws to actual conditions of life.

This approach, however has a serious drawback that renders it incapable of coping fully with the challenge of modernization. The drawback lies in the laws' complete lack of any societal framework needed to formulate an adequate response to the processes of change and the problems of life as manifested through these processes. Those laws remain casuistic in nature, relevant only to individual cases without clarifying the fundamental aspects of life besieged by the process of modernization, such as the relation between transcendental faith and empirical scientific reasoning. The laws that were intended to be the appropriate response to the challenge of modernization—a response that necessitates their adaptability to changing situations—become routinized and ossified into rigid rules with no capacity to adapt sensitively to human aspirations. What was a dynamic tool to remold society becomes a mass of formulas for the denial of creativity. A revitalizing process becomes an inert tradition, and the resulting adaptive legalism is transformed into legal traditionalism.

The Puritan Reaction

While the traditionalists were busy elaborating their casuistic laws, another development followed soon after. The inability of the traditionalists to provide a societal framework that could adequately respond to the challenge of modernization led to a reverse movement that campaigned in its fullest sense. According to this approach, Islam had to be purified from all aspects alien to its original character and purpose as a liberating religion for mankind as a whole. It had to be returned to its primary sources: the Qur'an and the Prophet's traditions. Human intervention, whether in the form of independent interpretative methods or some other form, had to be rejected for its deviationistic effects on Islam. Putting Islam on the right path meant a return to the original mission: to relive the golden age of the Prophet and his companions.

The simplicity of the faith should constitute the strength needed to face the onslaughts of modernization. The explicit injunction to use one's reasoning faculties should form the basic attitude toward the development of scientific knowledge. The injunctions for equality should be translated into egalitarian economic structures. The direct return to the fountainhead of religion would also diminish the dominant role of the religious scholars

in religious life. Innovation (*ijtihad*) symbolizes the direct relation between Allah and His worshipper, regardless of the degrees of the person's
religious knowledge.

The liberation from religious traditionalism means the elaboration of
a new societal framework and structure that could translate the basic
norms into social reality in the life of the Muslims. Stress on economic
undertakings, pursuit of nonreligious sciences, and establishment of health
services for the public, combined with charitable works for orphans, old
people, and the disabled, made up the main elements in the way of life
advocated by the puritanical movements such as Muhammadiyah and
Persis (Persatuan Islam or Islamic Unity). The first of these is now the
largest of the movements, having originated in West Sumatra and currently headquartered in the central Javanese town of Yogyakarta. With
a chain of thousands of schools and hundreds of health clinics, Muhammadiyah has left its imprint on the modern history of Indonesia. Persis,
a more locally situated movement and more narrowly oriented in its social
perspectives than Muhammadiyah, now takes a somewhat more militant
viewpoint in religious questions. Other movements of similar persuasion,
such as the organization of Indonesians of Arabic extraction, Al-Irshad,
have developed lesser variants of this basic puritanical strain.

The call for a more simplified religious belief combined with the
stress on developing a modernistic societal framework should work ideally as the logical response to the challenge of modernization. The actual
experience, however, shows that this is far from the reality. It is true
that the societal framework developed so far has been able to sustain
social activities quite extensive in range and scale, but difficulties abound
when trying to adapt this framework to respond to the main challenges
of modernization. The charitable character of their works fails to take into
account the structural nature of poverty. It is true that the strong emphasis
these movements place on educational programs has aided the establishment of both religious and modern secular schools throughout the country
and has facilitated the emergence of Muslim scientists and scholars in
practically all disciplines. From this, however, it would not be correct
to conclude that the movements have been successful in reconciling religious ideology with modern knowledge. The attitude toward the modern
empirical sciences is still ambivalent in that the approaches developed
so far are apologetic in describing the relationship between Islam and
modern science. As a result, a spurious reconciliation between the two
emerges in the most unfortunate form: whatever is good about the various
sciences is claimed to originate in Islam (or, at least, anticipated and
corroborated by this religion), whereas the undesired aspects of the same
sciences are blamed on the ''Western materialistic and secular civilization'' that produces them.

The failure of the puritanical movements to develop a viable response to the challenge of modernization originates in their insistence on purification. Such a demand stipulates the total acceptance of the Scripture and a noninterpretive adherence to it. What emerges is a literal approach to the understanding of religious teachings; strict Scripturalism becomes unavoidable. Although the pursuit of knowledge and egalitarian goals, a readiness to concretize the religious consciousness into a corresponding societal framework, and the liberation of individuals from the domination of religious scholars are the main pillars of modernistic puritanism in Islam, strict Scripturalism obstructs any significant new approaches to religious beliefs and, consequently, new ideological adaptations.

The transcendental concerns of these puritanical movements, despite their ostensible dynamism and modern orientation, lose their relevance in the face of the growing consciousness of the need for a humanism significantly different from the one developed so far by the traditional ideologies. The inability of the Islamic puritanical movements to put the whole religious experience in a sociohistorical perspective is exposed glaringly in their pet slogan of presenting the *zakat* (almsgiving) injunction as Islam's basic concern for social justice. Although they understand zakat's role as a redistributive tool to secure the basic needs of the poor, they remain unable to relate its nature to the social origins of poverty: the exploitative social structures that grow from a lack of any limit on individual property.

Although the Iranian revolution provides an opportunity to observe how a just society can be developed from a middle position that corresponds neither to the accepted capitalist model nor to the socialist one, the theoretical underpinnings of the undertaking are still shaky and seem somewhat artificial. How to transform the ideal frameworks developed so far into constitutional and societal ones remains a hard question to answer. Even if we grant that the Iranian revolution is committed to positive social goals—by accepting at face value the countervailing force it creates against the repressive nature of a Westernised type of modernization—Islamic puritanism still must find satisfying answers to the fact that many puritan Muslims collaborate with oppressive regimes in the Muslim countries to suppress the genuine aspirations of the people. The ideological contradictions in such situations are blatantly illustrated by the attitude of Pakistani Muslim purists toward the execution of Zulfikar Ali Bhutto. They have argued that the execution was feasible according to Islamic constitutional laws but at the same time are eager to claim that one of the basic political convictions of Islam is democracy.

The literal implementation of Qur'anic and Prophetic injunctions in the form in which they were elaborated in their original historical context and without modification by new humanitarian perceptions of the dignity of the human being as an individual has bizarre consequences. It leads to atrocities by law, such as cutting off the hands of thieves, stoning to death those guilty of adultery, or publicly beheading criminals sentenced to death. The same attitude continues to place woman in a position subordinate to man, at least in practice. At best, the Islamic puritanical approach provides only a partial reinterpretation of Qur'anic verses and the Prophet's traditions. Although it denounces slavery as un-Islamic according to the principle of the gradual approach of Islam to the aboliltion of slavery, based on the equality of human beings as explicitly upheld by the Qur'an and the Prophet's traditions, it fails to adopt a similar approach to the issue of a man having more than one wife. On this matter it merely prescribes moral injunctions to limit oneself voluntarily to one wife, but it does not give legal decisions at all. The same thing applies to the question of population control. Many eminent so-called modernist puritans reject the idea of family planning and see it as a plot to decrease the number of Muslims, even part of an alleged Christianization scheme.

Their views on inequality are equally superficial, since they do not go to the root of the matter, but merely accuse both capitalism and Marxism of being unable to eliminate inequality. These Muslims, however, purists themselves, are unable to provide more effective alternatives in terms of their own ideology. Their demand for equality consists only of protection of Muslim members of the middle class against the increasing economic power of Chinese businessmen and those of Chinese descent. It is not strange, then, that their main complaints are usually against what they term cultural penetration from the West, with its ensuing tendencies toward moral decadence among Indonesian Muslims, especially youth. A refinement on this theme is the persistent accusation that modern scientists still deify the natural sciences.

The failure of such Muslim modernists, as they are called by U.S. social scientists on dubious grounds, to respond positively to the challenge of the modernization process can be seen by comparing their views with what actually takes place in Indonesia. Registered acceptors or participants in national family-planning programs are increasing dramatically. They are still unable to combat so-called indicators of moral decadence, despite their concentration on indoctrinating the nation against it. Members of the younger generation of practicing Muslims increasingly express their dismay over their limited options to move within the confines of ethnic, religious, economic, cultural, and political barriers. The empty promises to bring ultimate justice and true democracy merely bore them. The speed with which the young reading public snapped up the recently published memoirs of the late young religious rebel, Ahmad Wahib, with its denunciation of so-called modernist puritanism, shows the extent of disappointment with this self-proclaimed reformation.

Modern Islamic education in Indonesia reflects the dilemma that now faces Indonesian Muslims. In need of far-ranging and complete acquisition of modern technology, institutions of Islamic education among the modernist Muslims are beset by two equally irrelevant issues: how to balance religious instructions against nonreligious ones, and how to explain modern sciences in a Qur'anic context. The best minds in physics, biology, medicine, chemistry, and astronomy are engaged in futile exercises that will give only shallow and short-lived relief. The modern Islamic education system, however, cannot afford to cut itself off from much needed natural scientists and experts despite their unconvincing endeavors. These endeavors at best succeed only in producing false or contrived explanations reconciling Islam with modern science and find expression in high-sounding terms such as "an Islamic framework of sciences." They present their religion in such terms as "Islam as scientific discipline" instead of trying to develop a new universal framework that can overcome sectarian and exclusive tendencies.

Whereas the adaptive legalism of the traditionalist religious scholars develops into a rigid traditionalism that fails to respond satisfactorily to the problems of modernization, Islamic modernist puritanism tends to be vague and amorphous in its ideology, without any coherent direction. As a result, its carefully elaborated basic framework of rationalization is readily used to support exploitative social structures and repressive military regimes throughout the Islamic world on the one hand, and the agents of change in an oppositional role on the other.

The Proliferation of Dissident Groups

It is not strange, then, that elements dissatisfied with that kind of puritanism, seeking to establish—as their own answer to the current splinter groups—a neo-orthodoxy with various objectives, have grown up in Indonesia. This is largely a result of the inconclusive efforts at puritanical reformation over the last seven decades, which at best can be characterized as a period of arrested development. The splinter groups that have emerged have only one characteristic in common: each claims for itself the title rightful Muslims. Each group views all other Muslims outside its own community as infidels, which has further intensified the fortress mentality and produced various psychological defense mechanisms such as forms of messianism, which are often found in many of these movements. These traits are often condemned by both the established movements—the traditionalists and puritans—but these splinter groups have shown their viability by surviving against all odds (including government bans instigated by the established movements).

Divisive in nature, the splinter groups become a haven for talented people who feel strangled in their religious expression by either the legalism of the traditionalists or the Scripturalism of the puritans. In this sense, the real contribution of these neo-orthodox splinter groups, such as the Islam Jama'ah movement in East Java and the Istiqamah Group in West Java, just disbanded by the government, is the fact that they provide opportunity for the critique of the established traditionalism and Scripturalism and offer some kind of alternative. Thus they become the last resorts for many people who are otherwise ready to abandon Islam altogether.

This role is evident in the development of a new phenomenon in the life of Islam in Indonesia today—that is, the use of the splinter groups as political tools by competing factions within the ruling circles. Each political faction feels the need to be included in the Islamic community (*ummah*) but without being identified with either the traditionalists or the modernist puritans. Their shallow Islamic identification, labeled by one observer "sociocultural Muslim," as opposed to the political (and fuller) one, makes it easier for these diverse political factions to patronize these splinter groups, albeit discreetly, so as not to antagonize the majority of the population. The splinter groups play one further important role: the countervailing function of containing the militant demands of the established movements for restrictive policies toward non-Muslims. By insisting on the necessity of consensus on the question of non-Muslims, the ruling circles can use these neo-orthodox splinter groups to stall the demands of the militants.

The emergence of short-lived splinter groups within the Islamic polity in Indonesia coincides also with another kind of neo-orthodoxy—the revival of Sufism. Although Sufi movements still have to seek legitimacy from Shari'ah juriconsults, religious scholars today exercise little control over them. The inability of the traditionalists to provide an appropriate response to the needs of development and modernization, as well as their inability to contain the puritanical movements and the neo-orthodox splinter groups, has given a new impetus to Sufi leaders to provide their own answers to the problems faced by Islam in Indonesia.

Sufism has a long tradition of absorbing outside influences into its unique spiritualism. By stressing the salvation of the individual worshipper through meditation, introspective personal piety, and other modes of inner reflection, Sufism has been able throughout its history to adapt its outer forms while retaining its total integrity. This absorptive capacity clearly attracts many people experiencing psychological strains in reconciling their needs in various contemporary life situations with their conventional religious morality and their formal faith. Sufism's spiritual core, the universal sharing of personal experiences in search of Ultimate Truth, gives its adherents the strong sense of belonging that is so intensely needed by modern man. Self-identification with a large, active brotherhood certainly helps to overcome the sense of alienation that is prevalent in modern life. This explains why a revival of Sufism seems to be likely in Indonesia now, despite the long-recognized backward-looking orientation of Sufism. Visits to sacred tombs, frequent voluntary self-withdrawals (*khalwat*), the personal allegiance (*bai'ah*) to the masters, and similar features of a Sufi's life in general constitute the orientation to the past so prevalent among Sufi movements.

The way Indonesian adherents of Sufism reconcile the conflicting demands of forward-looking modernization with the backward-looking orientation of its own tradition is a curious phenomenon in itself. Merchants, rich farmers, government employees, and other professionals are required by their respective professions to be dynamic and forward-looking in their life orientation. By observing pro forma outward manifestations of a backward-looking Sufi orientation, but still not allowing such an orientation to direct them in their occupations and their everyday life, they are able to retain the modern world view their professions demand. By visiting the sacred tombs and expressing openly their full allegiance to their masters, they can symbolically participate in Sufism while continuing to be the shrewd merchants, enterprising farmers, industrious employees they were before their conversion to Sufism. This kind of adaptation, though interesting, provides only a shallow understanding of the basic faith of Islam, which stresses the compatibility of the external secular life and the inner spiritual life of a Muslim. That is why Sufism still does not satisfy the religious scholars' intellectual needs. Hence the old problem of mutual distrust and recrimination between non-Sufi scholars and Sufi leaders, especially the nonscholar ones.

The politicization of Sufi movements, as in the case of the neo-orthodox splinter groups, is also revealing. Besides using local Sufi groups as political clients to back up their authority, local government officials are often converted to Sufism for the same reason that they relate to the splinter groups: while finding a spiritual refuge from their anxieties, they can still retain their loyalty to the government. Although the past history of Sufism in Indonesia is replete with cases of such messianistic and millenarianistic movements emerging and again rapidly declining and disintegrating—as is illustrated by the more than four hundred local rebellions against the Dutch colonial administration during the nineteenth century in Java alone—the present nonconfrontational character of the Sufi movements makes it easier for the government officals to relate to them. When politicization does occur in these movements, the process often furthers the initiative of the government and is beneficial to government policy as a whole. By declaring them nonpolitical, it can at the same use them for its own political purposes and show its attitude of acceptance toward the Islamic movement at large without having to encourage movements that are more clearly opposed to its policies.

Hence the emergence of the unique response of the ordinary traditionalist Muslims in Indonesia now, of having a double loyalty—to their Sufi masters and to the Shari'ah religious scholars at the same time. The Sufi masters provide them with spiritual salvation, and the non-Sufi scholars provide the channel through which they can express political views that diverge from those of the government! One can be tempted by this kind of dual approach in religious life—salvation seeking together with the practical need to bend religious injunctions here and there—to see the beginnings of an unformulated secularization process. The constant need to reconcile competing drives—the loyalties to the things of the past and the need to calculate the imperatives of the worldly present— can also be interpreted as the pragmatic dialogue between religion and development. This type of problem solving, however, by evading the hard process of making conscious choices in all their spiritual implications—not just as haphazard compromises undertaken by these new Sufists—brings with it serious dangers of being marooned in a spiritual middle ground, unable to compete fully in worldly matters because of minimal adherence to certain religious teachings, but at the same time also unable to get the deep satisfaction and peace of mind expected from spiritual affiliation with the Sufi movement. In a sense, then, what is achieved is not any meaningful solution to the central problem of defining one's identity in the modern context, in both the spiritual and secular sense.

Panchasila: The Primacy of Religion and the Modern State

This complex situation, which has witnessed the emergence of different types of responses to the process of modernization, is made even more complex by the issue of secularism, which has entered the scene in the last decade. Although Muslim intellectuals had been beset by the question of the separation of church and state since the establishment of formal Islamic organizations during the first three decades of this century, those organizations themselves did not feel an acute need to respond explicitly to the idea of a secular state until recent years. One reason was that those in favor of the idea never declared their ideology in clearly defined terms. They were satisfied merely to express a general need for a modern state viable for all sections of the society. Even when the need to decide the nature of the newly independent state arose in 1945, these nationalists—as distinguished from the Muslim ideologues—agreed to soft-pedal their secular aspirations by accepting a compromise with their Muslim counterparts in the form of the *panchasila* state philosophy, a set of five principles for guiding the life of the nation. The issue of a state philosophy, posed as a national problem for the religious scholars, was resolved in such a generalized way that eventually it came to be interpreted loosely in different ways for different purposes. The five *silas* or principles—namely, belief in one God, acceptance of humanitarianism, commitment to Indonesian nationality and social justice, and acceptance of people's sovereignty through representatives—could provide the formulation for keeping Islam free from a direct relationship with the state, without ever saying so. As a result, the Islamic movements at that time perceived no unacceptable contradiction between the state philosophy and their own politicoreligious aspirations.

This state philosophy declares belief in one God to be one of its basic tenets, which means no antireligious aspirations are given the right to grow in Indonesia. Nontheocratic acceptance of religion in the life of the nation provides Indonesia with a model of reconciliation between leading nonreligious and religious values, to be preserved and managed through a delicate act of balancing. Panchasila caters to the fundamental yearnings of the Muslim majority for a clearly pronounced religious participation in politics. This acceptance of the religious role in the political life of the nation differentiates panchasila from the exclusive ideologies of that time. How to provide for a society's religious aspirations by giving it a central role in the sharing of power, yet safeguard the system against the danger of a theocratic state, is the question panchasila seeks to answer.

Puritan Muslim intellectuals and traditionalist religious scholars challenged the state philosophy, not because they rejected it but because a crucial formula to maintain their political role in a leading position—namely, the phrase "with obligations to implement Islamic Law for adherents of Islam"—had been deleted from the preamble of the then prevailing version of the 1945 constitution. The Islamic challenge to promulgate the state philosophy and the constitution containing it resulted in a constitutional deadlock, which was overcome only by Sukarno's presidential decree to "return to the 1945 constitution" in July 1959. The dissolution of the constituent assembly and the elected parliament of 1955, together with the introduction of a guided democracy with fully or partially government-appointed legislative assemblies ever since—the present government's rejection of that kind of so-called democracy notwithstanding—made it impossible for even law scholars to discuss the question of secularism openly. At the same time the lack of meaningful discussions on the merits and dangers of separating state power from religious authority made it impossible for the government to adopt a clear policy on this matter. The government has been forced to maintain the status quo of noncommitment to secularism ever since.

This stalemate induced various Islamic organizations to pronounce their own cultural views of rejecting the atheistic ideology of secularism, introduced by capitalist and socialist ideologies as something alien to the nature of the Indonesian people and contradictory to the teachings of Islam. Various developmental policies were, and still are, branded as secular in character by those religious circles and accordingly opposed vehemently by the Islamic mass media. Should the government try to defend a particular policy branded as secularistic in nature by those people, the pointing finger is unfailingly directed to "certain secularist elements within the government." These recriminations against the secularists, which have continued for two decades, gathered such an intensity that President Suharto has been forced lately to declare that Indonesia is not a secular state and panchasila is not a secular ideology. One case proves this stalemate clearly. In 1973 the government tabled a marriage-act bill before the Parliament. It was perceived by religious scholars and nearly all sectors of Islamic movements as secular in nature. The opposition to it, including a temporary occupation of the plenary chamber of the Parliament, was so strong, that the government was forced to shelve the bill and adopt a more or less Islamic act instead—the one legally in force now.

From these accounts it is logical to compare the situation to the present one in Pakistan: the dismantling of Western laws and the promulgation of Islamic laws in their place. The tactics (and antics) of Islamic groups that oppose secularistic policies of the government, including such actions as walkouts from parliamentary voting sessions, clearly intimidate other sections of society to the extent that the latter are compelled to take a low profile for the time being. Further observation, however, reveals that dynamic forces are at work under this superficial conformity. It is here, beneath the surface, that the real developments take place. There was already partial adaptation to the thrust of modernization since colonial times, as is apparent from the responses of both traditionalist and puritan Muslims to the challenge of the Westernized school system. The modernist puritans adopted the Westernized school system in toto and developed a framework appropriate for that kind of undertaking. They were called Muslim modernists by Western historians and social scientists precisely because of this trait, and the name is applied to them even today, particularly when religious militants launch attacks against secularists. The traditionalists likewise developed an early response in the form of modifying their age-old religious systems, which evolved into the modified school system called the *madrasah* adopted by their pesantrens.

The Search for a Modernist Islamic Faith

This tradition, with its religious underpinnings, runs strongly in a steady—albeit nonverbal—manner. Sons and daughters of pious religious scholars gradually enter the modern world properly, either as graduates of modern and fully secularized universities or as professionals educated in specialized disciplines. True, there is a tendency toward militancy in an increasing number of modernized Muslims, but another important development has also occurred simultaneously. In the early 1970s a Muslim intellectual, formerly educated in the traditional pesantren way and subsequently graduated from the State Islamic University, called for a radical restructuring of the creed. Nurcholish Madjid spelled out the idea of secularization of nonsacral teachings of Islam developed throughout the ages. He argued that except for the essential beliefs constituting the central faith of Islam, all teachings should be reviewed to accommodate the ever changing human situation. He accepts the theologically acknowledged central position of man in the life of the universe (God creates man as His vice-regent on this earth and puts him in the best form of creation, so that he is able to pursue the righteous way of life beneficial to all other creatures and the universe as a whole) as the basis for his desacralization of the unsacral beliefs of Islam. This call, according to Madjid, is the way to secularize life without becoming secularist. Secularism and secularization of Islam are not identical, since in the very idea of secularization the basic adherence to Islam is still preserved. It is intended only to make Islam relevant to the contemporary world, not to abrogate its right to regulate human life.

A bitter backlash from the militant Muslim modernists followed Madjid's exposition, and he was forced to moderate his position to accommodate views closer to the general trends of Islamic thought. He has been able so far to resist pressure to retreat entirely from his main ideas, and he has modified his approach only to the extent that he admits that secularization is a misnomer while still maintaining the basic concept connoted by the word. In doing so, he is able to deflect the attacks of powerful critics and continues to enjoy the confidence and intellectual respect of tens of thousands of young Muslim university graduates and professionals beset by the problem of reconciling their basic religious beliefs with the demands of the professional roles assigned to them in a society undergoing a process of modernization.

Madjid's call to a modernistic Islamic faith is echoed in the responses of various groups of young intellectuals. A group of activists in rural development, for example, tries to formulate the framework of a movement to develop the traditional institution of pesantren as the base for the socioeconomic transformation of the rural areas. In this endeavour the group must develop its own viable religious ideology in the face of fatalism and the belief in predestined roles still prevalent among village religious communities. This type of effort to deal with problems of modernization in the name of Islam, as undertaken by different groups in various places, represents the diversified pattern of Islamic responses to the current situation in Indonesia.

The main point of contention between the puritan Muslim modernists and those who try to accommodate the demands of modernization lies in the methods of treating the very sources of Islam: the Qur'an and the traditions of the Prophet. For the puritan modernists, these two sources comprise the bulk of teachings to be implemented fully or partially in a literal way, whereas for the accommodating intellectuals, the Qur'anic verses and the traditions of the Prophet represent an ideological core, with the main function of providing an inspirational center for the responses Muslims must formulate in various individual or collective situations. In this approach, personalization of the different responses is inevitable, making a single pattern of religious thinking practically unattainable. Conformity of thought is not a desirable end in itself, and the plurality of opinions and religious views becomes the natural expression of the search for the truth.

This flexible framework for developing religious views is, however, anathema to the militant so-called modernists. One possible reason for the increasing militancy of their religious views, which express strong opposition to those government policies they deem secularistic, is a sense of being threatened by these loose, flexible methods of interpreting basic sources of Islamic faith. Hence the sigh of relief detected among them since Nurcholish Madjid has shown what they regard as a readiness to recant his mistakes. A comment on how these so-called heretics (a term of criticism in religious teachings employed by the majority of Muslims everywhere, since the traditions of the Prophet threaten such people with purgatorial punishments in the life hereafter) should pursue their aspirations is worthwhile here, although it falls outside the scope of this narration. These innovators cum reformers are expected to present their undertaking and reinterpretation not as a reformation, since such a presentation connotes that the literal interpretation of the Scripture is not adequate. Purification of religious teachings from un-Islamic elements—a process that took place over the past hundred years and has coalesced into the present ossified attitudes and militant tendencies—is proudly viewed by these so-called modernists as the one and only reformation (*tajdid*) needed to reinvigorate Islam. They regard further developments as merely heresies (*bid'ah*) that should be condemned categorically. Tactically, whatever the young intellectuals formulate should be presented as a continuation of the previous puritanical reformation, not as a departure from it.

The case of one young intellectual is noteworthy here. He works in the Ministry of Religious Affairs and for the past ten years was branded a deviationist for his tolerance toward the Ahmadiyah splinter group. A few years ago he argued that Islam should consider the sociohistorical context of the Prophetic traditions when formulating the framework needed to implement the Scripture. He brought up the question of the spirit of *zakat* (almsgiving to the poor) and inquired whether it should be kept in its present form of charitable deeds incorporated into the Islamic way of life. According to him, we should understand the historical background of this injunction. It was revealed to the Prophet during the time when the commercial activities of the Arabs in the market places were the main occupation of the ordinary people, and agriculture was the main field of work for the elite (the cost of claiming the arid lands and maintaining them agriculturally as viable production units was so high that only the elite could undertake agricultural enterprises). Consequently, Islam imposes zakat of between 5 and 10 percent of the harvests reaped as an egalitarian measure to redistribute wealth in a limited way in favor of the majority of the population, who are usually the poor traders. It was the rich agricultural elite, the minority in the community, who were taxed. This young intellectual questioned the continuance of this kind of imposition in a sociohistorical context that had changed entirely. Commerce is now concentrated in the hands of the few in Southeast Asia, and agriculture is dispersed among the poorest sections of the society—so much so that it is impossible to carry out the literal implementation of the zakat injunction without contradicting its previous egalitarian spirit.

To continue the imposition of a 10-percent zakat on the diminishing harvests of the poor, while letting the rich escape with only 2.5 percent of their yearly profits, constitutes a flagrant violation of the very sense of justice that Islam has nurtured from the beginning of its history. This restructuring of zakat naturally caused an uproar, not because the militants did not understand the basic issues involved, but because they were indignant at the call to discard the definite percentage already prescribed by the Prophet himself. When another young intellectual called for enlarging the zakat injunction to include professionals with their high incomes, as well as narrowing the application of the same injunction to a few types of farming jobs only, without changing a word from the Prophetic traditions, he was praised by the Islamic media as a resourceful intellectual worthy of the name reformer.

The basic contention of whether to follow a literal interpretation of the Qur'anic passages and Prophetic traditions relates to the attitude taken toward interpreting the Islamic heritage. According to the militants, the reigns of the Prophet and his subsequent first four Righteous Caliphs, regardless of their time span, represent a golden age to be emulated in its entirety—a period in which there was no separation of the power of the state from that of the religion. Islam has no church, but its laws should be the base of the state's life.

Intellectuals more accommodating to the modernization process think differently. The past heritage of Islam, according to them, should be recast in an entirely new context. The development of human history, with its full impact on human society and the personality of the individual, imposes its own laws beside the laws formulated by Islam in the past. One of these impacts is the need to separate the power of religious establishments from that of the state. The subjective nature of Islamic judgment of events should be tempered by the objective nature of scientific findings. Only by giving concessions to such an extent can Islam redefine its own priorities, reformulate its world view, and restructure its teachings—a process needed to place Islam in the mainstream of human development. It is natural, then, that a group of young Muslim activists believing in tolerance to different ideologies as well as religious affiliations emerged a few years ago, under the banner of working for humanitarian causes.

The new group, involving a considerable number of people, is led by a young Muslim intellectual. It seeks ways to make amends for the traumatic experience of the communists in the second half of the 1960s at the hands of Islamic groups. More than half a million people died—most of them innocent—and more than a hundred thousand were detained for long periods. More than ten thousand of these detainees were still in jail when the young Muslim intellectuals' institution was established. This institution began soliciting funds from society, mobilizing volunteers, and creating goodwill to secure the release of the remaining detainees, preparing their introduction into normal life after their release and helping them rehabilitate themselves on a self-reliant basis. In the process these active intellectuals find that an openness to attitudes that are different and even antagonistic to those they themselves hold is essential in enabling them to serve these unfortunate victims fully and satisfactorily. The nonconformist attitude of the detainees toward everything in the prevailing system, including religious beliefs held in high esteem by those helping them, is understood as the natural product of their own past ideology as well as the inhuman ordeal they had to undergo during their long detention period.

When extended to religious attitudes, this discipline of tolerance toward ideologies alien to Islamic teachings transforms itself into tolerance toward internal developments within Islam itself. Bold religious ideas and concepts began to get a hearing from these young intellectuals. Criticisms leveled against the religious establishment, such as indictments of its indifference to the exploitation of Islam by existing unjust structures for their own purposes, began to be circulated to a limited extent in printed form. A group of young professionals even began to publish a mimeographed journal questioning the validity of established theological doctrines such as the doctrine of the orthodoxy about predetermination and free will (*qadna* and *qadar*), which forms one of the *arkan al-iman* ("six principles of faith").

Much depends on the outcome of the dialogue between these contending schools of thought. The ideological consensus that will emerge as the agreed societal solutions to the central problems now faced by Islam will be crucial for the future of Indonesian society, since it will constitute the meeting ground needed for the creation and dynamic interaction between the Islamic center and other forces of change in Indonesian society.

Where the Dilemma Lies

The Ministry of Religious Affairs was born as a political compromise during the early days of independence. By accepting panchasila as the state philosophy, and the 1945 constitution based on it, Islamic groups got an institutional substitute for their former theocratic political aspirations in the form of this ministry. Although probably intended as a temporary compromise by more secularist groups, like the framework of the state philosophy as envisaged by the Islamic polity at that time, the ministry developed into a permanent fixture with a unique role.

In the beginning, it was concerned mainly with the promotion of Islamic education in its various systems and the supervision of religious life in general (including establishing the rights to officiate at marriages and divorces and to settle disputes concerning inheritance according to religious laws). The educational wing soon flowered into a full-fledged national program engaged in formulating guiding principles for modern religious education (including the use of the school system in the primary-secondary-tertiary levels, the maintenance of educational standards through state examination systems, and related matters); giving aid and assistance to private schools run by different organizations; and developing pilot projects to refine educational systems that already existed. At present, the religious-school system is one-fifth as large as the national education system. A dual national system of education inevitably emerged, with one-fifth of it under the jurisdiction of the ministry, including fourteen state Islamic universities in different provinces, whereas the rest comes under the jurisdiction of the Ministry of Education and Cultural Affairs. Another inevitable consequence is the ensuing confusion, which defies internally consistent solutions to the problems the dual system creates.

The supervision of religious life also developed into a miscellany of different kinds of activity, from the yearly task of organizing pilgrimages to Mecca for at least thirty thousand Muslims, to monitoring (and banning, if necessary) religious and intellectual trends that were contrary to the beliefs of the religions acknowledged by the state, including the ban on discussing openly the merits and dangers of atheism. This wing of the ministry developed into the present-day octopus with so many arms (information, planning, religious courts, supervision of endowments, maintenance of mosques and other places of religious worship, and so on) that it is difficult to find a government agency without its counterpart within the Ministry of Religious Affairs. The ministry now is hopelessly entangled in so many overlapping joint projects with other government agencies that it seems to act more and more as a state within a state, with these works resembling joint enterprises between two sovereign states. The ministry's activities in the health field can be used here to illustrate this kind of entanglement: nutrition education, public health, and family planning are all major fields in which the ministry is active with different types of programs in each.

The ministry's overlapping functions are apparent from the purposes formulated at the beginning of its life:

1. to promote religious life in general;
2. to safeguard acknowledged religions from elements detrimental to their existence;
3. to supervise nongovernmental activities in religious fields and provide them with necessary assistance.

The promotion of religious life now includes the mammoth undertakings of providing religious lectures and texts (including the preparation and printing of both the Qur'an and the Bible on a massive scale) and establishing agencies to organize and supervise pilgrimages to Mecca. Its works include the establishment of an Ulama Council of Indonesia at national, provincial, and subprovincial levels, as the meeting point between government agencies and nongovernmental religious organizations. From this point of view, the ministry plays a variety of positive roles for religious life in Indonesia, the most important being legitimizing both government and nongovernmental initiatives in the religious field; clarifying and expounding the aspirations of nongovernmental religious organizations to other government agencies; mediating in brief but potentially troublesome conflicts and misunderstandings among government and nongovernmental institutions about each other's intentions over sensitive matters such as the recently proposed Panca Agama (joint religious instructions in schools among adherents of different religions); and pioneering new forms of religious education, albeit still by presenting and implanting conventional religious views. The ministry forms a model of a moderating institution in a society troubled by deep cleavages in nearly every facet of life, including the religious one.

Nevertheless, a considered appraisal of the ministry's role shows that its negative effects on balance outweigh all these positive aspects. This is manifested in the ministry's present predicament. It is now embroiled in a bitter fight for survival between those who demand a more secular orientation toward religion and the so-called Muslim modernists described earlier. In the past the ministry acted only as a traffic officer in disputes between various sections of the community. It is now under pressure to develop a more active posture—that is, resisting ideas that run contrary to the wishes of the main religious nongovernmental establishment. The ministry has attempted to cope with this problem and to limit the articulation of ideas and opinions of the younger generation through an ingenious device: let diversity run in full force, if necessary by giving rights of expression to minority Islamic groups and splinter groups to carry out their activities. This Islamic pluralism, it is hoped, will liberate the Muslims from narrow conformity to the formal orthodox doctrines. This liberation is a necessary prelude to the emergence of healthy responses to the process of modernization, beyond the formalistic response that reiterates Islam's superiority to other systems of life without showing anything concrete to support that claim.

This kind of pluralism in the Islamic sphere, of course, runs counter to the institutionalized nature of the activity of the ministry. Although it is beneficial for the Islamic polity to have the ministry's legitimizing role and various forms of support, especially in the field of religious education (resulting, among other things, in the emergence of those young intellectuals who question the feasibility of retaining the ministry itself), the ministry's inherently bureaucratic approach to socioreligious developments is a formidable obstacle to this very pluralism. Moreover, the ministry's predilection for centralizing authority in itself in formulating religious policies—at least to the extent that they concern the religious perceptions of the Muslims—makes it impossible to develop an adequate and viable framework of Islamic pluralism in a governmental context.

Consequently the fundamental question is that of the very existence of the ministry itself. The following questions reflect the ethical dilemma inherent in maintaining a Ministry of Religious Affairs:

1. How can the ministry's symbolic role as guarantor of a religious orientation in national life be translated into a more functional role of promoting diversity—not only among different religions and cultural groupings but, more important, within the Islamic polity itself?

2. How can the ministry define in a holistic sense the role of religion in development, without merely making religion supportive of development in other sectors with their own nonreligious global and sectoral objectives?

3. How can the ministry shoulder the burden of giving religion a central role in development, while at the same time promoting the necessary processes of socioeconomic transformation and modernization—two things that often run counter to each other in the developing countries?

4. Is it possible to contain the tendency for religious bureaucratization within the ministry so as to fulfill the acute need to accommodate the creativity of the intellectuals, with their search for new insights and perceptions in the religious life?

It is increasingly felt that the ministry is not a part of the process of social transformation, but even becomes an obstacle to the changes needed to create more fertile ground for the religious aspirations that could give a more adequate response to the problems of modernization. The new religious conscience that presses for a just, democratic, and egalitarian society, free from any kind of exploitation and domination of one sector of the community by another—to take one example of a religiopolitical aspiration among the younger generation—is certainly anathema to a ministry ensconced within a government not yet fully democratic. Equally negative reactions can be expected in the case of other similar aspirations.

The institution has already fulfilled its original role of guaranteeing the acceptance of the role of religion in the life of the nation in a formal and definitive way, however deficient that role may be. Can it be transformed into an institutional framework that takes forward this acceptance into the more positive task of developing the rich, pluralistic religious conscience of Indonesian society, to respond to the need for socioeconomic change and the concomitant problems of modernization? Or has it fulfilled its life span and outlived its purpose, and must it now be removed from the scene to liberate the religious life from rigid institutional constraints?

3 The Quest for Equality: Protective Discrimination or Compensatory Justice?

Clarence J. Dias

In the Marathwada area of the state of Maharashtra, about 16 percent of the population comprises scheduled castes, of whom more than 80 percent live below the poverty line. In July 1978 a riot lasting sixty-seven days broke out, during which upper-caste Hindu capitalist landlords went on a rampage against scheduled-caste villagers. The riots affected some 1,200 villages, rendered some 5,000 villagers homeless, and affected some 25,000 scheduled-caste villagers. Violence, destruction, and rape were successfully employed in an effort to terrorize the villagers; the police and other official protectors of law and order were either passive spectators or actually participated in the attacks. Such was the horror of the atrocities resulting from the caste frenzy that even after the riots had ended, several of those who fled were reluctant to return to their villages—even though the alternative was semistarvation in the nearby jungles or abject poverty in the nearby towns.[1]

This instance of carnage against untouchables is by no means unique. The list of instances of the organized use of violence to terrorize lower castes is too long to enumerate here. An indication of the gravity of the problem is provided by the fact that at least one state (Bihar) has found the situation so desperate as to announce plans for providing arms to untouchables to enable them to survive predatory attacks from caste Hindus.[2]

In Bihar, which has been the scene of some of the worst atrocities, the Adivasis are meeting violence with violence. In Ramgarh they killed a usurious money lender who had reduced them to becoming sharecroppers on their own lands.[3] In Khunti, when the local schoolteacher was arrested (on the grounds that he was in default by a few months in repayment of a government loan) some ten thousand Adivasis stormed the local official's office and demanded and obtained the release of the teacher.[4] In Simdega they set ablaze the offices of forest officials against whom they had individual and collective grievances.[5] The growing militancy underlying the demands of India's scheduled-caste population and the growing rate of atrocities being perpetrated against them forces a critical appraisal of government programs for their development.

The problem confronting India is one shared by many of the other countries of Asia that have pluralistic societies and historically disadvantaged groups and communities that seek to be fully integrated into the national mainstream of economic, social, cultural, and human development. The formidable task ahead is to achieve national integration by reducing cultural differences rooted in structural segmentation.

The Constitutional Affirmation of Equality

The preamble to the Constitution of India presents the goals that the people of India set for themselves on achieving independence thirty years ago. In that preamble the people of India solemnly resolved to secure to all citizens:

> *Justice:* social, economic, and political;

> *Liberty:* of thought, expression, belief, faith, and worship;

> *Equality:* of status and of opportunity;

and to promote among them all:

> *Fraternity:* assuring the dignity of the individual and the unity of the nation.

These were ambitious goals indeed, since they were meant to be secured to all citizens, including some sixty million untouchables suffering from two thousand years of exploitation and discrimination.

The emphasis on building an egalitarian society meant an acceptance of two types of policies aimed at equality: vertical policies aimed at lessening gaps between existing stratified levels of social hierarchy, and horizontal policies aimed at lessening gaps among the pluralistic elements in the society. Since the high proportion of untouchables were landless agricultural workers, inevitably there would often be a merging of the horizontal and vertical policies.

The concept of *equality* was in itself an innovation that the makers of the Constitution sought to introduce into Indian society, since at independence India was a highly stratified, rigidly hierarchical social polity. The ascriptive status of caste was viewed as an important source of reciprocal rights and duties. The caste system carried with it its own ethical framework within which rights to equality were assigned lesser importance than obligations between unequals. Caste was viewed as one of the main unifying forces of the heterogenous Indian polity and, there-

fore, was not seen as posing the same kind of potential threat to the
nation state that tribes, religious communities, and linguistic groups did.[6]
Several social scientists took the view that the caste system in India would
respond to changes in its political and economic environment and was
capable of transforming itself from below and within.[7]

There was thus some ambiguity about what the secular concept of
equality enshrined in the independence constitution was meant to be.
Would it serve a normative, standard-setting function? Was it meant to
provide evaluative criteria for securing the social accountability of public-
and private-sector actors? Was it meant to be an aspirational declaration
or a source of real (as distinct from paper) rights and obligations? From
strictly a legalistic perspective it could be argued that there was no ambiguity, since equality was declared to be a fundamental right. Such a
perspective, however, would ignore the distinction between declaring
that fundamental rights exist and effectively securing the realization of
such rights.

India's policy of protective discrimination was developed by the British over several decades in the preindependence period. The British listed
in a schedule to the Government of India Act, 1935, the lowest-ranking
Hindu castes, who would be the beneficiaries of statutory safeguards and
other benefits. This was the origin of the term *scheduled castes,* a bit of
legal jargon appropriate only in the context of legal provisions and government action. Otherwise, the term is meaningless since it designates
not a single, undifferentiated group but a large, diverse population (estimated in 1971 at approximately 80 million). The postindependence
government has expanded and modified both the policy and the list since
1947 with a view to enlarging the groups entitled to protective discrimination. Although the initial focus of attention in the Constituent Assembly was on untouchables, the focus broadened to backward castes and
tribes—that is, historically disadvantaged groups with a distinct ethnic
identity. The beneficiary group has widened as the basis for inclusion
has moved away from the ascriptive status of caste to objective criteria
of social and economic deprivation, exclusion, and exploitation. Thus
by 1980 a third category of socially and educationally backward castes
or classes (SEBC) was added to the two earlier categories of scheduled
castes (SC) and scheduled tribes (ST). This category covers eighty-two
communities, including a few Muslim communities.

**Untouchability during Colonial Rule
and the National Struggle**

The protective-discrimination policies adopted by India on attainment of
independence have their roots in those adopted by the British colonial

government in India. As mentioned earlier, the Government of India Act, 1935, listed several castes in a schedule. These castes became beneficiaries of statutory safeguards and benefits. The colonial government's interest at the time was to ameliorate the misery and some of the objective conditions of deprivation rather than to attack social and other ritual disabilities resulting from caste. Therefore, the policies did not forcefully assert *equality* as a preferred value.

The period of Indian history leading to the enactment of the independence constitution witnessed a clash between two disparate and conflicting sets of values and beliefs. The old value system rooted in Hindu religious thought provided the basis for support of the caste system and the untouchables' inferior position within that system. A new, secular value system established by the independence constitution asserted the principle of social and political equality for all.

One of the earliest movements away from British policy and toward equality came in the 1917 Congress Resolution, which placed "upon the people of India the necessity, justice and righteousness of removing *all disabilities* imposed on the Depressed Classes."[8] The Congress Resolution came after an earlier meeting in Bombay of the depressed classes, who sought this resolution in return for supporting the 1916 Congress–Muslim League constitutional scheme for self-government.

The Congress Resolution set the stage for members of the depressed castes to participate in the formulation and initiation of the new scheme. In the period before independence two national leaders—Gandhi and Ambedkar—influenced greatly the new scheme that was to be adopted. These two individuals brought to their leadership very different styles, approaches, objectives, and ethical frameworks.

Gandhi, though himself of a high-born caste, nevertheless saw himself as the leader of the *Harijans* (depressed castes). In Gandhi's policy toward untouchability is reflected the dilemma of a dual personal role: *political leader* of India's national struggle for independence, and *mahatma*—social and religious reformer. His task as political leader was to weave divergent interests in India into a unified opposition to the British. One of the main unifying forces, however, was caste; his challenge as *mahatma* was to pursue a course of social reform without tearing apart the prevailing social fabric of India. Not surprisingly, therefore, Gandhi firmly reiterated the law of *varna*. He denounced untouchability, however, and tried to change caste Hindu thinking about the lower castes by preaching and by personal example.

As Gandhi stressed, "*Swaraj* is unattainable without the removal of the sin of untouchability as it is without Hindu-Muslim unity." He reiterated that the treatment of castes below the *shudra* level as unclean is "not only inhumane but harmful to Hinduism," and he denounced disabilities based on untouchability as "an excrescence on Hinduism, a hydra-headed monster, a device of Satan." At the same time Gandhi also reaffirmed the law of varna, which prescribes that "a person should, for his living, follow the lawful occupation of his forefathers"; but he urged that all varnas possess equality of status and all occupations are equally honorable. "One born a scavenger must earn his livelihood by being a scavenger and then doing whatever else he likes," but "a scavenger is as worthy of hire as your President. That according to me is Hinduism."

Gandhi translated the foregoing approach into the following lines of action. First, he would constantly assert, "I do not want to be reborn but if I have to be reborn I should be born an untouchable" and would, at every opportunity, give tangible proof of this belief by commingling with untouchables. Second, he insisted that all volunteers for his non-cooperation campaign against the British in 1921 sign a pledge that placed responsibility on the individual to eradicate untouchability. His emphasis here was constantly on the caste Hindu's obligations to untouchables; consistent with this approach, he founded an organization to serve untouchables.

Gandhi's ambivalence about caste is perhaps best evident when on the one hand he stresses, "I would persuade all caste Hindu girls coming under my influence to select Harijan husbands," and yet on the other hand he supports other caste-based practices, saying, "interdrinking, interdining and intermarrying is not essential for the promotion of the spirit of democracy."

Gandhi's approach to untouchability refects the dilemma of one who sees value in preserving the traditional social order but who is also committed to reform of certain abhorrent aspects of such order: reform that might well, if successful, have the effect of not just creating a rift in the social fabric but of rending it apart.

The other major Indian leader who helped shape India's policies toward untouchability was B.R. Ambedkar. Like Gandhi, he was a London-trained barrister; but unlike Gandhi he was a member of a scheduled caste (the *Mahars*). The Mahars were a caste group whose traditional occupation was maintaining cremation grounds, hauling away dead cattle, and other menial tasks short of scavenging. With the establishment of British rule in the presidency of Bombay, several of the Mahars sought out opportunities for army service or employment in mills, munitions factories, or as servants in British households. They were heavily influenced by the opportunities for education they received in the army or domestic service; and later (in 1880) several Mahars sought to escape from caste disabilities by claiming a higher status based on the assertion that their ancestors were in fact from the warrior-caste group. Ambedkar never sought this solution to the problem and never urged claims for higher-caste status for untouchables. He had several caste Hindu patrons, one of whom, the Maharaja Gaikwad of Baroda, as part of a policy of educating untouchables, gave him financial help to secure M.A. and Ph.D. degrees from Columbia University (New York), a D.Sc. degree from London, and the Bar at Grey's Inn. On his return to India, most of Ambedkar's closest associates were high-caste Hindu reformers who condemned not only untouchability but the very concept of varna as well. Not surprisingly, to Ambedkar, Gandhi's denunciations of untouchability seemed hardly radical. His own caste Hindu associates backed Ambedkar in more militant and assertive stances. Thus Ambedkar, with their support, registered one of his most dramatic protests in rejection of Hindu orthodoxy: the burning of the ancient book *Manusmriti* in 1927 as a protest against traditional caste restrictions.

For Gandhi, equality meant equal status of all varnas. For Ambedkar it meant equal social, political, and economic opportunity for all. His approach sought to awaken in untouchables an awareness of their debased condition and common interests that would promote their mobilization into effective organizations for mass action. He advocated a separatist policy accentuating caste distinctions as an initial stage in creating a society in which identities would be unimportant. He directed his own efforts toward programs to bring the untouchable from a state of dehumanization and slavery into one of equality through the use of modern methods based on education and the exercise of legal and political rights. His emphasis on education was the result of his own personal experience of the value to be derived from education. His emphasis on political rights was hardly surprising, since he had witnessed representation of untouchables grow from one appointed member to the Bombay Provincial Legislative in 1921 to full-fledged elected representation on the basis of reserved seats by the 1940s.

Ambedkar firmly believed in the power of representative political bodies to correct social and economic injustices and reiterated that political power must be assured the untouchable even if separatism is fostered by the granting of such power. Ambedkar sought to adapt Western forms of government and Western concepts to the Indian scene. He thus based his claims for political rights for untouchables on concepts such as democracy, fraternity, and liberty. In his Marathi speeches, however, he tried to bring to his caste the implications of these concepts in the word familiar to his community, *mansuki*, which conveys the ideas of humanness, feelings of self-respect, and humane attitudes toward one's fellow man. By 1935 he had rejected Hinduism, and even earlier he was leading nonviolent direct action in protest of existing practices of untouchability. Thus in 1927 in Mahad, Bombay, he led several thousand members of his caste en masse to a water tank in the Brahmin sections of town, and the leaders stooped and drank water from the tank. The Brahmins later ritually purified the tank. Ambedkar's commitment to legalism created self-imposed dilemmas for him, however. When a court injunction was issued prohibiting nonviolent direct action (*satyagraha*) for water rights, he chose to comply with the injunction and fight and win a ten-year court battle rather than to take to the streets again.

Ambedkar was also caught up in the freedom struggle. Unlike Gandhi, however, his role as national leader did not create constraints on his struggle against untouchability. In fact, he saw linkages between the two struggles: only *swaraj* would bring the possibility of equality to the Depressed Classes. He argued with Congress leaders that no country is good enough to rule another but would tell Congress point blank that it is equally true that no class is good enough to rule over another class.[9]

Ambedkar's efforts in the preindependence period focused around securing political rights for untouchables. Although initially he did not press for a separate electorate (one in which untouchables could vote for their candidates independently of the caste Hindu vote), by the First Round Table Conference (1930), he reversed his position, since by then the Muslim demand for separate electorates had already become unalterable. At the Second Round Table Conference (1932) the inevitable clash between him and Gandhi occurred, with Gandhi not only refusing to consider separate electorates but also opposing any form of special representation involving reserved seats.

On 20 September 1932 Gandhi went on a "fast unto death," objecting to separate electorates. His reasons were partly those of a politician:

> These poor fellows will ask why I who claim to be their friend should offer *Satyagraha* simply because they were granted some privileges; they would vote separately but vote with me. They do not realize that the separate electorate will create division among Hindus so much that it will lead to bloodshed. "Untouchable" hooligans will make common cause with Muslim hooligans and kill caste-Hindus. Has the British Government no idea of all this? I do not think so.

His reasons were also partly moral, however:

> I have not the slightest shadow of doubt that it [separate electorates] will prevent the natural growth for the suppressed classes and will remove the incentive to honorable amends from the suppressors. What I am aiming at is a heart understanding between the two, the greatest opportunity of repentance and reparation on the part of the suppressors. I am certain that the movement is ripe for the change of heart among them. I would therefore favor widest possible franchise for the suppressed and establish a convention between the two sections for securing proper election of representatives of the suppressed.[10]

Gandhi's fast came as a response to the compromise formula offered by the British government at the Third Round Table Conference when they suggested giving the depressed classes a double vote—one in a separate constituency for a modest number of reserved seats and one in the general electorate.

Ambedkar was adamant that political separation from the Hindus in the electoral system was necessary for the attainment of untouchable political rights. Faced with Gandhi's continuing fast, the British government insisted that a solution to the representation of the depressed classes had to be settled within the Hindu community itself. In the historic Poona Pact, Ambedkar drove a hard bargain, trading a separate electorate for a separate primary election plus an increase in reserved seats from 78 to 148.

After this conflict both leaders intensified their efforts, each adopting his own approach. Gandhi continued trying to change the hearts of the caste Hindu by moral pressure within the framework of Hindu tradition. In 1932 he founded the Harijan Sevak Sangh to use peaceful persuasion to secure access to all public wells, schools, temples, roads, and cremation grounds. Gandhi's efforts at moral persuasion, however, failed either to appease the untouchables or to conciliate orthodox Hindus.

Ambedkar concentrated his efforts in the fields of education and politics in an attempt to gain legal rights for the untouchable in a secular world. His efforts to secure a separate electorate failed when in 1943 the Cripps Mission provided only for reserved seats and not separate electorates. By then the decision to create Pakistan had meant that the Muslims no longer demanded separate electorates; as a result, all hopes for a scheduled-caste separate electorate came to an end.

After independence, Ambedkar became law minister and chairman of the committee drafting the Indian Constitution. On 28 November 1948 the Constituent Assembly enacted a provision legally abolishing untouchability. The House resounded with cries of "Mahatma Gandhi Ki Jai"— a tribute to Gandhi's thirty-year efforts to remove the practice of untouchability. The moment was tinged with dual irony, however. A legalistic measure was being taken in the name of Gandhi, who had no use for legalism. There was no recognition of the efforts of Ambedkar, who had drafted the measure and had bitterly fought Gandhi to secure legalistic solutions to the problems of untouchability.[11] In 1956, just before his death, Ambedkar took two actions that stressed once again his belief that separatist action was necessary for eventual integration. On 14 October 1956 he converted to Buddhism, starting a movement of some three million conversions. These conversions represented not only a rejection of Hinduism but also a voluntary forfeiting of several of the legally provided measures for protective discrimination. Ambedkar also formed the Republican party, which he hoped would be the instrument of political power for untouchables—a hope that was never to be fulfilled. Ambedkar's approach, however—based on concepts of self-respect and self-help—was to have far greater impact over the years than any of the more specific, tangible victories he gained.

The Strategy of Protective Discrimination

The program adopted by the government of India seeks to synthesize the ways of Gandhi and Ambedkar. The main instruments of the program relate to:

1.   reserved seats in all legislative bodies;
2.   reservation of government jobs;
3.   reservation of seats in educational institutions;
4.   prizes to villages demonstrating equality;
5.   money gifts for mixed marriages;
6.   support for housing projects;
7.   legal machinery for suits against discriminative practices.

Although the goal of the makers of India's constitution was one of achieving equality and of complete integration and assimilation of historically disadvantaged groups into the larger Indian community, paradoxically enough the strategy chosen was one of protective discrimination: a strategy that reinforces concepts of separateness and tends to perpetuate an ideology of discrimination. The strategy chosen had several closely related components. First, there was an attempt to establish new norms that would emphasize egalitarianism. Hence the constitution itself proscribed untouchability in any form and created a fundamental right for every citizen to be protected against discrimination on grounds only of race, religion, caste, sex, or place of birth. The constitution also guaranteed equality of opportunity to all citizens in matters relating to public employment and, going further, guaranteed to all persons equality before the law and equal protection of the laws within the territory of India. The secular, egalitarian values underlying these norms were meant to displace the traditional values in Indian society that had led to the creation of a caste system and other forms of social stratification.

The mere enactment of norms, however, though a necessary first step, is not very effective unless backed by machinery for implementation. Hence subsequent legislation was enacted to provide for punishment of offenses of untouchability. The constitution contained its own provisions of remedies against discrimination.

A second component of the strategy was a scheme of state-sanctioned protective discrimination in favor of the backward classes. The benefits under this scheme are of two main types: first, *reservations,* applied to political representation, government employment, and higher-educational admissions; and second, *financial assistance,* administered through a variety of welfare schemes. In theory the protective discrimination is used to guarantee members of the lowest castes a share of power and opportunity for advancement until they can hold their own without it. The scheme is by definition temporary and is supposed to last only as long as it is needed.

A third component of the strategy was geared toward securing vertical equality. General development and welfare programs (of clearly redistributional intent) were established to aid landless agricultural laborers, municipal slum dwellers, or other low-income groups. These programs would also benefit scheduled-caste individuals, since they are found in large numbers in such populations. Some states in India have also enacted special legislation to deal with particular problems involving scheduled-caste individuals. Thus, for example, Maharashtra has enacted law to check or prohibit the alienation of Adivasi lands into non-Adivasi hands and also to restore lands already alienated in contravention of law.

Basically, the strategy chosen was one of benign, state-sponsored paternalism. This strategy was ahistorical and essentially conservative. It largely ignored deep-rooted structural inequalities that reinforced and perpetuated the present-day system of discrimination and exploitation and assumed, in much too facile a fashion, the possibility of a clean break with tradition. It is conservative in that it emphasizes the *caste*-conflict aspects of some of the problems wherein the *class*-conflict aspects are perhaps more significant. It is paternalistic (especially in its origins during British colonial rule over India) and not sufficiently sensitive to the thin dividing line between protection and the creation of dependency relationships. The process of policy formulation can hardly be termed participatory and at best represents what a well-meaning elite thought should be done for and to the downtrodden. The strategy assumes equal access to law and assumes the effectiveness of state law as an instrument through which redistribution of power and of essential resources can be effectuated.

The Implementation of the Strategy
and its Social Impact

Detailed critical evaluations of the operation of the strategy outlined here have already been undertaken, and this chapter will not seek to duplicate them.[12] Some observations drawn from experience with attempting to work the foregoing strategy, however, are needed both to make a critical assessment of the strategy of protective discrimination and to stimulate the search for alternative approaches.

The strategy of protective discrimination has three main components: first, the establishment of new norms on untouchability and the right to nondiscrimination; second, a program of state-sanctioned protective discrimination through (1) reservations in political representation, employment, and education, and (2) financial assistance and welfare programs; and third, a program designed to achieve vertical equality through welfare measures directed toward low-income groups.

As far as the norm-articulation, standard-setting component of the strategy of protective discrimination is concerned, there were definitional problems from the outset. Ironically, it needed the First Amendment to clarify that the constitutional prohibition against discrimination did not bar discrimination in *favor* of backward castes and classes. Moreover, the fundamental-rights provisions securing equality have met with a similar fate as those securing property: repeated litigation to clarify meaning, judicial attitudes ranging from conservative to reactionary, and constitutional amendments to provide further clarifications. The use of caste for definitional purposes has also had serious shortcomings, and the Supreme Court has had to interpret *backwardness* as not necessarily being synonymous with caste. In the first place, there are non-Hindu backward communities that have no castes. Even with respect to Hindus, caste

> may be a relevant factor to consider in determining . . . social backwardness . . . [but] it cannot be made the sole or the dominant test. . . . Social backwardness is in the ultimate analysis the result of poverty, to a very large extent . . . social backwardness which results from poverty is likely to be aggravated by considerations of caste to which the poor citizens may belong, but that only shows the relevance of both caste and poverty in determining the backwardness of citizens.[13]

Problems were also encountered in defining *untouchability*. Neither Article 17 of the Constitution nor the Untouchability Offenses Act (1955) nor the Protection of Civil Rights Act (1976) attempts to define untouchability. As long as the term remains undefined, serious difficulties will persist in attempting to enforce proscription of the practice of untouchability.

Turning to the second component of the strategy, it appears that the system of protective discrimination through reservations has created new structures of discrimination that are becoming increasingly inequitable in a modern context in which poverty, income inequality, and destitution cut across the traditional forms of discrimination. The reserved-seat system in electorates has created special political roles and led to a process of fragmentation of scheduled-caste politics. Reservations in political representation were intended as a means of redistribution of political power. They were intended to have a limited existence of ten years but have instead been regularly renewed for further periods of ten years each. After thirty years of their existence, there still does not exist a single scheduled-caste political party. Instead, scheduled-caste and tribal politicians continue to be regularly coopted into the dominant political groups. The reserved-electoral-seat system (unlike the system of separate electorates that was rejected) has tended to operate in practice as follows. All that is required to qualify for election from a reserved seat is membership in a scheduled caste. This has led political parties to coopt some of the more competent politicans from among the scheduled-caste communities. Thus to be in the political mainstream it helps to belong to a scheduled caste. The price for belonging to such a caste, however, is prejudice and discrimination at a social and cultural level. A good scheduled-caste politician (in the absence of separate electorates) must depend on high-caste Hindu votes. This fact leads to a process of depoliticization of scheduled-caste politicians. A similar trend has been evident with reservations of public-employment opportunities. Educated, able, scheduled-caste youths are drawn into civil-service jobs under the system of reservations. In such jobs they are rendered politically sterile by civil-service rules. Moreover, in the face of continuing hostility and discrimination based on caste from their superiors, they are forced to shed, or at least attenuate, their scheduled-caste identity. This is how the process of professional socialization of bureaucrats and politician legislators operates in modern India. Thus reservations, which were intended as a strategy of redistribution of power, have degenerated into instruments of control by elites of depressed groups.

Protective discrimination as a whole seems to have fostered the growth of a new class. The kind of people who can avail themselves of the opportunities offered by protective discrimination (running for a legislative seat, seeking admission to college, applying for a government clerkship) have already reached a level of education, prosperity, and influence well above that of the vast majority of the intended beneficiary group. With the operation of the system over the years, the gap within castes between the more fortunate minority and the rest has widened. Also, benefits tend to be unevenly distributed between backward castes and classes. Those who belong to large caste aggregates with organized politics secure a distinct advantage under the prevailing system of preferences.

Reservation of employment opportunities has fostered a sense of dependency on handouts or, worse, of personal inadequacy. Such reservations have also at times proved disruptive of the morale of the rest of the worker or student community. There have inevitably been abuses, with false certification of caste membership. Perhaps the most trouble-some aspect of protective discrimination, however, has been the pres-sures it generates for self-perpetuation. Several ways have been suggested over the years for eliminating protective discrimination (shifting the concessions to bases other than caste, imposing time limits on castes to be protected, stratifying castes into less and more backward, taking the more advanced castes off the lists of those eligible for benefits); but none of these seems likely to be adopted in the foreseeable future, for obvious political reasons.

The third component of the strategy of protective discrimination con-sisted of welfare measures directed toward low-income groups and de-signed to achieve vertical equality. General measures of agrarian reform and other welfare programs have, paradoxically, at times produced in-equality of results. The redistributional benefits have ended up at the upper strata of the depressed groups and have failed to reach the poorest and most exploited members of these groups. This process is prevalent in many redistributional programs.[14] The caste system overlaps the class structure to a large extent.[15] The purpose of the welfare programs is to make certain aspects of life, such as land ownership, occupation, and so on, less dependent on caste than before. The importance of such an approach was borne out by a study of villages in Mysore, where provision of reserved seats for untouchables on the village panchayat did not mean real power for them since they continued to be dependent on their peasant masters.[16] Several states in India have enacted special laws intended to benefit scheduled castes. Thus, for example, Maharashtra has enacted legislation to prohibit alienation of Adivasi lands into the hands of non-Adivasis and to restore lands already alienated. Several deficiencies and loopholes in the law have reduced its effectiveness, however. Some states have attempted to allot land to Harijans, but often these efforts end as mere allotment orders on papers. The Harijans have either never been given possession, or, as happened in Kannadia (Madhya Pradesh), Hari-jans have been killed attempting to till the land allotted to them by the government.[17] Beating and killings of Harijans, forcible occupation of lands allotted to them, and destruction of houses and crops occur with increasing frequency.[18] Not all this violence comes from caste Hindus. For example, the murder of nine Harijans in Belchchi (Bihar) in 1977 was perpetrated by members of a few so-called backward castes that held enormous economic and political power in an effort to tighten their feudal hold over castes that were below them.[19]

Several other measures have been enacted to alleviate economic ex-ploitation of rural scheduled-caste communities, such as debt-relief leg-islation and legislation seeking to abolish bonded labor. Such laws, however, remain unimplemented or underimplemented.

The state-sponsored program of protective discrimination does place heavy reliance on the coercive power of the state through police and courts. At least so far as the police are concerned, the dilemma is that ruthless enforcement of such laws will inevitably result in a ruthless erosion of their own power base. The state program also does place heavy reliance on the institutions of state law for the implementation of the program. The very character and nature of state law and state institutions for administration of justice, however, render them at times inappropriate and more often than not very burdensome vehicles through which the intended beneficiaries of the program must seek effectuation of the program's goals and objectives.

State-sponsored efforts to combat ritual aspects of caste discrimination have met with little greater success than their efforts to combat the nonritual aspects of caste discrimination. The Untouchability Offenses Act, 1955, sought to provide the implementing framework for Article 17 of the Indian Constitution, which abolished untouchability in any form. Between 1955 and 1971 in all of India only 8,819 cases were registered with the police under the act, of which only 1,870 resulted in convictions.[20] There are several factors that have contributed to this situation. The legislation does not define *untouchability*. Thus, although the victims of the practice of untouchability know quite unambiguously when such practice has occurred, lawyers and judges have had to struggle with burdens of proof, legal presumptions, rebuttable presumptions, and other legal niceties to establish the fact of an offense. Moreover, the system for implementing the act has also been found wanting in several respects. It places too much burden on the victim and presumes the victim to have access to lawyer intermediaries who are, more often than not, lacking. It is not proactive in its reach and is plagued by delays in its operation. Moreover, the costs (psychological as well as economic) of invoking the protection of the act have tended to serve as a deterrent to its use. It employs the typical structure of criminal courts of the state law system—institutions about which rural villages have generally negative perceptions. Moreover, the adversarial nature of the proceedings seems inappropriate since they assume a level of assertiveness that is largely nonexistent in the victim's community. The Untouchability Offenses Act, 1955, was replaced recently by the Protection of Civil Rights Act (CRA). During the deliberation of a joint select committee of Parliament involved in revision of the law, the type of administrative structure necessary to support an effective drive against the practice of untouchability was one of the key issues that arose. Regrettably, the CRA as it emerged from these deliberations embodies an administrative structure that, at best, is geared to incremental change.[21] Although the CRA does represent an improvement over its predecessor, there is still considerable scope for further improvement. Untouchability remains undefined even in the new legislation. There is still no appropriate central agency charged with the responsibility of enforcing the law. The act does, however, empower the various states, at their discretion, to take special measures, such as setting up special courts for trial of CRA offenses, declaring areas of disability, and conducting surveys of the impact of the law.[22] The CRA has introduced several worthy innovations, such as identifying new categories of behavior involving untouchability (for example, discrimination in job or employment); providing for minimum punishments and also forms of punishment in addition to fines and imprisonment; and making new categories of persons (such as company officials) liable to punishment. The highly discretionary and decentralized nature of its implementation structure, however, will inevitably limit the effectiveness of the act.

One particular aspect of the practice of untouchability in rural India that serves to highlight some of the problems involved is the question of access to water. The CRA prohibits enforcement of any disability on the ground of untouchability against any person with regard to "the use of or access to any river, stream, spring, tank, cistern, water tap or other watering place." Nevertheless, user restrictions that clearly indicate the practice of untouchability persist. A few states, like Gujarat, have sought to confront the problem through a tough-minded approach to the enforcement of the law. Several other states, however, have chosen to provide separate wells and taps for untouchables. Although this approach does ensure that untouchables will no longer be dependent on higher-caste tolerance in meeting so basic a need as water, it nevertheless creates problems of accepting double standards and of selective nonenforcement of the provisions of CRA.

Two quite divergent assessments of the state program are usually offered. Supporters of the program claim that despite its imperfections it has enabled affected groups to play a more prominent role than they otherwise might have in public life. Opponents denigrate it as a tool of those who in fact control it and argue that, from its inception, the politicians of the Congress party have learned to dominate it and through it control a majority that might otherwise have become troublesome.

The existence (even if only on the books) of a comprehensive scheme of state programs has:

1. inhibited the emergence of a new mahatma championing against remaining injustices;
2. forestalled the emergence of a separatist untouchable leader attempting to build a national movement outside the walls of government privilege and patronage;

3.   deadened Indian consciousness regarding the continuing problems of the untouchable.

Moreover, the majority of untouchables today are landless villagers. Economic dependence on others continues to restrict their development and raises problems that relate to secular rather than ritual deprivation.

Self-Reliant Action for Compensatory Justice

The foregoing description of problems and failures of state-sponsored programs of protective discrimination projects a gloomy picture of the progress since independence in the quest for equality. Simultaneous with the state-sponsored programs, however, there has gradually emerged an alternative approach that may perhaps be termed the compensatory-justice approach. As the term connotes, the approach is based on perceptions of rights (for example, to compensation rather than benign charity, or to justice rather than to protection). This approach emphasizes self-help and self-reliance and is concerned with bringing about the structural transformations needed to demolish historical modes of exploitation and discrimination. Over the years in different parts of rural India, there have emerged spontaneous self-help, participatory rural organizations of Adivasis and other backward caste populations: Chipko, Bhoomi Sena, Rangpur, the Santhal Jhar Khand movement.

B.R. Ambedkar repeatedly expressed the view that political power was the key to all progress and that the scheduled castes could achieve betterment only if they captured political power by organizing themselves into a separate party. Through political action he wanted to force the caste Hindus to ameliorate the conditions in which the scheduled castes were living. Ambedkar's dream of a separate scheduled-caste political party was never to come true; and, moreover, the device of reservation in political representation served not as a source of gaining political power but as source of depoliticization and cooptation of scheduled-caste politicians. Yet Ambedkar's thesis that only when they had achieved political power could the social and economic conditions of the scheduled castes be improved, remains valid even today. The participatory rural organizations of Adivasi and other backward-caste communities, mentioned earlier, deserve closer scrutiny since they represent a vehicle through which these communities can aggregate and exercise political power. Some of these organizations function virtually as parallel local governments. They carry out developmental activities in their region, settle intraorganization disputes, they plan and implement local economic activity, and even virtually develop their own legal norms governing group activity. In a sense they represent the achievement of decentralization. These nonstate organizations enter into linkages and have relationships (sometimes mutually reinforcing and at other times antagonistic) with state agencies and political structures. Admittedly, these organizations are mainly a rural phenomenon and are of limited relevance to the problems of urban backward classes. Nevertheless, they merit close analysis as representing a possible alternative avenue for the backward classes to secure a redistribution of political power.

The *Bhoomi Sena* ("land army") is an organization of historically depressed, landless, rural workers in Maharashtra.[23] They became mobilized for organized action when they learned that the government was failing to enforce legislation that declared, in effect, that agricultural workers should enjoy various rights to minimum wages and security in their employment and in possession of land leased to them by their employers—rights that amount to the very rights of these people to existence. This knowledge led to mobilization—a consensus to work together to redress perceived wrongs. Through modes of participatory decision making, they agreed on various courses of collective action and group-sponsored efforts to force officials to interpret and apply relevant laws and to force landlords, moneylenders, and others to obey them. These tactics included group letters and deputations to officials; demonstrations and public appeals; and refusal to accept the legitimacy of traditional leases, loans, and contracts of employment. Pursuit of these objectives led to other activities: the creation of a group-managed credit institution, child-care centers, and schools, and the building of community facilities.

The *Chipko* groups comprise villagers in some of the most backward hill districts in Uttar Pradesh in India.[24] These groups came together in a struggle for survival. They live in villages at the foothills of the Himalayan mountains, where reckless deforestation of the hill slopes had led to a mounting toll of lives and property from landslides that annually buried their villages under crashing rock and rubble. The Chipko villagers originally mobilized to prevent the felling of adjacent forests by literally clutching on to the trees and stating, "If the axe must fall, it should fall on us before the trees are felled." Over the years the Chipko movement has grown. It has now become both an ecological movement for the preservation of the environment and a people's organization to foster self-help, development, adult education, and functional-literacy programs.

The *Rangpur Ashram* and *Lok Adalat* in Baroda serve as the epicenter for the socioeconomic development of an adjoining region comprising about a thousand villages.[25] The Rangpur Ashram was established in 1949 by Harivallabh Parikh, a Gandhian social worker. The ashram stands on sixteen acres of land and serves as a group-managed training and demonstration farm. It has a trained cadre of around seventy rural workers who provide education and relevant skills for groups in the region desiring to undertake rural self-help activities. The ashram provides technical help, credit, sale, and purchase facilities for surrounding villages that have decided to set up cooperative societies through which they pursue self-help and self-development projects. A major achievement in Rangpur has been the irrigation program, which has brought some fifty thousand acres of land under irrigation. Other achievements are the adult literacy programs and the social-welfare programs such as *sharab mukti* (liberation from liquor). Over a thousand Rangpur villages have set up their own common participatory, governmental, and bureaucratic structures centered around the institution of the *lok adalat* (people's court).

The *Santhal* movement in Bihar has passed through several phases.[26] During its first phase, in 1950, the Santhal Jharkand—a political party— was formed by the tribal Santhals. This party contested the national elections in 1952 and emerged as the main opposition party in the state legislature. In 1955 the party presented to the government a demand for a separate Santhal state. The second phase of the Santhal movement came with a rejection of this demand and the merger of the party with the Congress. The third phase, up to 1969, saw a weakening of the Santhal movement due to the presence of factions and cleavages among the Santhal leaders. The fourth and present phase witnesses a resurgence of the movement under strong Santhal leadership. The Santhals have established measures to prevent alienation of tribal land and have repossessed land that has fallen into the hands of moneylenders. (The moneylenders are allowed to keep the land if they cultivate it themselves and become ex-moneylenders.) The land reclaimed from the moneylenders is distributed among the landless Santhals. The land is cultivated by what is called *samuhikheti:* individual ownership but with labor and farming implements pooled into a team. A grain *gola* (common storehouse) is maintained, with each farmer making contributions to five accounts: to pay for labor used, to set aside seed for replanting, to run a village-level night-school system, to support political activities of the organization, and to provide hospitality to visitors. The Santhal organizations have set up their own courts, called *baishi,* assemblies of about twenty villagers. The Santhals do not go to regular courts but prefer the cheaper and speedier justice meted out by the *baishi.* The Santhals have adopted the policy of selective use of violence. As one of their leaders, Shibu Soren, explains the policy, they will meet violence with violence.

The *Shramik Sanghatana* is a movement and organization of rural Adivasi workers in Maharashtra State.[27] The Sanghatana directs activities to repossess Adivasi land in the hands of moneylenders, to enforce minimum wage and other labor welfare laws, to fight repression, to improve the conditions of particularly disadvantaged groups such as women, and to organize a variety of cultural and educational activities.

In Andhra Pradesh, peasant organizations called *ryot coolie san-*

ghams have been springing up to fight exploitation by higher-caste landlords.[28]

These rural movements and organizations have all been born out of conditions of impoverishment, destitution, and discrimination. Caste has been a unifying factor—an asset. These rural groups represent an alternative, bottom-up response from within the disadvantaged communities to their own problems. They are born not out of despair or acquiescence but rather out of hope and conviction—conviction that by collective effort those exploited can take steps to improve their lot. They represent hope in a better future that is obtained through unified action and self-help, through finding a new identity: one in which discrimination can truly become a thing of the past and equality a dream of the not-too-distant future. The remarkable achievements of the rural Adivasi groups are documented elsewhere. Their problems and difficulties have been legion, too, but they have grappled with these problems with a will to overcome. They are still a relatively new and not very carefully studied phenomena. They do, however, represent an alternative strategy to protective discrimination—a vehicle through which a backward community seeks to establish new and mutually beneficial two-way relationships with the community at large. To the extent that they seek to confront caste inequalities as well as those of class, they will inevitably have to resist suppression by vested interests seeking to preserve the status quo. Rangpur provides a good example. The Rangpur lok adalat for nearly three decades has provided the people from the villages of Rangpur with a popular forum in which their disputes could be settled through a process that was participatory and encouraged consensus. As the lok adalat grew in strength, it provided the villagers with a means of securing the accountability of corrupt local police, officials, and administrators—a means through which they could collectively confront many clusters of dominant structures of power in the region and the state. In doing so, however, and by failing to protect itself in cases of jurisdictional overlap, the lok adalat has come under heavy attack, with several of its leaders facing criminal charges (of complicity in concealing murder) for the way they settled a dispute involving the death of one of the Rangpur villagers. The people of Rangpur, however, will not give up without a struggle or abandon what they have fought so hard to establish. The story of the most recent phase of their struggle is perhaps best told in the words of a scholar who has worked very closely with and for Rangpur:

On July 5, 1959 a historic event occurred in Bhakha, near Naswadi in Baroda district of Gujarat. At a mass meeting thousands of adivasis [tribals] and villagers, subscribed by acclamation to a resolution which, in part read:

It is our democratic right to operate the Lok Adalat. All kinds of questions and problems concerning us arise. It is the foun-

dation of people's government for us to have the power to deal
with them and solve them. We shall brook no interference in
the matter. We do not interfere with the social organization or
the "life-style" of the "advanced" classes. Similarly, they
should not interfere with our social organization which has
traditions going back to many centuries. We shall not tolerate
any interference.

Two days later, a much bigger mass meeting at Dhanpuri village also
solemnly reiterated this right to self-determination.

The event is historic because it is for the first time in Independent India
that a group of historically and contemporaneously disadvantaged and
depressed people assembled together to assert their "democratic right"
to preserve and protect their own system of adjudication and self-government. Significantly, they did this in the title of democracy in terms
of "people's government" whose prime function it is to preserve the
autonomy of group life, its legal culture and traditions. The claim for
self-determination was also supported by a plea for equality. They
asserted that they do not presume to interfere in the manner in which
the higher strata of Indian society deals with its disputes and conflicts
through a legal system of their making and choice. They demanded
reciprocity: an equal respect for their autonomy to maintain a legal
system of their own choice and making, without any interference. They
went further to serve notice on to the other side: the institutions of the
formal policy, administration and adjudication. The message was clear
and simple: "We shall not tolerate any interference with our social
organization."

What made this miracle possible? For, it is nothing short of a miracle
for thousands of illiterate, poor, and depressed people to assert such a
unique right. The answer generally lies in their commitment to the
survival of the institution known as Lok Adalat [People's Court] which
has been functioning in and around Rangpur for well over the last
quarter century under the leadership of a stalwart Sarvodaya worker,
Harivallabh Parekh.[29]

Spontaneous, endogenous self-help organizations of the backward
classes represent an alternative to state-sponsored programs of protective
discrimination. They represent perhaps a movement away from a strategy
that emphasizes protective discrimination toward one founded on principles of compensatory justice. The emergent strategy would seek to
combine and reconcile state intervention with spontaneous self-help and
would use instruments of state law as well as those of peoples' law. The
emergence of such a strategy inevitably will witness a reconciliation of
a plurality of prevailing (and at times competing) ethical systems: those
underlying the traditional caste systems, the modern state-sponsored system of egalitarianism, the emerging ethical systems of self-help groups,
the systems underlying various subgroups in India's highly pluralistic

polity. The process will inevitably pose dilemmas for those who have devised, operate, or are beneficiaries of the state-sponsored system of protective discrimination. The resolution of these dilemmas might well prove decisive for the people of India in their quest for equality.

The Changing Configuration of Caste and Class

As asserted at the outset of this chapter, there has been a clear trend of increasing violence in caste relations in present-day India. Much of this violence, however, needs to be analyzed in terms of class struggle, rather than caste conflict. In the words of two dissenting members of the joint select committee of Parliament charged with a comprehensive revision of the law, the problems of caste discrimination were products of "feudal and semi-feudal relations in rural areas and the religious and ideological superstructure of bourgeois-landlord power structure in the country in general." In their view the problem could not be seriously addressed within the "capitalist path of development pursued by the bourgeois landlord state." Not surprisingly, they ended up recommending "radical land redistribution, spread of literacy and the guarantee of employment."[30] When the strategy of protective discrimination was first articulated in British India, there was indeed a very strong correlation between the ritual status of castes and the secular condition of their members. In India today, however, there is a growing discrepancy between caste and class variables.

The dissent and views outlined heretofore are useful in that they do seek to locate the problems of protective discrimination within the larger context of national-development strategy. The Indian concept of development has always claimed to emphasize several dimensions: political, economic, technological, and cultural. The development strategy adopted, however, has tended to be heavily influenced by shifting trends at the center, toward and away from centralization. The trend toward centralist modernization reached its zenith during Mrs. Indira Gandhi's emergency rule. Prime Minister Gandhi repeatedly asserted that she would secure disproportionately large benefits to the weaker sections of Indian society through centralized bureaucratic programs. Despite attempts, at times genuine, to redistribute resources, during her eleven years in office the position of the bottom third of Indian society deteriorated at a faster rate than it had previously. The trend toward decentralization reached its apex during the short-lived and largely ineffectual Janata regime. The national-plan document issued by the Janata government states:

Critical for the success of all redistributive laws, policies and programmes is that the poor be organized and made conscious of the

benefits intended for them. Organized tenants have to see that the ten-
ancy laws are implemented. Organizations of the landless have to see
that surplus lands are identified and distributed to them in accordance
with the law within five years. . . . The general lesson of the experience so far is that because of leakages in delivery systems and ineffective administration, rural programmes fail to improve the distribution
of income. The Planning Commission is proposing a massive shift of
resources in favor of rural areas with an in-built redistributive character
in almost every programme. But whether these larger resources will
have the desired equalizing effect will depend on the extent to which
the organized pressure of the beneficiaries counteracts the weaknesses
of the administration and the opposition of vested interests.

The record of the Janata government and the subsequent strongly voiced
sentiments of the Indian electorate, however, provided ample evidence
of the gap between promise and performance.

More recently, trends toward centralization have again begun to be
evident. These trends will undoubtedly influence significantly the balance
between strategies of protective discrimination and strategies of compensatory justice, and ultimately the very quest of the peoples of India for
equality.

State programs implemented through state institutions have enjoyed
their limited successes only regarding ritual aspects of discrimination by
sanctioning proscribed behavior and by providing incentives to induce
desired behavior. Even here, however, state action carries with it its own
constraints. In present-day India, ruthless enforcement of penal laws
proscribing untouchability would mean in effect ruthless erosion of the
existing power base. Not surprisingly, the police and courts are failing
in their roles as deployer, on behalf of the state, of the legitimate coercive
power that the state program not only sanctions but really commands and
needs if it is to be effective. Moreover, state instruments of redistribution
are increasingly degenerating into instruments of control. State programs
are also unable to assimilate and integrate tribal members of protected
castes without requiring a loss of tribal and cultural identity.

Increasingly in India today, the secular aspects of deprivation are not
aspects of caste as such but rather reflect the class characteristics of the
caste's members at any given point in time: their actual distribution of
occupations and related roles; their levels of literacy and education, wealth,
income, and debt; their health and living conditions; their individual and
collective social prestige; and their positions of political dominance or
dependence. The nonstate self-help movements described earlier seek to
address these secular attributes of deprivation. They provide a vehicle
for development without loss of tribal and cultural identity. The emergence of people's law and its institutions provide an alternative avenue

both for disadvantaged groups to secure rights, remedies, and redress, and for the deployment on behalf of the state of the legitimate coercive power that state institutions (police and courts) are failing to exercise effectively. The environment of state law within which self-help groups and movements operate does affect their capacity to redress secular aspects of deprivation. Laws prohibiting bonded labor or prescribing minimum wages have been invoked by organizations of agricultural labor. Self-help groups have also attempted to implement land-reform laws (such as tiller's-day statutes), debt-relief laws, and laws prohibiting alienation of Adivasi land. One must be realistic about the potential and limitations of such self-help groups. After all, these groups do operate within a larger political-economy context that may constrain their viability. Some self-help groups have lost their initial dynamism and meaning. Self-help movements in India have been, so far, essentially a rural phenomenon, although there are a few instances of mobilization among urban depressed classes. As for the most depressed groups (such as scavengers), the backwardness of the individual is often a reflection of the social backwardness of his group. There is some skepticism that self-reliant movements can contribute significantly to overall structural change. Despite all these caveats and limitations, however, self-reliant groups in India are playing important roles in alleviating deprivation. Not all such groups are antagonistic toward the power structure, and some (such as the Bhoomi Sena) have been very skillful in neutralizing bureaucratic opposition and even political opposition by constantly asserting that the group's activities are meant to assist and facilitate implementation of state programs. Some of these self-help groups have also been successful in establishing a network of supporting relationships with sympathetic bureaucrats, politicians, law-enforcement personnel, and judges.

During the last few years, five interrelated and alarming trends have emerged:

1. a decline of liberal values and, in particular, of the values of social equality among higher-caste Hindus;
2. an increase in the incidence of ritual discrimination on the basis of caste;[31]
3. an increase in the incidence of violence directed against scheduled castes;[32]
4. an increase in social tensions and violence between untouchables and other social classes that are categorized as scheduled castes;
5. a growing antireservation movement and the establishment of a national organization to fight against the concept and system of reservations.[33]

These trends force a reassessment of state policies of protective discrimination and of the very role of state programs to fight discrimination. State efforts to abolish ritual disabilities based on caste and to protect and realize civil rights for all remain less than satisfactory. An official study of the enforcement of the Protection of Civil Rights Act in the state of Tamil Nadu finds the incidence of offenses under the act to be "on a significant and growing scale." These offenses include denial of access to drinking-water facilities, stipulation of separate utensils and eating places in hotels, denial of entry to temples, and prevention of the use of *chappals* and shoulder cloths by scheduled-caste members. In certain panchayats, scheduled-caste members are made to remain standing while the meetings are in progress.[34] The study concludes that one of the factors that hamper the scheduled castes in asserting their basic civil rights is their continued economic dependence on the perpetrators of the social discrimination. This creates a particularly poignant dilemma because efforts on their part to break free from such economic dependence are met with violence and repression. Social tension between scheduled castes may have been an unintended consequence of the decision in 1980 to extend protective discrimination to a category of "socially and educationally backward castes or classes." At the top and bottom of the hierarchy, caste and class do tend to coincide. At levels in between, however, there is considerable divergence. In the process of competing for limited employment and educational opportunities made available by the system of reservation, it is inevitable that the less backward classes will tend to dominate and discriminate against the more backward classes. Nevertheless, reservation of educational and employment opportunities provides a vital avenue for social mobility, and criticism of the malfunctioning of such reservations systems is directed toward correcting such malfunctions. Such criticism is not intended to imply that the system of reservation of educational and employment opportunities should be abolished. The present wave of antireservation sentiment reflects increasing competition for limited opportunities; in such an environment of increasing competition and increasing scarcity, the reservation system becomes all the more important to the most deprived. The struggle is to ensure that such systems of redistribution do not degenerate into patronage systems that themselves perpetrate fresh inequalities.

Reservations with respect to political representation are another matter. There is growing dissatisfaction against such a system, even among the Harijan community. There is an increasing gulf between the scheduled-caste politician and his community,[35] and there remain grave doubts that the emerging Harijan elite will provide the leadership to enable the political reservations system genuinely to benefit the scheduled castes.[36] Nevertheless, the attainment of political power is a vital prerequisite for such groups to combat their deprivations effectively and attain true social and economic equality. In this respect self-help organizations may be the most likely vehicle through which such groups can develop desperately needed countervailing political power.

A new relationship between state and nonstate approaches to redressing inequality, along with a cooperative rather than confrontational relationship between participatory self-help organizations and centralized committed bureaucracy, seems essential if India's quest for equality is not to remain unfulfilled.

Notes

1. *Economic and Political Weekly,* 12 May 1979, p. 865.

2. Upendra Baxi, *Untouchability: Constitution, Law and Plan—an Examination of Some Socio-Legal Aspects,* (New Delhi 1979), p. 15. For a more recent statement by Home Minister Zail Singh, see *India Now* (January 1982).

3. *Economic and Political Weekly,* 9 September 1978, p. 1544.

4. Ibid.

5. Ibid.

6. Lloyd I. Rudolph and Susanne Hoebler Rudolph, *The Modernity of Tradition: Political Development in India* (Chicago 1967), p. 67.

7. See, for example, Harold Gould, "The Adaptive Functions of Caste in Contemporary Indian Society," *Asian Survey* 3 (September 1963), and Rajni Kothari, ed., *Caste in Indian Politics* (New Delhi 1970).

8. S. Natarajan, *A Century of Social Reform in India* (Bombay, 1962), at 144.

9. Above discussion drawn from Eleanor Zelliot, "Gandhi and Ambedkar—A Study in Leadership," in J. Michael Mahar, ed., *The Untouchables in Contemporary India* (Arizona 1972), p. 69, at 72.

10. Mahadeo Desai, *The Diary of Mahadeo Desai* (Ahmedabad, 1953), p. 301.

11. Zelliot, "Gandhi and Ambedkar," note 9 at 92.

12. See, for example, Eleanor Zelliot, "Bibliography on Untouchability," in M. Mahar, *Untouchables,* pp. 431–481, note, and Sachchidananda, *The Harijan Elite* (New Delhi 1977), pp. 205–210.

13. This rule enumerated in Balaji's case was further developed in Chitralekha's case; see *M.R. Balaji v. State of Mysore,* A.I.R. (1963), s.c. at 702, and *Chitralekha and State of Mysore,* A.I.R. (1964), s.c. at 1823.

14. Baxi, *Untouchability,* p. 1, n. 2.

15. See, for example, Andre Beteille, *Caste, Class and Power: Changing Patterns of Stratification in a Tanjore Village* (Bombay 1966).

16. Scarlett Epstein, *Economic Development and Social Change in India* (Manchester 1962).

17. *Economic and Political Weekly,* 24 September 1977, p. 1673.

18. In Khanjawal (not far from the country's capital, Delhi), for example, 120 acres of village grazing land were allotted for a five-year period to 120 low-caste families. High-caste landowners have formed an organization to fight this measure with force (for example, in October 1977 they destroyed the standing crops) through law (for example, they obtained a judgment from the Delhi High Court allowing them to retain the land as village-grazing land), and with political rallies (staged in front of the prime minister's residence and Parliament and protesting "governmental pampering of Harijans"). See *Economic and Political Weekly,* 3 February 1979, p. 184.

19. *Economic and Political Weekly,* 18 June 1977, p. 974. Similar incidents have occurred at Papri in Sasaram. See *Economic and Political Weekly,* 16 September 1978, p. 1580.

20. Baxi, *Untouchability,* p. 13, n. 2.

21. Ibid., p. 15.

22. The state of Maharashtra has, in fact, exercised such discretion and has appointed district-level vigilance committees to oversee the implementation of the law.

23. For a detailed account of the Bhoomi Sena movement, see N. Mehta, A. Rahman, G.V.S. deSilva, and P. Wignaraja, "Bhoomi Sena: A Struggle for People's Power," *Development Dialogue* 2 (1979). For an assessment of the movement, see A. Rahman, *Some Dimensions of People's Participation in the Bhoomi Sena Movement* (Geneva: UNRISD, 1981).

24. For a detailed account of the Chipko movement, see A. Mishra and S. Tripathi, *Chipko Movement: Uttarakhand Women's Bid to Save Forest Wealth* (New Delhi: Gandhi Peace Foundation, 1978), and Upendra Baxi, "Dialectics of Law and Direct Action," in *National Law Review,* 12 January 1981; 19 January 1981.

25. See Avadh Prashad, *Lok Adalat* (Sterling Publishers: 1977); and Upendra Baxi, "From Takrar to Karar: the Lok Adalat at Rangpur," *Journal of Constitutional and Parliamentary Studies* (1976):54–116. For an account of some of Rangpur's political linkages, see Upendra Baxi, "Popular Justice, Participatory Development and Power Politics: the *Lok Adalat* in Turmoil," unpublished, 1979.

26. A brief account of the Santhal movement is given in W. Haque, N. Mehta, A. Rahman, and P. Wignaraja, "Towards a Theory of Rural Development," *Development Dialogue* 2 (1977):25–27. See also *Economic and Political Weekly,* 10 January 1976, p. 37; 9 September 1978, p. 1544.

27. For a detailed account, see P.V. Paranjape, V. Kanhere, N. Sathe, S. Kulkarni, and S. Gothoskar, *Grass-Roots Self-Reliance in Shramik Sanghatana, Dhulia District, India,* ILO Working Paper, WEP 10/WP22 (1981).

28. *Economic and Political Weekly,* 1 September 1979, p. 1493.

29. Upendra Baxi, "Popular Justice," n. 26.

30. *Joint Committee on the Untouchability (Offenses) Amendment and Miscellaneous Provision Bill,* 1972, pp. xii–xiv (Lok Sabha Secretariat, 1974).

31. A survey conducted by the Union Home Ministry to examine the implementation of the Protection of Civil Rights Act in one state in India (Tamil Nadir) reports a "distinctly upward trend" in offenses under the act during the period 1975–1978. See *Economic and Political Weekly,* 1 December 1979, p. 1944.

32. In the state of Uttar Pradesh, for example, it is alleged that over 4,000 Harijans were recently killed. See *India News,* January 1982, p. 1.

33. I.P. Desai, "Gujarat Agitation in the Perspective of Social Change," unpublished (1981), p. 26, analyzes the recent antireservation agitation in the state of Gujarat.

34. See *India News* (January 1982).

35. C. Parvathamma, "The Case for Untouchables," *United Asia* 20:279–286, describes this frustration of scheduled castes with their own present leadership or lack thereof.

36. For a less pessimistic view of the potential of the Harijan elite, see Sachchidananda, *Harijan Elite,* n. 12.

4 Intercommunal Relations and Problems of Social-Economic Development: The Malaysian Dilemma

Viswanathan Selvaratnam

Because of its location, peninsular Malaysia (earlier known as the Malay Peninsula and later as West Malaysia), with an area of 51,000 square miles, has for many centuries been subject to the direct influence of diverse social and cultural forces from India, China, Indonesia, and the Middle East, and from the fifteenth century onward, predominantly from the West.[1] Before the introduction of indirect British rule in the latter part of the nineteenth century, the peninsula was divided into states. At the head of each of these states was a sultan, who protected his subjects, conducted the state's relations with other states, and in times of war organized its territorial defense. The state was divided into districts, each of which was headed by a chief. Despite the fact that the chiefs had to pay regular obeisance to the sultan, they enjoyed a great deal of autonomy in raising revenue and running the day-to-day affairs of their respective districts. The chief also administered justice within his district and had the right to demand free labor (*kerah*) from the peasantry (*rakyat*). This limited the sultan's real political control despite his ceremonial and social preeminence.

British rule worked far-reaching changes on this traditional Malay polity, however. Under the efficient and penetrating indirect rule of the British advisors and residents, the British established administrative structures that controlled law and order, administered justice, collected taxes, and built public works. This gradually eliminated the traditional administrative role and power of the feudal hierarchy except in those matters pertaining to Islam and Malay customary practices (*adat*).This helped the Malay rulers retain the traditional character of Malay society, particularly the ascriptive stratification and the deference that went along with it.

British hegemony also ushered the country into a dependent economy based on the production of raw materials for export, with foodstuffs and manufactured goods imported from the metropolitan centers. The main raw materials exported are rubber, timber, palm oil, tin, and crude petroleum, which together account for more than 70 percent of the value of peninsular Malaysia's exports. Until recently the ownership and control of this was predominantly in European hands.[2] The local Malay population, for various political and cultural reasons, either was not prepared to enter or was prevented from entering into these rapidly expanding export-oriented industries. Therefore, to man these export-oriented primary sectors, cheap Chinese and Indian immigrant laborers were brought in large numbers from the economically depressed areas of China and India, especially between the 1850s and 1920s, under a "new system of slavery."[3]

Thus a multiethnic society was created: the Malays, the Chinese, the Indians, and others, working in different jobs and cohabitating side by side in apparent harmony for over a century. Today the Malay peninsula has almost 11.84 million people. The Malays form 53.9 percent, the Chinese communities 34.9 percent, and the Indian and other communities (such as the Pakistanis, Ceylonese, Eurasians, and Europeans) 11.2 percent.[4] Although there were some cultural exchanges, in social reality there were major ethnic cleavages as each of these communities had its own distinct religion, language, educational system, customs, and habits, and still continues to maintain them.

Ethnic Differentiations under the Colonial System

The ethnic differences in Malaysian society were further accentuated by the political tactics deriving from the British policy of divide and rule.[5] The British not only encouraged the different communities to organize communally but also isolated them from one another culturally, economically, and politically. In other words, the policy was to keep the immigrant communities transient and alien. Thus an overall political consensus among the different ethnic groups was difficult to achieve, and cooperation was absent. Intercommunal conflicts and overt political consciousness and expression were contained by the strong law-and-order machinery operated by the colonial power.[6]

Communal heterogeneity was reinforced by considerable communal specialization in economic activity and by its related geographical isolation. For example, on the eve of independence only about 20 percent of the 4.2 million Malays lived in urban areas, where a sizable number of them were and are still conspicuous in the civil and administrative services and in the lower ranks of the public services such as the police and armed forces. The remaining Malays live in rural communities and are engaged in subsistence agriculture and related industries.[7] The 3 million Chinese were and still are in wholesale and retail trade, a sizable number as petty traders, artisans, wage laborers in the urban and rural sectors, vegetable farmers, and in recent years in the manufacturing and formal industrial sectors as well. The Indians, numbering a little over a million, were and still are largely wage laborers in the predominantly European-owned and managed rubber and oil-palm plantations; in the public-utility services, railways, and public-works departments; and as casual contract workers in the building industry. A small section of them are wholesale and retail traders, petty traders, and white-collar professionals and semiprofessionals in the public sector. The members of the smaller communities, such as the Ceylonese and Eurasians, are essentially white-collar workers in the towns. Of the former group, however, a sizable proportion availed themselves of the English education provided in the urban centers and thus managed to give their offspring a head start in entering into both professional and semiprofessional occupations in sizable numbers in relation to their population ratio in the total Malaysian population.

A congenial and efficient British political and administrative framework provided for the European (mainly British) private enterprise much of the infrastructure of a modern economy: railways, public utilities, agricultural-research stations, educational and health services. The early roads and railways were largely intended to serve the tin and rubber-plantation industries and the population associated with them, rather than the rural Malay population.[8] Under such favorable conditions, the European entrepreneurs inevitably dominated the ownership and control of plantation agriculture, the tin mines, the industries, and the numerous agency houses that still handle much of the region's export and import business. Wherever there was European economic interest, there was also economic expansion and income generation. The people other than the Europeans who benefited from this economic prosperity were the upper class of the Malay population and the Chinese, Indian, and other other communities who lived in the urban centers of the west- and east-coast states. The apparent Chinese control of commerce and trade in the Malaysian economy owes as much to their high degree of urbanization as to any special skills they might have brought with them, and to the social solidarity of the clan associations as well as the secret societies that took care of them from the day of their arrival in peninsular Malaysia.

Despite the fact that the British followed a pro-Malay policy toward the Malay rulers and their subjects, the bulk of the Malays, who are essentially rural and whose economic, social, and cultural activities are closely interwoven with the land, were largely neglected except for a series of legal enactments to protect them against the ''more rigorous economic drive of the other ethnic groups,'' especially the Chinese.[9] The British officials realized that otherwise the country would soon cease to be a country of the Malays and become, instead, another province of

China. Thus the Malay Reservations Enactments were passed by the respective legislative councils of the different states from 1913 to the beginning of World War II. The main aim of these enactments was, and still is, to protect the economic status of the Malays and to set aside certain areas of state land for alienation only to "natives of the soil."[10] It is undeniable that this piecemeal legislation did not raise the standard of living of the predominantly rural Malay population, but instead gave rise to the forbidding evils of economic isolation. The Malays were neither permitted to share in the predominantly European-owned and managed plantation and tin industries, nor encouraged to participate in the prosperity generated by these extractive industries. This prevented the formation of capitalist and working classes among the Malays. Instead, the official British policy was to maintain intact the feudal nature of Malay society. In order to further reinforce this, a Malay college known as the Eden of the East was established in 1905 to institutionalize a system of educational training for the Malay elite. The products of this institution were reserved administrative positions in the exclusively Malay Administrative Service (MAS); and a section of the rakyat who were given rudimentary education at primary schools in the Malay medium were admitted to occupy humble positions in the public services, as messenger boys, drivers, policemen, soldiers, and the like. The Malay Administrative Service later became the recruiting ground for the present Malay political elite. This so-called pro-Malay political, educational, and cultural policy of the British, however, benefited only the upper crust of the Malay population and left the bulk of the Malays in a state of relative economic deprivation.

One important phenomenon that resulted from this was that there was a close coincidence between ethnic differences, occupations, income distribution, and geographical location. Even as late as 1970 the agricultural sector had the greatest incidence of poverty, and the majority of those engaged in this sector were Malays (68 percent), compared with the Chinese (21 percent). In contrast, in the key sectors of the modern economy, which generated most of the wealth, the Chinese were over-represented (66 percent), whereas the Malays held only 26 percent. A big disparity in income existed between the traditional subsistence-agricultural sector and the rest of the economy in peninsular Malaysia. This continued to widen from about 1:2.5 in 1960 to more than 1:3 in the 1970s, despite the apparent success of the government's development program for small-scale agriculture.[11] It was not surprising that even as late as 1976 the incidence of poverty among Malays was 65 percent, among Indians 37 percent, and among Chinese 39 percent.[12] In other words, the dilemma of the continued widening of income disparity between the predominantly rural Malay community and the predominantly urban Chinese community continued, despite the pro-Malay policies formulated by the colonial and postcolonial states.

The Politics of Intercommunal Accommodation

In the early 1950s an alliance was formed by the marriage of convenience between the political parties representing the country's three major communities, namely the United Malay National Organization (UMNO) as the senior and dominant partner, together with the Malaysian Chinese Association (MCA) and the Malaysian Indian Congress (MIC) as junior partners in order of importance. It was this alliance that took the country through a peaceful transition to independence in August 1957, although the country was and continues to be an ethnically plural society.[13] It was important to realize that this coalition did not bring either the peasant-proletariat base or the middle classes of the different communities together, but instead was a coalition of the core of the business leadership of the MCA and the core of the professional intelligentsia of the MIC. Its main thrust was to cope with communal accommodation. This, as was seen earlier, was largely due to the development and politicization of the British colonial policy of divide and rule and its inevitable carry-over into the postcolonial period. As a result, one sees the development and continuance of marked and varied economic, political, and cultural differences and cleavages between the different ethnic groups and within the ethnic groups themselves. Even the rural peasantry in the countryside is a heterogeneous, undifferentiated mass. These obvious differences and a lack of overall political consensus among the different communal groups was one of the foremost dilemmas that the governing alliance led by Tunku Abdul Rahman faced, on the eve of independence and during subsequent years. Despite this and a number of outbreaks of communal violence since the end of World War II, however,[14] the studies dominated by metropolitan and metropolitan-trained scientific and value-free social scientists of the Third World,[15] who have consistently used race as a category for social analysis, have described peninsular Malaysia as a classic model of a viable democracy, with a united and harmonious multiethnic society to be envied and possibly emulated. For example, one U.S. academic concludes in his analysis:

> Malaysia's most significant achievement is in racial cooperation. Combining communal parties into an Alliance has worked effectively. A similar compromise on the explosive issue of national language has avoided the violence that occurs in many countries. Malaysia seems to have discovered a way of permitting three ancient cultures to continue

their great traditions but to work together in harmony. It is this that
makes Malaysia so significant to the world.[16]

On 10 May 1969, in the country's third parliamentary and state
elections since independence, the ruling Alliance party suffered setbacks
to its intracommunal electoral arrangements for the first time. In this
third election the Alliance was returned with a total of 66 of the 104
parliamentary seats in peninsular Malaysia, whereas in the 1959 and 1964
elections it had won 74 and 89 seats, respectively.[17]

Despite these setbacks, the Alliance secured a majority in the federal
Parliament, although it did not have the crucial two-thirds majority needed
to bring about constitutional amendments or changes. In the state elections, too, the ruling party for the first time lost control of the northern
state of Penang to the more recently formed Gerakan Rakyat Malaysia
(Malaysian People's Movement, popularly known as Gerakan); in Perak,
another northern state, it won only nineteen out of the forty seats; and
in the important central state of Selangor, it won fourteen out of twenty-
eight seats. In both these states it became a possibility that the predominantly non-Malay opposition parties would dominate the government.

The Islamic-oriented and Malay-dominated right-wing Pan-Malayan
Islamic Party (PMIP), now known as Partai Islam Se Malaysia (PAS),
retained the predominantly Malay-dominated east-coast state of Kelan-
tan. In addition, PAS made considerable inroads in Malay-dominated
rural constituencies of the northern states of Perak, Kedah, and Perlis,
and in the eastern states of Trengganu and Pahang.

In the urban areas the boycott of the elections by the opposition left-
wing Labour party, and a common election pact solely for the purpose
of vote catching between the opposition parties, gave considerable gains
to the racially oriented and Chinese-dominated Democratic Action party
(DAP) and Peoples Progressive party (PPP), and to the multiracial Gerakan. These opposition parties themselves were surprised at their election
success. The jubilant opposition supporters celebrated their electoral success jointly with massive parades. During some of these victory parades
on 11 and 12 May, in the Malaysian capital, Kuala Lumpur, bands of
overjubilant youthful supporters booed and jeered at Malays, using of-
fensive language against them and asking them to return to the *kampongs*
(villages). The election setbacks suffered by the Alliance, especially by
the MCA, and the opposition victory parades were interpreted by the
Malay elite leadership—especially by the so-called ultra section of the
UMNO—as a considerable weakening of their own political power and
that of Malays generally in favor of non-Malays, namely the Chinese.
The ruling elite had always emphasized to the Malay and non-Malay
population at large that only through Malay political leadership and spe-

cial position could general Malay economic deprivation ultimately be ended in order for them to cope with the other races economically.[18]

On 13 May a section of the ultra group of the UMNO, led by the then UMNO youth leader and former chief minister of Selangor, Dato Haji Harun Idris, organized counter victory parades with UMNO supporters from all over the state.[19] These demonstrations in Kuala Lumpur disintegrated for the first time into communal violence of an unprecedented nature between Malays and Chinese. Subsequently, on 28 June, Malay violence was directed toward Indians in Sentul.[20] Although violence did not spread throughout the country, the conflict broadened and became a straightforward Malay versus non-Malay confrontation throughout the country. In other words, racial polarization became the order of the day.

Thus the events of May 1969 exposed the superficiality of the intercommunal harmony and national solidarity that was perceived to exist, and detonated the long-standing, covert conflict between the Malay and non-Malay communities. Second, within UMNO in particular, they considerably weakened the Tunku Abdul Rahman–led moderate section of the traditional and conservative political elite, which had been ruling the country since independence in August 1957 without any serious political crisis or challenge. Third, they revealed that there was considerable dissatisfaction in the country, on the part of both the bulk of the Malay peasants and the Malay and non-Malay proletariat, with the policies and especially the economic programs of the ruling order.[21] Fourth, it transforms the diverse and disoriented masses of the different culturally heterogeneous categories into rigid communal blocks; thus, instead of intercommunal integration, it catalyzed false consciousness, communal polarization, and aggravated tensions. This has helped to maintain and intensify cultural and political pluralism. Finally, the conflict united the different groups, especially the Malays and later the Chinese and Indians, into expressing actively their resentment of the existing order. Malay extremists in particular were disillusioned with Tunku's leadership and expressed a strong desire for a change in leadership. This led to considerable political realignment and finally to an asymmetrical transformation of the Malaysian social order, with the Malay ruling elite under the leadership of the then deputy and former prime minister, the late Tun Abdul Razak, as the paramount head.

As a result of the serious nature of the May violence in Kuala Lumpur, and to avoid violence engulfing the entire country, the government proclaimed a state of emergency on 14 May 1969, and imposed a twenty-four-hour curfew throughout the country.[22] An eight-man National Operation Council (NOC) was formed under the directorship of the late Tun Abdul Razak.[23] It was to carry out "the exercise of the executive authority of Malaysia.''[24] The NOC suspended parliamentary democracy. The late Tun Dr Ismail, a member of the NOC and subsequently deputy prime minister and minister of home affairs, said: ''[D]emocracy is dead in this country. It died in the hands of the opposition parties who triggered off the events leading to this violence.'' Thus Malaysia, which was considered by Western observers, investors, and social scientists to be a relatively stable and successful multiracial parliamentary democratic political system, suddenly lost this image after more than a decade. Parliamentary rule was restored in February 1971, however, in the form of a so-called guided democracy.

The Problems of National Identity in a Pluralistic Society

The pertinent question to pose at this juncture, therefore, is: What were the central issues of conflict that became significant since the transfer of power by the British to the local elite, especially in the light of the growth of Malaysian, and in particular Malay, nationalism and the development of the aspirations of the large and youthful Malaysian population (both Malay and non-Malay) who were entering into the labor market? Since independence, political leaders, foreign observers, and academic pundits asserted that the dilemma that faced the country was the marked coincidence of social divergences with economic differences between the Malay and non-Malay population. This, they determined, was the primary reason that conflict existed and continues to exist. They argued that the only significant way to face this dilemma was to compensate for this imbalance through a political process—that is, to weigh political power in favor of the indigenous population from whom the British had wrested political power, and guard jealously the rights of the Malays to have priority in the politics of their country until the economic disparities between the Malay and non-Malay population are redressed—in other words, until a higher condition of well-being is achieved by the Malays.

UMNO pointed out to its non-Malay partners in the Alliance that if the parliamentary process was to work satisfactorily in favor of the Alliance, then it was faced with a dilemma—namely, it had to meet the primary aspirations of Malay political, economic, and cultural demands (for the Malay voters were dominant and the constituencies were weighted in favor of rural Malays) or else there would be a danger of the predominantly rural Malay voting population consolidating political power in the hands of the PAS. This in turn would lead to their political and cultural hegemony over the country's non-Malay population. The PAS has always accused the UMNO leadership of betraying Malay political, economic, and—most important—Malay cultural values to the non-Malay immigrant races and especially to the Chinese.

At the same time, the MCA too was faced with a dilemma. The MCA expressed the view within Alliance circles, that if it wanted to retain its own power base as it had done in the 1955, 1959, and 1964 elections in the majority of the predominantly Chinese-dominated urban constituencies, then it would have to work for Chinese political and economic rights and the general betterment of the Chinese community. Otherwise, the more vociferous Chinese communal parties such as the PPP and the DAP and the more radical parties like the Socialist Front (coalition of the Malay-based Partai Rakyat and the Labour party) would take the initiative. It thus appeared that the Alliance leadership, in order to retain its political power, had consciously or unconsciously divorced itself from the dilemmas of the political and economic realities faced by the population at large. The MCA leaders in particular, in order to protect and enhance their personal economic interests, channeled most of their efforts toward the dilemma of merely minimizing racial conflict and maintaining racial harmony through a process of asymmetrical political patronage, artificial consensus, and superficial accommodation, and until 1969 Tunku Abdul Rahman was at the apex of this asymmetrical patronage system. The Alliance government's efforts to build a united Malaysian nation depended on the premise that intracommunal unity had to be consolidated to achieve a wider unity of all Malaysians. This considerably inhibited the development of intercommunal ties and linkages at the base of the population however; all that was protected and safeguarded were the interests and positions of a small minority, comprising the elites of the ruling class and the foreign interests.

On the other hand, the Alliance and UMNO in particular drove home the viewpoint that in order to achieve a single Malaysian nation, a linguistic distinctiveness and a unified Malaysian-oriented dynamic system of education would be necessary.[25] This could only be achieved if Malay, which has been the lingua franca of the country and the region, should become in due course the sole official language. This should be reinforced with national schools that would have a common syllabus and a uniform system of education, with Malay and English as compulsory subjects. Instruction in the language of the other communities would be made available wherever there was a demand for it by more than fifteen pupils. Chinese and Tamil primary schools were to continue to exist, but in these schools both Malay and English would be compulsory subjects. At the secondary-school level, only national schools, in which either Malay or English would be the medium of instruction, were to be made available to all races. The recommendations of the report regarded a proficiency in Malay as a prerequisite for entry into secondary schools, for the award of scholarships, and for entry into the civil service. These policies were formulated by the Razak Report of 1956, formed the basis of the National Education Bill of 1957, and were gradually implemented.[26] Under the British, however, different communities had been given the right to determine the form of education their children should receive; this policy had reinforced the existing divisions among the different ethnic groups.

The non-Malays protested that the language and education policy as enunciated in the Razak Report was a curb not only on their communal aspirations but also on their fundamental rights. They held the view that it would not only handicap them but would give the Malays an undue advantage over them in avenues of employment, especially in the public sector. A large section of the Chinese community in particular considered this (education) policy anti-Chinese and claimed that it "has sounded the death-knell of the Chinese language and will result in Chinese being relegated to a second class status."[27] An editorial in *The Straits Times* in 1956 pointed out that although the Razak plan had been adopted unanimously by the legislature, it was being challenged by a large section of the Chinese community.[28]

Whereas the non-Malays agitated for the adoption of multilingualism, whereby Chinese and Tamil would be accorded official status, as in Singapore (where English, Malay, Chinese, and Tamil are the official languages), the Malays protested that the government was not taking enough steps to implement Malay as the country's sole language, as had been stipulated in the 1957 federal constitution. The Malays in UMNO were of the view that they had agreed to accept non-Malays as citizens only on the understanding that the non-Malays would accept Malay as the national and sole official language of the country, and also accord the Malays special privileges in the field of employment and economic activity, as laid down in Article 153 of the constitution.

The main champions of the Malay language were and are largely the rural-based Malay schoolteachers (who have tremendous influence over many rural branches of UMNO), the Malay Language Society of the University of Malaya, and GAPENA (the national writers' association). Teachers expressed their dissatisfaction with the implementation of the language policy through their Federation of Malay School Teachers' Association (FMSTA) and subsequently through the Barisan Bertindak Bahasa Kebangsaan (National Language Action Front, popularly known as NLAF), which is composed of members from FMSTA, the University of Malaya's Malay Language Society, GAPENA, and a number of UMNO members (including some Alliance parliamentarians). In addition, the PAS had always criticized the slow implementation of the national language policy by the government and the continued importance given to

English as a sellout of the Malays to non-Malays and as a further disadvantage imposed on the Malay population, who continued to be the economically backward group, albeit in their own country.

Between September 1963 and August 1966, Malaysia was in confrontation with Indonesia. This overshadowed many domestic issues, including that of language, in the 1964 general election; therefore, the Alliance, as expected, was returned to power with overwhelming majorities. The language issue reemerged as a crucial issue in West Malaysian domestic politics, however, when in August 1967 steps were taken to make Malay the sole official language. By this time there was a considerable consensus among Alliance leaders that Malay should be accorded the status of sole official language; but there was also a good deal of opposition from some of the constituent bodies of the Alliance, especially in the branches of the MCA. Toward the end of 1966 an extremist faction developed within the MCA that endeavored to influence the party to agitate for official status for the Chinese language. In fact, in the Penang branch of the MCA in October 1966, a resolution was passed "that Chinese should be respected and accepted as a language for official and extensive use throughout the country."[29] This resolution was rejected by the MCA's Central Working Committee, which instead "pledged its support for the more liberal use of Chinese language in selected fields and in Government notices, forms and so on."[30]

The first prime minister of the country, Tunku 'Abdul Rahman, appreciated the sensitivity of the language issue and decided to effect a pragmatic solution to the problem that would satisfy both the Malay and the non-Malay population. As a result, the 1967 Language Act was introduced, which made Malay the sole official language except in certain departments.[31] For example, it allowed the continued use of English in court proceedings, in parliament, and in state legislatures with the Speaker's approval.[32] It also allowed English to be used in "any translations of official documents or communications in the language of any other community in the Federation for such purposes as may be deemed necessary in the public interest."[33] The Yang di-Pertuan Agong (King) was vested with powers to "permit the continued use of English language for such official purpose as may be deemed fit."[34]

With this enactment, despite the qualifications, the position of Malay as the official language was considerably improved. Malay was used extensively by the government for correspondence with both business houses and other private institutions. Steps were also taken to extend the use of Malay as the medium of instruction in English-medium primary schools to teach music, arts and crafts, physical education, and local history.

Opposition to the act was voiced both by the Malay and the non-

Malay sections of the population. The late D.R. Seenivasagam,[35] the leader of the then Chinese-dominated opposition PPP, said in Parliament that the bill was a "betrayal of the four million non-Malays in this country."[36] The other opposition parties, such as the DAP and the United Democratic Party, held similar views that the country's policies should reflect a "Malaysian Malaysia" character. On the other hand, Malays were divided on the issue. The more liberal Malays viewed the act as a rational and sensible solution to the problem. The ultras, however, represented by the NALF, strongly objected, not so much to Chinese and Tamil translations being allowed whenever they were necessary, but to the continued use of English as specified in the Language Act. They wished to see the immediate enforcement of Malay as the sole official language of the country. Therefore, until 1969 the language issue remained one of the most sensitive areas of intercommunal relations in the country.

Citizenship and the Non-Malay Population

In matters of citizenship, all Malays and the subjects of the Malay rulers were by law deemed to be citizens of the country. On the other hand, non-Malays, even those born in a Malay state, had to apply for citizenship. Thus large sections of the Chinese and Indian communities who had been born in Malaysia and had lived there for at least a generation realized that they were not automatically citizens. They had to acquire citizenship; if they did not do so, they would ultimately face discrimination, not only in employment and education but, more important, politically. They would not have the political power necessary to control and protect their vast economic resources and the vital economic activity that accompanies them. Therefore:

> by 1952 the need to give the non-Malay communities a permanent Malayan identity had become clear beyond question. This meant that a Malayan community had to be created, embracing Malays and non-Malays alike, and identifiable by a similarity and unity more deep-rooted than provided by the mere presence of a common legal classification. Common citizenship is admittedly a vital prerequisite for the emergence of such a unity. . . . [37]

On the other hand, the Malays held the view that citizenship qualifications for non-Malays should not be overliberalized. This was due to two basic fears:

Firstly, they will have very strong doubts regarding the professed loyalty of the non-Malay communities; for this reason they consider liberalization to be a political risk of the first magnitude. Secondly, they realized that since the non-Malays are now admitted to citizenship on a large scale, their own community as a matter of course will have to relinquish gradually *even* the *minimum* privileges which it has hitherto enjoyed.[38]

Thus from the beginning the Malays, through the UMNO, have tended to make citizenship qualifications for non-Malays very complex and restrictive, even more so than the provisions of the Malayan Union Scheme.[39] After 1948 the UMNO was able to bring significant changes in the granting of citizenship to non-Malays born in West Malaysia, who were now deemed to be eligible for citizenship only if both their parents were born in the country and if the applicants had lived there for fifteen years continuously. Non-Malays, particularly the Chinese who were unable to return to China after 1945, found the restricted qualifications for federal citizenship a major obstacle.[40] In 1952, however, the Malays were persuaded to compromise on new citizenship laws. Accordingly, a new federal ordinance and the nine Malay States Nationality Enactments in the respective Malay states were introduced. Under this ordinance and these state enactments, non-Malays were by law eligible to become subjects of one of the sultans if they were born in one of the states and if additionally one of their parents had been born in the country and had completed a period of fifteen years' residence. This enabled a large section of the second-generation non-Malays to become citizens. It also enabled non-Malays who were born outside the country to acquire citizenship by naturalization, if the applicant had resided in the country for a total period of ten out of the twelve preceding years, including the two years immediately preceding the date of application, and was reasonably proficient in Malay or English. When the ordinance and enactments came into force, it was agreed to relax the language qualification for a period of five years whenever it was felt that an applicant, in the opinion of the Language Board, had not had a reasonable opportunity to learn Malay or English but was otherwise a suitable person for registration as a subject of a ruler.[41]

Independence brought a further modification in citizenship laws. The constitution divided citizenship acquisition into three categories—citizenship by operation of law, citizenship by registration, and citizenship by naturalization. As a result, citizenship was automatically conferred on anyone born in the country after Merdeka Day (Independence Day, 31 August 1957) if one of his or her parents was a permanent resident of the country. Under the registration clauses a woman married to a citizen could acquire citizenship if she had resided in the country throughout the two years preceding the date of application, provided the marriage was subsisting and registered, and she was of good character. An individual over eighteen years of age born in the country before Merdeka Day was entitled to be registered as a citizen if he or she demonstrated residence in the country for an aggregate period of five years during the seven years immediately preceding the application, and showed that he or she intended to make the country his or her permanent home, that he or she was of good character, and that he or she had an elementary knowledge of Malay. For one year after Merdeka Day, however, the requirement of passing the elementary Malay-language test was dispensed with.

Citizenship by naturalization was chiefly designed for those who were born outside the country but chose to make Malaysia their home. Many Chinese and Indians fell into this category, and they were required to show that they had resided in the country for an aggregate of ten out of the twelve years immediately preceding the application, that they intended to make Malaysia their permanent home, that they were of good character, and that they had an adequate knowledge of Malay. These liberal citizenship provisions to some extent appeased the non-Malays temporarily.

Subsequent amendments to the citizenship laws, however, in 1962, 1965, and 1966, have been directed toward making citizenship harder to acquire and easier to lose.[42] In addition, they have enlarged the powers of executive authorities—that is, of the ministers—and widened the scope of their discretion in determining matters of citizenship. These laws have further aggravated non-Malay grievances and on several occasions threatened the fragile marriage of convenience of the Alliance.

The Ethnic Dimension of Inequality

One of the most important pieces of legislation that the UMNO was able to retain in the 1957 constitution in favor of the Malay community is Article 153 of the constitution. The British, however, had always emphasized the special position of the Malays, and this was provided for in the 1948 Federation of Malaya agreement. Before this legislation became incorporated in the 1957 constitution, Tun Tan Siew Sin, the leader of the MCA, said:

> In the first place, the principle of the special position of the Malays has already been embodied in the Federation of Malays Agreement [the Agreement of 1948, which was in operation until 1957]. The Malays

therefore cannot be expected to give up what they already have in the same way that they do not expect the other communities to give up their existing rights. Far more important, however, is the indisputable fact that as a race the Malays are economically backward and well behind the other races in this field. . . . An economically depressed Malay community in a prosperous Malaya will not mean a peaceful Malaya. An economically depressed Malay community will never be able to achieve the desired degree of cooperation with the substantially more prosperous non-Malay communities.[43]

Article 153, while protecting the legitimate interests of the other ethnic groups in the country, not only safeguards the special position of the Malays but provides special remedies to ensure for Malays the reservation of such proportion as may be deemed reasonable of positions in the public service, scholarships, exhibitions, and other similar educational or training privileges. This also applies to permits or licences for the operation of any trade or business.[44] It was also decreed that at least 50 percent of the land in each state be held under Malay ownership perpetually. This legislation has been included, say the Alliance leaders, to enable the Malays to catch up with the non-Malays, particularly the Chinese, who had had a head start during the colonial period. This piece of legislation cannot be amended or abolished by Parliament without the consent of the Yang di-Pertuan Agong.[45]

To remove inequality of opportunity and raise the standard of living of the predominantly rural-based Malay population to the level of other communities, the government designed a national economic program with employment-generating policies within the framework of a laissez-faire free-market economy. The Second Five-Year Plan, 1961–1965, and subsequent plans gave particular emphasis to the development of rural areas.[46] Therefore, these areas are subject to large development schemes under the direction of the Ministry of National and Rural Development.[47] Under the guidance of this ministry, the Federal Land Development Authority (FELDA) had been opening up new land-settlement schemes. In addition, the respective state governments had been developing fringe alienation land schemes. The main aim of these schemes is to make land available to deserving and suitably qualified farmers who are operating uneconomic units and to others who are landless.[48] In addition, Malays in both rural and urban areas, in order that they might catch up with the relatively better off non-Malays, were and are still given special privileges in certain types of trade, businesses, and occupations. In order to promote Malay participation in commerce and industry, a specific organization known as Majlis Amanah Rakyat (MARA) was set up.[49] With regard to recruitment to the Malaysian civil and foreign service, the policy of 4 to 1 is applied; that is, for every four Malays employed, one non-Malay would become eligible for appointment. Although this precise ratio does not apply to other services, the government does give preference to Malays, especially in the technical and professional fields, in order to redress the historic imbalance operating against the Malays.

The privileges for Malays established by legislation have been one of the main sources of contention between the Malay and non-Malay communities. The marked neglect of the Malay rural population during the period of colonial rule and the rise of compradore capitalism among certain sections of non-Malays, especially the Chinese, has led the Malays to believe in the generalization that non-Malays, especially the Chinese, are wealthy and Malays poor.[50] Therefore, the problem of poverty has been treated, especially prior to the Second Malaysian Plan, as though it were exclusively a Malay problem. In addition, it was popularly believed by the Malays that the Chinese, because of their dominance as middlemen, exploit the rural Malay population by manipulating commodity prices to their own advantage.[51] The dilemma was that resentment was directed against all Chinese, regardless of whether they were rich or poor, rather than against those Europeans and Chinese who do own, control, and exploit the economy to their continuous advantage.

The opposition political parties—particularly the former Labour party, the predominantly Malay Parti Socialis Rakyat, and other non-Malay parties—though agreeing that major priority must be given to the elimination of Malay rural poverty, view the problem of poverty and economic backwardness as a class problem, not an exclusively ethnic one. The left has always pointed out that the invisible capitalist mode of production dominated by the British and other foreign interests in collaboration with local Chinese capitalists, and accompanied by a feudal mode of production in rural areas, has been the greatest obstacle to economic redress of the bulk of the rural Malay population. Leftists also believe that the ruling party's rural-development policies have benefited the rich peasants at the expense of the poor peasants. In addition, these parties have pointed out that the ethnocentric economic policies established under the special-privilege clause have not brought any real economic benefits to the Malay rakyat at large over the past two or more decades, but instead have increased, and continue to increase, the wealth of a closed circle of upper-class Malays in both urban and rural areas.[52] In addition, the policy has created a small class of the newly rich and a class of privileged and powerful bureaucrats and technocrats. What has happened is in effect the creation and perpetuation of a clientele social class of local bourgeois, bureacratic, and technocratic elite, with local and foreign capitalist interest.

The Impact of Socioeconomic Policies on Ethnic Conflict

Rural areas have benefited by the provision of infrastructural amenities such as bridges, water supplies, irrigation canals, community halls and mosques, health services, and the like; but there has been no significant change in the economic well-being of the ordinary Malay peasant vis-à-vis his urban counterpart who is a bureaucrat or technocrat.[53] For example, Ungku Aziz points out "that these schemes are good in themselves is absolutely 'undeniable.' However, without other steps, they may bring about further increases in inequality inside the rural areas."[54] The great majority of these peasants are dominated and exploited by a relatively small class of large landowners. In addition, the land-development schemes, particularly before 1970, have not been rapid enough to meet the demand of a large section of the landless Malay population. In 1967, out of the total of 5,459 applicants interviewed (the land schemes are multiethnic but predominantly Malay), the FELDA was able to grant land to only 1,670 families.[55] Up to 1967 the various land-development schemes of FELDA were able to resettle only 12,390 families on a total acreage of 201,651 acres, although according to the First Malaysia Plan, the target was to settle 22,000 families by the end of 1970.[56] Those peasants fortunate to obtain a place in one of the FELDA schemes have been saddled with a loan repayment ranging from M$15,000 to M$25,000.[57]

As mentioned earlier, the dilemma was that the ruling elite, although it perceived the economic realities and contradictions facing the mass of the population, was unable to design the right type of development strategies to help solve the economic disparities facing the Malaysian population at large.[58] Of course, in relation to other Third World Southeast Asian countries, Malaysia has achieved a substantial growth ratio and has one of the highest per capita gross national products (GNPs). As indicated earlier, however, the distribution of the gains from this growth has been lopsided. A high population growth of more than 3 percent per annum during the 1960s has not only depressed per capita living standards but also diverted government expenditure into unproductive uses. At the same time it has substantially increased the numbers moving into the labor market. At the beginning of the 1960s unemployment was 6 percent, but it increased to 8 percent by the time of the election in 1969.[59]

In the five big urban centers, unemployment became acute, with levels double the national average. There was also a considerable amount of underemployment in both rural and urban areas. Although the country did embark on a formalized industrial program involving foreign and local collaboration, the employment growth rate was only 2.6 percent

per annum; therefore, the surplus labor force was far greater than that
which the capital-intensive industrial sector could absorb. There has been
and still is considerable unemployment, particularly among youths—the
school leavers and the dropouts—in both rural and urban areas.[60]

The laissez-faire economic policies, with liberal tax concessions and
benefits to foreign investors, that were a part of the government's in-
dustrial-development policies, in effect protected and advanced certain
class interests. Some of the income gains made flowed out as profits,
but whatever remained was unevenly distributed. According to Bhanoji
Rao, the increase in per capita gross national income at constant prices
was estimated to be only 2.6 percent per annum between 1957 and 1972.
This is a very slight improvement over the period 1947–1958, when the
increase was 2.3 percent per annum.[61] The economic well-being of the
urban proletariat did not improve because of the low wages. On the other
hand, the benefits of economic development and growth were concentrated in the high-income groups in both rural and urban areas.[62] The
government failed to realize that growth is not necessarily accompanied
by an equitable distribution of the gains. Therefore, in the 1969 elections
all these crucial political, economic, and cultural issues were reexamined
in both Malay and non-Malay communities. These debates were further
vitalized by the participation of the People's Action Party (PAP) of Singapore, for a brief two-year period, in the politics of the peninsula.
During this period the PAP leadership emphasized that Malaysia was for
all Malaysians regardless of race and that those who subscribed to this
concept should openly declare their loyalty to it. This appealed particularly to the younger generation of non-Malays, who could not compre-
hend the discrimination against them, particularly in employment, vis-à-
vis the Malays. According to R.K. Vasil, during this period "the PAP
succeeded in awakening and articulating the entire non-Malay communities to a degree that the entire non-Malay opposition had failed to
achieve over a much longer period of its existence and efforts."[63] This
alarmed the Malays as well. Questions of income disparities, lack of
employment and economic opportunities for the growing young Malay
and non-Malay population, political and cultural insecurity among non-
Malays, and the Malay community's fear of an ascendancy of non-Malay
political power came to the forefront in the election campaigns. This
contributed to the Alliance's setbacks in the 1969 elections and the subsequent intercommunal conflict.

The aftermath of the elections of 13 May 1969 was the serious and
widespread disenchantment of the Malays with Tunku Abdul Rahman's
leadership of the Alliance and the UMNO in particular. There was there-

fore a sudden proliferation of unstructured Malay racial sentiments, articulated by individuals or groups of so-called young Turks drawn from Malay intellectual, bureaucratic, and student circles. These groups attributed the UMNO's election setbacks to the PAS, and the Chinese and Indian electorate's rejection of the MCA and the MIC in support of chauvinistic parties like the DAP and the PPP, as an unprecedented threat to Malay political dominance and as a Malay dilemma. To Dato Seri Dr. Mahathir, the present prime minister of the country:

> the Malays seem to be teetering between the desire to assert their rights and arrogate to themselves what they consider to be theirs, and the overwhelming desire to be polite, courteous and thoughtful of the rights and demands of others. Deep within them there is a conviction that no matter what they decide to do, things will continue to slip from their control, that slowly but surely they are becoming the dispossessed in their own land.[64]

In the light of this, they made a number of demands. These included a call for the resignation of the Tunku—chief architect of Malaysian independence and the communal-political framework of the Alliance, and undisputed father of the nation—as leader of UMNO and prime minister of the country.[65] In addition, they wanted UMNO to reject the existing Alliance framework and parliamentary democracy; they held the view that the country should continue to be ruled by the Malay-dominated NOC.

Later, a more moderate group of intellectuals under the leadership of Inche Senu bin Abdul Rahman, the secretary-general of UMNO, brought out a book called *Revolusi Mental* in which they presented the Malay personality as responsible for the economic backwardness of the community.[66] The book is a self-critical reappraisal of Malay economic ethics in contrast to those of the Chinese. Chinese success is attributed to Chinese self-reliance, diligence, and acquisitive drive; the Malay psychology is presented as lacking in these qualities. In addition, the book asserts, Malays have certain misconceptions of religious beliefs and are easily contented. This leads to a lack of persistent effort in work and to dependency on others, chiefly on government agencies. The book states that the Malay's economic dilemma is due not to the existing exploitative social and economic structure, but to his lack of the rationality and modernity that are vital to economic advancement. Thus progress could be achieved only through a revolution in mental attitudes, leading in turn toward economic advancement through self-reliance.[67] In other words, the Malays would have to change from a culture-oriented to an economic-oriented society.

Rukunegara and the New Policy Framework

The May conflict and the events that followed undoubtedly helped to influence a change in the existing order; and the Malay ruling elite under the leadership of Tun Abdul Razak, Tun Ismail, Tan Sri Ghazali Shafi, and Dato Hussein Onn steered through the crisis without any further communal upheavals and established a new political order. The new ruling group had to take stock of these various ethical issues and views and restore national unity through the democratic process. In addition, the leadership was anxious to restore the parliamentary image of the country and wanted to return it to the pre-May-1969 status quo. In its view, this would reverse the setbacks to foreign investment that occurred after the May 1969 events and would also attract much-needed foreign investment to boost economic growth and employment.[68] This foreign capital would not be forthcoming in a divided society with acute political instability. The leaders looked to the newly created Department of National Unity, which was advised by foreign social scientists, to study the communal tension in depth and devise a set of strategies to deal with it.[69] These strategies were to prove effective; they regulated the conflict by lowering the rate of political participation; thus, by shifting power away from the political process and institutionalizing the more important aspects of the Malaysian political system in a strong and efficient bureaucracy,[70] they sought to make them independent of the parliamentary political process.[71] The wisdom of this is that in a multiethnic society active politicking on sensitive issues will unduly exacerbate racial tensions and hostility. Therefore, communal conflict could be minimized by enacting laws to prevent people from making provocative speeches about sensitive issues.

Tan Sri Ghazali Shafi, who has been minister with special functions, minister of home affairs, and currently minister of foreign affairs, stated in a speech that, for national survival, national harmony, unity, and progress, racial sensitivities must never again be trampled on by the different ethnic groups.[72] He stressed that the major reason for the riots of 13 May was the flouting of the gentlemen's agreement between the Malays and the non-Malays, especially the Chinese, when independence was achieved. Under this agreement the Chinese were given citizenship; in return it was agreed that the Malays should retain and safeguard their special position and maintain the Malay-Muslim character of the country. This tacit agreement was embodied in the view that the UMNO always asserted itself as the senior and dominant partner of the Alliance, whereas the MCA and the MIC played a secondary role. In the elections the Chinese-dominated opposition parties had challenged the Malay position, and this had infuriated the Malays.[73] Hence the Malay elite held the view that the entire base of the politics of the country had to be revamped. From 1970 a program of action began to be executed by the NOC.

The Rukunegara (rukun: a principle or basis; negara: nation) was proclaimed by the Yang Di-Pertuan Agong in the name of God on 13 August 1971 and embodied a number of crucial aims and principles to guide Malaysia toward national unity. The emphasis was that ''our nation, Malaysia, being dedicated to achieving a greater unity of all her peoples; to maintaining a democratic way of life; to creating a just society in which the wealth of the nation shall be equitably shared; to ensuring a liberal approach to her rich and diverse cultural traditions; to building a progressive society, shall be oriented to modern science and technology.'' Every Malaysian's pledge is to achieve these ends, and in this they should be guided by the five principles—namely, ''Belief in God; loyalty to the King and Country; Upholding of the Constitution; Rule of Law; and Good Behaviour and Morality.'' The Rukunegara was considered by the ruling elite to reflect the predominant trend in the political and philosophical thinking of the Malaysian nation.[74]

The new minister for education, Datuk Abdul Rahman (later chief minister of Sarawak and currently the Yang Di-Pertua Negeri Sarawak), spelled out a new educational policy. From January 1970 a timetable was specified for the conversion of all English-medium schools to national schools, with Malay as the sole medium of instruction for all subjects and with English as a compulsory second language. This process was to be extended gradually to university levels by 1982. Malay was also made the sole official language, as entrenched in Article 152 of the constitution. This phasing in of Bahasa Malaysia (Malay) as the medium of instruction was considered by the late Tun Razak as the vital thrust to strengthen national unity. In the 1973 Merdeka celebration speech, Tun Razak emphasized that the basis of Malaysian culture will be the indigenous culture of the people of the region. He added, ''I want this to be properly understood so that there will be no more doubts and anxiety.''[75]

As soon as Parliament was convened in February 1971, the first bill to be passed was the Constitutional Amendment and Sedition Act.[76] Briefly, this act severely curtailed freedom of speech in the interest of security or public order, especially if such speech or speeches questioned the 1957 constitution's articles relating to Bahasa Malaysia as the national and official language, the special position of the Malays and other indigenous people, the economic policies related to the upliftment of the

Malay and indigenous communities, the sovereignty of the Malay rulers, and the citizenship rights of the non-Malays. The amendments do not grant the defense of privilege to members of Parliament and legislative assemblies of the states with respect to anything said in either houses or assemblies, as had been the case in the past. Under these constitutional amendments, provisions have also been made to empower the Yang di-Pertuan Agong to reserve a reasonable proportion of seats in universities, colleges, and other educational institutions of higher learning for Malays and natives of Sabah and Sarawak in order to give them a greater access to educational and training opportunities. The purpose of the act, according to the late Tun Abdul Razak, was twofold: first, to remove paramountly sensitive political issues from the realm of public discussion in order to ensure the smooth and continuing function of the parliamentary form of government, and second, to ensure the smooth implementation of policies designed to correct the racial imbalance in certain sectors of the nation's life.[77]

Malay Participation in the Economy

Simultaneously, on the economic front there was a concerted attempt by the leadership to implement a program that would enable the Malays to participate in an equitable share of economic and commercial activities, as well as woo non-Malay voters. With these factors in mind, the government launched the comprehensive and ambitious Second Malaysia Five-Year Plan (SMP), with an expenditure of M$14,350 million and a projected annual growth target of 6.5 percent.[78] The plan shifted emphasis from mere growth to an egalitarian growth-distribution policy to create a united, socially just, economically equitable, and progressive Malaysian nation. The strategy of the plan was "a two-pronged, New Economic Policy (NEP) for development" which would first reduce and eventually eradicate poverty by raising income levels and increasing employment opportunities for all Malaysians, irrespective of ethnic identity—that is, the have-nots of all races. Second, the NEP aimed to correct the prevailing economic imbalance by restructuring Malaysian society and thus ultimately eliminating the present economic specialization along ethnic lines. The SMP stated explicitly that the government, in order to achieve the targets set in the NEP, would devise and influence policies that would reflect at all levels the multiethnic composition of the country. The NEP specifically aimed to reduce the existing income imbalance between Malays and non-Malays by restructuring the ownership and control of wealth in the modern sector, by reducing Malay participation in traditional low-income activities, and by increasing Malays' role in the urban sector. The SMP envisages that this can be achieved through a process of modernization of rural life and the creation of a Malay commercial and industrial community at all levels of activity. It is hoped that by 1990 Malays and other indigenous people will own and manage at least 30 percent of the total commercial and industrial assets and thus will be true partners in all aspects of the economic life of the nation. Interestingly, the SMP hopes to achieve this target, not by the transfer of any existing property to Malays, but by expanding the economy, with Malays playing the dominant role in this expansion.[79] The Third Malaysia Plan constituted the second stage in the implementation of the NEP.[80] The Malay ruling elite considered the achievement of these goals to be the paramount prerequisite for national unity in the future of a multiethnic society like Malaysia. In addition, according to the Third Malaysia Plan, the continuation of these policies, programs, and objects "will also contribute to the task of assuring national security for all its people."[81]

In 1970, however, 62 percent of the country's corporate investment was directly owned and another 10 percent indirectly controlled by foreign hands, but the SMP did not suggest a gradual transfer of economic control from foreign to Malay hands. Instead, the SMP spelled out incentives to encourage large-scale foreign investors to invest further in the country.

The government created new institutions in addition to MARA to carry out the NEP. In 1969 Perbadanan Nasional Berhad (PERNAS) was established as a private company to spearhead the creation of a Malay entrepreneurial community by directly encouraging Malays to participate in industrial and commercial activities. PERNAS is a holding company with wholly owned subsidiaries operating in the fields of construction, property development, insurance, manufacturing, securities, and trading. In addition, a new stock exchange was established to build up Malay and indigenous ownership of capital assets. In the field of trading, PERNAS started a joint venture with the well-known and then predominantly British-owned and managed trading house, Sime Darby. In addition, an Urban Development Authority (UDA) was established to develop urban projects for Malay participation. UDA's main function is to develop urban properties specifically geared to provide incentives through loans and the like in order to encourage Malays to participate in urban trading and related sectors.[82] These policies, it was hoped, would gradually increase the Malay share in corporate ownership and control and in commerce. The creation of these agencies and institutions has, in fact, helped the Malays in particular to penetrate into areas unknown to their forefathers. These populist policies have considerably enhanced the political prestige of the Malay ruling elite and have also aroused some apprehension among the Chinese business community. For example, when PER-

NAS opened trading relations with mainland China, the Chinese business community protested that PERNAS was encroaching on their traditional import trade. However, despite the mammoth efforts toward consolidating a greater Malay equity share in economic enterprises, progress so far has been unspectacular. Nearly a decade later *The New Straits Times* of 30 May 1980 pointed out in an editorial that "From 1971 to 1978 bumiputra interest in the corporate sector increased from 4.3 per cent to 10.3 per cent. The corresponding non-bumiputra percentage increased from 3.4 per cent to 43.7 per cent."[83] It appears that although there was an increase in bumiputra activities in retailing, transportation, and service industries, bumiputra participation in manufacturing, wholesaling, and financing was extremely limited.

The question one must raise with regard to the Malaysian situation is whether economic growth and development in an ethnically divided society can be achieved with the NEP or with a policy with a broad front—that is, where all sections of the population have a genuine stake in its rewards. It is therefore essential to look into the questions not only of incentives for investors, but more important of incentives for the vast majority of those sections of the population who are farmers, fishermen, agricultural workers, and so on. Greater conscious participation by the majority of the population in government development plans presupposes changes in the ownership and control of the means of production, and redistribution of income in favor of the low-income groups. The overall eradication of poverty would necessarily include the eradication of Malay poverty and the consequent elimination of a major source of communal tension. On the other hand, if the disparities are maintained, vested interest groups, especially the ultras among Malays and non-Malays, will wish to exploit and sustain the notion of race consciousness, evolved around primordial ties of language, religion, and race. In this situation, as the late Tun Razak himself admitted in a press conference, national unity will remain an elusive concept.[84]

Communal Political Parties and the Pursuit of National Goals

The ruling elite, especially the more moderate elements in whose hands political power is presently concentrated, are very concerned with questions of national unity and communal harmony. They realize the dangers of pursuing lopsided economic, political, and cultural policies. They reject the view of the ultras that Malay interests can be safeguarded by the political and cultural hegemony of the Malays over the non-Malays, through the creation of a Malaysian Malaysia. This is demonstrated by the fact that since 1974 the leadership has formed a Barisan Nasional (National Front) government to replace the Alliance. This multiracial government included PAS and other predominantly non-Malay parties, the PPP, and Gerakan. PAS has since left the National Front, however, and has once again joined the ranks of the opposition, which includes the DAP and Partai Rakyat Malaysia.

The dilemma facing the Malay ruling elite is that their very political survival is dependent on the pursual of a Malaysian-Malaysia policy. Even under the current limited parliamentary framework, it is not possible for the Malay ruling elite to adopt an open policy in employment, economic opportunities, and cultural policies. Their room for maneuvering has been severely curtailed by the ultras, who since May 1969 have demonstrated their ability to manipulate the majority of the rural Malay population in the election to censure the leadership (as PAS did in the 1969 elections) if too many concessions are made to the non-Malays in these areas. This ability has been further strengthened with the formation and operation in recent years of extreme Islamic underground movements in the country, such as the Pertubuhan Angkatan Sabilullah (PAS), whose main objective is to make Malaysia a true Islamic nation with Malay support. The aim of movements like this is to ensure that non-Muslims will be deprived of many of their economic and political rights.

Thus to some extent one must consider the question of ethnic relations, national unity, and development strategies in peninsular Malaysia in the light of the dilemma that faces not only the moderate ruling Malay elite who now lead the UMNO, but also the ruling National Front, who are continuously under the scrutiny of the ultra group and are therefore obliged to guard and preserve, through the constitution, communal symbols such as the dignity and prestige of the Malay rulers, the special position relating to the Muslim religion and customs, Bahasa Malaysia, and (most important) the special position and privileges of the Malays until they are liberated from their economic backwardness. It also has pledged to promote the "advancement of Islam and to foster its growth as the *modus vivendi* for Muslims living in the country."[85] It has been argued that this pledge by the elite binds the Tanah Melayu (Malay country) to serve the Malay community and preserve the Malay-Muslim character of the country first; only after their obligations to the Malays have been met can they turn their attention to the demands of the non-Malay communities. At the same time the extremely vocal group of young Turks also began to question and challenge the established Chinese leadership, and this roused Chinese resentment.

The strategy of developing major political parties along communal lines has contributed to the nation's remaining culturally and politically plural. In fact, the coalition of the UMNO, the MCA, and the MIC to form the Alliance and later the National Front has "tended to define, on a pan-Malaysian basis, ethnic blocks which in former times were merely categories. Paradoxically with nationalism and independence, the Malaysian society's plural nature is more marked today than ever before."[86] This strategy survived in the country because the dispossessed urban or rural proletariat were unable to form an interethnic alliance as a class challenge to the ruling elite. Hence ethnic politics still dominates the Malaysian political milieu.

The question one might raise is why antagonistic communal relations remained covert in Malaysia until May 1969, with the exception of a few isolated incidents of violence, although there has been deep-rooted communal dissatisfaction. The explanation is that the special relationship between the various communal elite groups within the Alliance enabled them to minimize overt conflict through subtle political arrangements of consensus and accommodation. By tacit agreement the UMNO had the dominant voice; and the other partners in the government, the MCA and the MIC, had to defer to the wishes of the senior Alliance partner.

It is a paradox, however, that the National Front, a noncommunal alliance, cannot attempt to resolve internal differences arising from the conflict of interests between communal groups for fear of being accused of indulging in communal politics. Although individually the majority of the present National Front parties are frankly and openly communal, their joint membership in the noncommunal National Front government imposes on each of them, especially on those representing the non-Malay groups, severe restraints in expressing their grievances. The moderate leadership is faced with the dilemma of retaining political power and trying to integrate the different vested groups and communities, both Malay and non-Malay, who have diverse and discrete cultural, political, and economic loyalties, into a united Malaysian nation.

The political process since 1969 further strengthened Malay political supremacy when the leadership in the UMNO was able to forge an alliance with the PAS, which had secured significant rural Malay support in the 1969 elections. This unity provided a strong core of Malay backing for the Malay leadership in the UMNO and, not surprisingly, further eroded whatever political leverage the MCA, the MIC, and other members of the Barisan Nasional had thus far possessed. The MCA and the MIC have progressively weakened; not only do they face a stronger Malay leadership, but they also have lost their ability to mobilize and deliver the Chinese and Indian votes, respectively, as was demonstrated in the 1969 election results. Hence the bargaining power of non-Malay political organizations has become minimal, despite the fact that PAS has since withdrawn from the Barisan Nasional. The UMNO leadership, through its post-1969 policies, has marshaled substantial Malay electoral support and does not need non-Malay electorate support to keep it in power because post-1969 changes in the delimitation of electoral constituencies have further reinforced the Malay electoral constituencies and Malay voting power.

Notes

1.   The Malaysia Agreement was signed on 9 July 1963 between the United Kingdom, the Federation of Malaya (today known as peninsular Malaysia), North Borneo (now known as Sabah), Sarawak, and Singapore. The Malaysian Federation came into being on 16 September 1963. Singapore left the federation on 9 August 1965.

2.   See J.J. Puthucheary, *Ownership and Control in Malayan Economy* (Singapore: Eastern University Press, 1960), and Malaysia, *The Second Malaysia Plan, 1971–75,* (Kuala Lumpur: Government Printers, 1971). According to the tables on page 40 of this plan, the Ownership of Share Capital of Limited Companies is as follows: Malays and Malay interest, 1.5 percent; Chinese, 22.8 percent; Indians, 0.9 percent; federal and state governments, 0.5 percent; foreign interests, 62.1 percent; and others, 12.2 percent.

3.   Hugh Tinker, *A New Form of Slavery: The Export of Indian Labour Overseas, 1830–1920* (London: Oxford University Press, 1974). For a historical account of immigrant labor flow and the colonial policy related to it, see R.N. Jackson, *Immigrant Labour and the Development of Malays, 1786–1920* (Kuala Lumpur: Government Press, 1961); J. Norman Parmer, *Colonial Labour Policy and Administration* (New York: J.J. Augustin, 1960); and Kernail Singh Sandhu, *Indians in Malaya: Immigration and Settlement, 1786–1957* (Cambridge: Cambridge University Press, 1967).

4.   Malaysia, *Fourth Malaysia Plan, 1981–1985* (Kuala Lumpur: National Printing Department, 1981), p. 74.

5.   See Richard Morrock, "Heritage of Strife: The Effects of Colonialist 'Divide and Rule' Strategy upon the Colonized Peoples," *Science and Society* 37, no. 2 (Summer 1973): 129–151.

6.   Overt conflict based on the color line has not been experienced except during the colonial period, when the white bureaucratic and business community maintained a social distance from the nonwhite population. See, for example, Mona Brand, "Strangers in the Land," in *Two Plays about Malaya* (London: Lawrence and Wishart, 1954).

7.   Ginsberg Norton and Chester F. Roberts, *Malaya* (Seattle: University of Washington Press, 1958), p. 369.

8. V. Selvaratnam, "A History of Western European Enterprise in the State of Selangor from 1874 to 1894," B.A. Hons. Academic Exercise, University of Malaya, Singapore, 1960, chap. 6.

9. Raja Mohar Bib Raja Badiozaman, "Malay Land Reservation and Alienation," *Intisari* 1, no. 2 (1963): 20.

10. Ibid.

11. Kevin Young, William C.F. Bussink, and Parvez Hasan, *Malaysia: Growth and Equity in a Multiracial Society*, A World Bank Country Economic Report (Baltimore: Johns Hopkins University Press, 1980), p. 31.

12. See Malaysia, *Third Malaysia Plan, 1976–80* (Kuala Lumpur: Government Press, 1976), p. 5.

13. See J.S. Furnivall, *Colonial Policy and Practice* (London: Cambridge University Press, 1948).

14. Sino-Malay clashes have taken place in Teluk Anson (Perak) and Batu Pahat (Johore) in 1945–1946; in Penang in 1957 and 1959; in Pangkor (an island off the coast of Perak, where the Pangkor Engagement of 1874 was signed, resulting in the introduction of British rule in the country) in 1964; and in 1968 in Bukit Mertajam (Province Wellesly) and Penang. See Nancy L. Snyder, "What Happened in Penang," *Asian Survey* 8, no. 12 (December 1968): 960–975.

15. See A.W. Singham and N.L. Singham, "Cultural Domination and Political Subordination: Notes towards a Theory of the Caribbean Political System," *Comparative Studies in Society and History* 15, no. 3 (June 1973): 258–288.

16. James W. Gould, *The United States and Malaysia* (Cambridge, Mass.: Harvard University Press, 1969), p. 241.

17. UMNO won fifty-one out of the sixty-seven seats it was allocated to contest in the intracommunal constituency and voting framework, whereas MCA retained only thirteen out of its thirty-three allocated seats. In 1964 it won twenty-four seats. The MIC retained two seats out of its three, but only by a slender margin. See also Judith Goldman, "Party Support in Western Malaysia: Results of the First Stage of an Ecological Enquiry," *Asian Survey* 11, no. 6 (June 1971): 582–609. Out of the 2.1 million voters, 49.1 percent cast their votes for the Alliance, whereas the combined opposition parties secured 50.9 percent. In 1964 the Alliance secured 58.5 percent of the votes cast.

18. There have been a number of documents, articles, and books, both from the official side and from individuals, giving reasons for the May riots. Some of them are: Tunku Abdul Rahman, *May 13: Before and After* (Kuala Lumpur: Utsan Melayu Press, 1969); National Opera-

tions Council, *The May 13 Tragedy: A Report* (Kuala Lumpur: Government Press, 1969); John Slimming, *Malaysia: Death of a Democracy* (London: John Murray, 1969); and Cheng Teik Goh, *The May Thirteenth Incident and Democracy in Malaysia* (Kuala Lumpur: Oxford University Press, 1971).

19. Dato Haji Harun Idris subsequently served a jail sentence of six years for corruption while in office. While serving his sentence he was given a royal remission and freed. After his release he was elected one of UMNO's vice-presidents.

20. Sentul is a suburb of Kuala Lumpur.

21. See Derek Davies, "The Racial Balance Sheet," *Far Eastern Economic Review,* 10 July 1969, p. 119. Davies says: "Tun Razak appears to have decided that the root cause of the May riots was Malay economic resentment."

22. The proclamation of emergency was made on 15 May 1969.

23. It was established under the Emergency (Essential Powers) Ordinance no. 2 of 1969.

24. Ibid., section 2(1). However, he "shall act in accordance with the advice of the Prime Minister," that is, Tunku Abdul Rahman. In September 1970, however, Tun Abdul Razak became the prime minister when the Tunku stepped down.

25. Margaret Roff, "The Politics of Language in Malaya," *Asian Survey* 7, no. 5 (May 1967): 317.

26. *Report of the Educational Committee, 1956* (Kuala Lumpur: Government Printers, 1956). The chairman of this committee was the present prime minister.

27. Leon Comber, "Chinese Education—Perennial Malayan Problem," *Asian Survey* 1, no. 8 (October 1961): 30.

28. *The Straits Times,* 13 August 1957, as quoted in Margaret Clark, "The Malayan Alliance and Its Accommodation of Communal Pressures, 1952–62," M.A. thesis, University of Malaya, 1964, p. 143.

29. Roff, "Politics of Language," p. 323.

30. Ibid.

31. *National Language Act, 1967* (Act of Parliament no. 7, 1967).

32. Ibid., sections 5, 6, and 8.

33. Ibid., section 3.

34. Ibid., section 4.

35. Of Ceylon Tamil origin and a lawyer by profession.

36. Roff, "Politics of Language," p. 326.

37. K.J. Ratnam, *Communal and Political Process in Malaya* (Kuala Lumpur: University of Malaya Press, 1965), p. 89.

38. Ibid., p. 67.

39. Mills, op.cit. p. 37.

40. Ibid., p. 81.

41. *State Nationality Enactments, 1952*, Article 5(2) (Kuala Lumpur: Printing Press, 1952).

42. See Nik A. Rashid, "Selected Cases on Constitutional and Administrative Law," Mimeograph (Kuala Lumpur: Faculty of Economics and Administration, April 1969), pp. 18–19.

43. As quoted in Ratnam, *Communal and Political Process,* p. 115.

44. Malaysia, *Federal Constitution* (Kuala Lumpur: Government Press, 1968), Article 153.

45. Ibid., Article 159, Clause 5.

46. Federation of Malaya, *Second Five-Year Plan, 1961–65* (Kuala Lumpur: Government Printers, 1960), pp. 17, 18, 28–36.

47. This ministry was set up in 1959. It ceased to operate as a ministry for some time, but under the prime ministership of Dato Seri Dr Mahathir Mohamed, it was reestablished as an independent ministry.

48. *Kongress Ekonomik Bumiputra Malaysia Kertas 2 Kerja* (Kuala Lumpur: Government Printers, 1965), p. 111.

49. Majlis Amanah Rakyat is the Council of Indigenous People, an important Malaysian development authority, particularly to uplift the economic backwardness of Malays.

50. Puthucheary, *Ownership and Control,* p. 174.

51. Ibid. For an interesting discussion on rural poverty and the monopoly-monopsony system, see Ungku Aziz, "Poverty and Rural Development in Malaysia," *Kajian Ekonomi* 1 (June 1964): 70–79.

52. See *Eastern Sun,* 24 March 1968. For an interesting comment on this, see Ungku A. Aziz, "Facts and Fallacies about Malay Economy," *Kajian Ekonomi* 3, no. 1 (December 1966); E.L. Wheelwright, *Industrialization in Malaysia* (Melbourne: University Press, 1965), pp. 134–135; and S. Husin Ali, "Some Aspects of Change, Mobility and Conflict in Post Merdeka Malaysia," *Manusia Dan Masyarakat* 1 (1972): 51–60.

53. Bob Reece, "Dare The Tunku Go?" *Far Eastern Economic Review* December 1969; pp. 550–553.

54. Aziz, "Facts and Fallacies," p. 82.

55. Federal Land Development Authority, *Annual Report, 1967* (Kuala Lumpur: Perchetakan MAS Sendirian Berhad, 1968), p. 57.

56. Ibid., p. 51.

57. Ibid., p. 53.

58. See Frank Peacock, "The Failure of Rural Development in Pen-

insular Malaysia,'' in *Issues in Malaysian Development,* ed. James C. Jackson and Martin Rudner (Singapore: Heinemann Educational Books (Asia), 1979), pp. 375–395.

59. Unemployment was a problem in the 1960s and still is. In 1967 the Malay rate of employment was 91.2 percent, the Chinese 92 percent, and the Indian 87.7 percent. See International Confederation of Free Trade Unions, *First Asian Conference on Unemployment* (New Delhi: ICFTU).

60. Tun Abdul Razak, ''Malaysia's Prosperity Is for All,'' Speech over radio and television Malaysia, 1 July 1969. Reproduced in *The Straits Times,* 2 July 1969.

61. Bhanoji V.V. Rao, *National Accounts of West Malaysia, 1947– 71* (Singapore: Heinemann Educational Books, 1976), p. 83.

62. For an overall critical evaluation of the development program of the 1960s, see Herman Hatzfeldt, *Economic Development Planning in Malaysia* (Bangkok: Ford Foundation, 1970).

63. R.K. Vasil, *Ethnic Politics in Malaysia* (New Delhi: Radiant Publishers, 1980), p. 158.

64. For an account of Dr. Mahathir's views, see *The Malay Dilemma* (Singapore: Asia Pacific Press, 1970).

65. The Tunku subsequently resigned as prime minister on 30 August 1970. Up to the end of 1973 he held the post of secretary-general of the Islamic Conference in Jeddah, Saudi Arabia. He was the first person in the Islamic world to hold this position.

66. Senu Abdul Rahman, ed. *Revolusi Mental* (Kuala Lumpur: Penerbitan Utusan Malaya, 1971).

67. Ibid.

68. Domestic capital, it is said, is not really scarce. Interest rates in Malaysia have been rather low, and the country was a net exporter of capital in the 1960s. See Lutz Haffman and Tan Siew Ee, *Industrial Growth, Employment and Foreign Investment in Peninsular Malaysia* (Kuala Lumpur: Oxford University Press, 1980), p. 209.

69. See R.S. Milne, ''National Ideology'' and ''Nation-Building in Malaysia,'' *Asian Survey* 10, no. 7 (July 1970): 565.

70. See Eric A. Nordlinger, *Conflict Regulation in Divided Societies,* Studies in International Affairs, no. 29 (Cambridge, Mass.: Harvard University Press, 1972).

71. Ibid.

72. See *Far Eastern Economic Review,* 31 July 1969, p. 278.

73. Ibid.

74. See Seyed Hussain Alates, ''The Rukunegara and the Return to

Democracy in Malaysia,'' *Pacific Community* 3, no. 3 (April 1972): 800–808.

75. *The Straits Times,* 31 August 1973. See the speech of the prime minister on the eve of the Merdeka anniversary.

76. *The Constitutional Amendment and Sedition Act 1971* (Kuala Lumpur: Government Printers, 1972).

77. *The Straits Times,* 31 August 1973.

78. Malaysia, *Second Malaysia Five-Year Plan (1971–75)* (Kuala Lumpur: Government Printers, 1971).

79. Ibid., p. 40.

80. See Malaysia, *Third Malaysia Plan (1976–80)* (Kuala Lumpur: Government Printers, 1976).

81. Ibid.

82. *Far Eastern Economic Review,* 15 January 1973, p. 18.

83. *New Straits Times,* 30 May 1980.

84. See *New Straits Times,* 2 April 1980.

85. Margaret Clark, ''The Malayan Alliance and Its Accommodation of Communal Pressures, 1952–62,'' M.A. thesis, University of Malaya, 1964, pp. 167–168.

86. Maurice Freedman, ''The Growth of a Plural Society in Malaya,'' *Pacific Affairs* 33, no. 2 (1960):167.

5

Violence and Development in Sri Lanka: Conceptual Issues

Godfrey Gunatilleke,
Neelan Tiruchelvam,
and *Radhika Coomaraswamy*

The issues selected for analysis in this study encompass a wide range of sociopolitical phenomena. Therefore, at the outset it is necessary to provide some working definition of the concept of violence as used in the study, in order to distinguish the forms and manifestations of violence that fall within its framework from those types of disorderly and criminal activity that are outside its scope. The phenomenon of violence examined in the study could initially be defined as the use of force for the resolution of conflicts in society that mainly originate from sociopolitical, economic, ethnic, and cultural causes and that find expression in various forms of collective action.

This definition excludes from the study a whole category of criminal acts of violence of individuals or groups that do not form part of any larger social or political action but are primarily directed toward personal objectives. This distinction itself raises numerous problems, which anticipate some of the fundamental dilemmas inherent in issues relating to violence and development. First, it must be pointed out that the changing patterns of crime and socially deviant behavior most often serve as a useful index of the quality of life achieved in the process of development. Rapid urbanization, the breakdown of traditional value systems, and the erosion of community life generate new types of violence and a different pathology of crime, ranging from the organized criminal underworld in big cities, to seemingly irrational acts of inhumanity and violence. Next, some aspects of the emerging problems directly impinge on questions relating to development and the underlying patterns of structural change. In the growing urban centers of developing countries in particular, problems of urban poverty and of a dual society begin to merge with problems of crime and violence. From the dark side of the disadvantaged urban world of slums and shanties, the existing system would be perceived as

The authors wish to acknowledge the invaluable contribution of Noel Tittawella to this chapter, especially with regard to the analysis of the instruments used to contain violence.

one that defends the structures of inequality and the unequal distribution of assets, producing affluence for a few and desperate poverty for many. The types of violence generated within such a system, although they may all originate in underlying social conflicts, can assume diverse forms and express themselves in varying degrees of inhumanity. The manifestations of violence may be part of an effort to survive within the inequities of the system by those who have no legitimate opportunity to participate in it. On the other hand, violence is sometimes a mode of social action directed at the radical transformation of the system. There is also the indiscriminate use of violence and the infliction of suffering on other human beings, which differ from both of the former types and are the product of life-styles that have cut themselves adrift from any center of human values or moral foundations.

These various forms of violence are not always distinct from each other. The value systems that are implicit in these different types of violence, with their specific expressions of inhumanity, merge into each other and draw on each other in given situations. Purely criminal violence, for example, takes advantage of political disorders to pursue its own objectives. Similarly, political violence, as in the case of terrorism, can become indistinguishable from indiscriminate acts of aggression against humanity. The problems posed here become crucial when we move to violence that is adopted as one of the necessary instruments in the pursuit of social objectives and in promoting socioeconomic and political change.[1]

The case of Sri Lanka has been selected for this study because the postindependence history of the country provides an appropriate framework for conceptualizing the main issues relating to the sociopolitical manifestations of violence in the process of development and for exploring the broad typology of violence that could be observed in many developing countries. First, Sri Lanka offers the example of a multiparty parliamentary system based on universal franchise that has shown a capacity to sustain the democratic process while coping with social conflict. It has had to manage both actual eruptions of violence and a deep-seated propensity to violence in a pluralistic developing society. Sri Lanka's experience is helpful in identifying some of the essential elements of a normative framework within which we could consider issues pertaining to violence and development and inquire what the preconditions are for minimizing the propensity to violence and for managing violence when it occurs with the least cost to human values and to the democratic process as a whole.

Second, Sri Lanka provides a fair sample of the forms of sociopolitical violence that take place in the process of development. The Marxist-led militant working-class movement, which struggled hard for the recognition and establishment of the rights of the working population, contained a potential for violence that occasionally erupted in violent incidents and demonstrations against authority. The postindependence period has had an ugly record of violence and brutality arising out of ethnic conflict. Outbreaks of violence and clashes between political parties and their following have been another disturbing feature of political life in this period. Finally, there have been two efforts at coups d'etat by small elite groups and one armed insurrection, each aimed at overthrowing the existing system and either imposing its preferred pattern of socioeconomic change or causing a reversal of ongoing trends. The events that are discussed in the study would therefore cover the main sources of conflict in Sri Lankan society as well as the different modes of action, including the participation of organized social groups, revolutionary and counterrevolutionary responses to socioeconomic problems, and mob violence.

One of the underlying assumptions in the study is that the propensity to violence and rapid discontinuous change are inherent in the process of development. Development would inevitably result in the continuous disturbance of the prevailing social balance; in the emergence of new social classes and the formation of new interest groups that threaten the existing distribution of power and assets; in the release of forces that break up the ideological bases that had promoted a broad social consensus with respect to the prevailing order; in forms of national integration that are inimical to long-standing regional and ethnic identities. Development therefore acquires a pervasive character of instability, disequilibrium, and conflict. The conditions exert strong pressures that tend to push a society in the direction of force and violence. Such force and violence might be used either for establishing order, suppressing conflict, and reducing instability, or for seeking a radical and lasting resolution of the conflicts themselves. The former would normally fall into the category of counterrevolutionary violence—violence for the preservation of the status quo; the latter might be described as revolutionary violence. Viewed in this perspective, the problems of violence and development raise a number of conceptual issues that are related to our understanding of man and society.

From one ideological position it might be argued that violence in the process of development does not lend itself to ethical consideration or analysis, that the question of whether violence is good or bad is by itself irrelevant, that violence itself is a necessary outcome of a particular convergence of historical forces wherein an old system does not give way to an emerging new system.[2] The relevant question, then, is whether the violence releases new creative and productive social forces or suppresses them. In such a formulation violence is accepted as a concomitant—and even an essential—instrument of the rapid structural changes that are needed in a developing society.

This study adopts a different analytical framework, however. The one basic underlying assumption here is that within the limits of any given historical situation, a society has the latitude to choose between several alternatives, and that this applies equally to the choice of violence as a means to achieve given ends. The problem is to define the limits and the space for choice within a given historical situation. Violence, for the purpose of the study, includes both the violence implicit in an established system for enforcement of law and order and the violence of those acting outside the system and in opposition to it. The former is violence that is internalized and implicit in the structures of domination and inequality in a society, structures that are legitimized by the prevailing juridical order and sociopolitical and economic institutions. The character of this violence, often defined as *structural violence,* will vary from society to society.[3] Its intensity will depend on the structure of inequality in a society, the degree of disparities in power and resources between a small affluent minority and a large disadvantaged majority, and the pattern of domination needed to sustain the inequalities. Again, its repressive character will vary, depending on the success with which the prevailing ideology has gained acceptance for the system from the society as a whole. The extent of the structural violence in any society will largely determine the propensity to violence in the whole of that society, as well as tendencies within it to generate violent responses and create a vicious circle of violence.

In contrast, the society in which the propensity to violence is controlled is one that has already succeeded in reducing structural violence or is in the process of lessening it rapidly. Such a society is moving toward equality; is lowering disparities in power, wealth, and income; and has progressively less need for systems of coercion, suppression, and intensive internal security. It could then evolve systems that create the opportunity for the surfacing of the conflicts already present in the existing social structures and for the expression of opposition and dissent. At the same time it could provide the mechanisms for resolution of such conflict through social bargaining, eventually leading to a rearrangement of social relations and a new sharing of power. The equity-oriented patterns of development and the systems for negotiated settlement of conflict are complementary processes that create conditions both for minimizing recourse to violence and for managing violence in a manner that does not permanently impair the democratic polity and the framework of civil liberty and human rights. As the Sri Lankan study tries to demonstrate, the management of violence, even in a democratic polity, results in each case in the suspension of certain parts or the whole of the normal civil order and civic rights that go with that order. The duration of this suspension, the extent to which certain inalienable human values and rights are protected during that period, and the speed with which the system is restored to normality will depend on the processes that have been discussed. At best the systems will have built-in mechanisms that will impart an automatic self-correcting character to the resumption of normality.

The line of argument adduced here leads to the general conclusion that a society with high inequality and rigid, inflexible political structures that leave little room for the ventilation of conflicts and the negotiation of their resolution has a high propensity for violence, whereas societies that have an equity-oriented pattern of development, with systems that provide space for the expression of conflict and opposition and that evolve mechanisms for negotiated settlements of conflicts, have a relatively low propensity for violence. It would then be possible theoretically to locate a developing society on the trajectory as it moves from the high-violence societal pattern to the low-violence pattern. Of course, the actual social and political reality is much more complex than is assumed in such a neat categorization. The firm exercise of governmental authority, even harsh systems of political repression, may go with equity-oriented development. South Korea, and to some extent Singapore, may fall into this category. The effective enforcement of law and order, though containing a large element of what has been defined as structural violence, may be successful in preventing open violence and creating stable social and political systems over long periods. So-called soft governments, on the other hand, which are less repressive, may not have the capacity to cope with the violence generated by internal dissension and struggle.[4] Furthermore, they may not be able to mobilize the collective effort for growth and augmentation of resources and as a result may exacerbate internal conflict. Socialist countries would fall into a special category in which equity-based policies are counterbalanced by ideological and political systems that do not accommodate political opposition and have few mechanisms for promoting the expression of latent internal conflicts and negotiating their resolution. Most of them, however, have a long record of a stable social order in which sociopolitical violence is minimal.

The problems of violence and development therefore manifest themselves in a wide variety of combinations resulting from the different patterns of development that are pursued. They need to be understood in relation to the specific historical evolution of each society and the balance of power between contending social forces at any given time. At least three major clusters of development goals appear to influence these combinations—the cluster of goals relating to freedom and the political space for dissent and social bargaining; the cluster relating to equity and the reduction of disparities in income, wealth, and power;

and the cluster relating to growth and the increase of productive capacity. The weight of each of these in the development strategy, the equilibrium that is achieved in relation to each, will determine the character and extent of the structural and other forms of violence in a society. The Sri Lanka study expects to throw some light on how the pursuit of these three goals and the way they are balanced have a bearing on the problems of violence and development. For the purpose of this study, the general assumption that the absence of open violence could be the result of an efficient apparatus of repression with a high degree of structural violence is a useful point of departure. The criterion of a social order free of violence then refers not merely to the absence of open violence, but also to the absence of violence in a deeper, more comprehensive sense. Here, violence includes the ever present threat of force in the structures of established authority, the constant readiness to use force to suppress opposition and dissent and perpetuate the existing disposition of power in society.

This bring us to a more fundamental question concerning the ideological framework within which violence is perceived. The mainstream of traditional ideology regarded violence as a natural human attribute. This would be true of ideological systems derived from Christian beliefs, Hinduism, Islam, or the Chinese philosophical tradition. Obviously it would not be possible within the scope of this chapter to explore the traditional concepts of the sources of power and authority and the value systems governing the relationship of the ruler and the ruled. It would also be totally misleading to talk about traditional concepts as though they constituted a single consistent body of thought on these subjects. This would be to ignore the diversity and complexity of traditional philosophical inquiry. For the purpose of this study, however, in order to understand the conflict of tradition and modernity in the evolution of political systems in developing societies, some of the main ideological frames within which the problem of violence and authority was viewed in traditional civilizations do have some relevance.

It is possible to distinguish two opposing but coexistent ideological positions in many of the traditional systems. One position places the emphasis on human imperfection and the natural human proclivity to sin. In its extreme form this approach would lead to the position of Hobbes in European thought, of the *matsya nyaya* (''law of the fish'') in Hindu thought, or the philosophy of Hsun Tsu in the Chinese tradition.[5] This position is best stated in Hsun Tsu's treatise ''The Nature of Man is Evil.''

The nature of man is evil. Whatever is good in him is the result of acquired training. Men are born with love of gain. . . . They are filled with envy and hatred of others. . . . Clearly then to accord with man's original nature and to act as instinct dictates must lead to contention, rapacity and disorder and cause humanity to revert to a state of violence. For this reason it is essential that men be transformed by teachers and laws and guided by li and justice . . . only then is good order possible . . . It is clear that man's original nature is evil and that he becomes good only through acquired training.[6]

This line of argument is not far from the principal traditions of Christian or Hindu thinking. The Christian notion of man flawed by original sin, and the recognition of the innate human tendency to engage in internecine conflict found in Hindu political thought, are essentially in accord with Hsun Tsu's formulation.

Within this conceptual framework, authority has an indispensable positive role—whether it be the authority of the sages, of the state, or of the church. To overcome the violence and dissension that characterize the natural order, there must be an exogenous integrating force—whether it be the redemptive grace of the church, the wisdom of the sages, or the all-powerful *chakravarti* of Hindu political theory.[7] Man, the polymorphous pervert of Freudian psychology, has to be civilized; the process of civilization itself is a violent transformation of nature. In this scheme of things, the firm exercise of power, strong government, the disciplining of instinctual behavior, and the coercive socialization of man are all part of the redemptive process. The ruler, the priest, the teacher, the elite create the structure of domination in this process of socialization; and it is this structure that welds conflicting social groups into a stable civil order. Such a structure functions essentially on charismatic leadership, authority, tutelage, and indoctrination. In such a scheme, authority flows from above; the validity of the civil order derives from the fact that it is also the temporal manifestation of the divine order. The dominant ideology is therefore nonparticipatory, far removed from what would be defined as democratic. The main problem in such a structure is that of combining power with goodness; of linking secular authority to an overriding moral order; of establishing the right relationship between the religious leaders, the custodians of the moral order, on the one hand, and the secular power holders on the other. The search is for the philosopher king, the Confucian emperor, the Dharma chakravarti, the righteous ruler.

Closely interwoven with this dominant ideology, however, was another strand of traditional thought that emphasized man's innate goodness, his worth as a moral being. This dichotomy of man as a creature with an innate propensity to evil and man as created in the image of God, which was illustrated in the great controversies of the earlier Christian Church—for example, the conflict between the Augustinian and

Pelagian view of human nature—finds expression in the Asian setting as well. The *athman* resided in every being (Hinduism); enlightenment was within reach of all (Buddhism); every man was a vice-regent of Allah on earth (Islam); man was essentially a social being. In this way of thinking the community and the people had a central place in the total social and moral order. The exercise of power was for the common good; there were inviolable moral constraints on such power, and the right to rule was forfeited where fundamental moral laws were violated.[8] In such situations the "decree of heaven" passed to the people who then claimed the right to revolt.[9] Here, the underlying concepts relating to the disposition of power in society were democratic and participatory in direction. The consent of the people in terms of just government was also a necessary source of the ruler's authority and power.

If force and violence were an inalienable part of the natural order and their use was an essential element in the art of effective government, then love and understanding, tutelage for self-realization, constituted the base of the spiritual or transcendental order. In the traditional ideological framework, good government had to be perceived within the continuing dialectical tension between these two orders. In Hindu political writing, *saman* (gentleness, peaceful dealing, negotiation) was an important ingredient of good rule, along with *danda* (firmness, the rod, severity in chastisement).[10]

Among the powerful symbolic elements that nourished the culture of these societies were the symbols of profound renunciation—monarchs who became *sanyasis,* hermits or religious teachers. Gautama Buddha himself is the supreme symbol of this tradition: the prince who renounced earthly power to seek spiritual deliverance. Dharma Asoka, the righteous emperor, filled with remorse at the violence and destruction he had caused, stopped his career of conquest, became a convert to Buddhism, and attempted to base his government on the doctrine of compassion and nonviolence. King Vessantara was the symbol of *dhana*—charity and self-sacrifice.[11] In Sri Lankan history the warrior king Duttugemunu, after his great victory, was overcome with sorrow and despair at the human slaughter for which he had been responsible and had been consoled by the clergy. In true ecclesiastical fashion, the monks persuaded him that of all those who were killed, only two deserved to be regarded as human—one *arahat,* an individual who had achieved spiritual deliverance, and one *samenera,* a person who had taken vows of the religious order.[12] The incident itself poignantly illustrates the dilemma of power and violence. The solution is in the tradition that accepts imperfection. This dilemma of the historical necessity of violent action and the spiritual purification of the motive of the actor is best exemplified in the Bhagavadgita and in Krishna's exhortation to Arjuna in the battlefield. Siri

Sangabo, the Sri Lankan king, sacrificed himself when a reward had been offered by the usurper, rather than have innocent persons killed. Once again the story becomes part of the traditional symbolism and mythology shaping the spiritual consciousness of the community.[13]

One important mode of political action that was derived from this thinking was *ahimsa,* the nonviolent struggle for liberation. The political philosophy of Gandhi made this the main instrument in the Indian movement for independence. An effective nonviolent methodology of political struggle was evolved, in which noncooperation, passive resistance to authority, withdrawal from civic action, courting of imprisonment, and civil disobedience became the principal modes of action. Nonviolent resistance sought to expose the violence of the state and assert the moral and spiritual force of the righteous oppressed. Thereby it sought to undermine the legitimacy and moral authority of those in power. As a method of resistance to the wrongs of established systems, it has inspired movements outside South Asia, such as the opposition to apartheid in South Africa and the civil-rights struggle of the black opposition in the United States. Its success has depended on the profound moral commitment of the leadership and its capacity to mobilize a following who have full allegiance to the spiritual discipline demanded by this mode of action—"the method of securing rights by personal suffering."[14] The values sustaining the ideology of nonviolence regard human society as one. Its advocates seek a methodology of struggle, change, and social transformation that is nondivisive in its final outcome and that integrates society. In such an approach, violence—the use of force against another social group and its physical liquidation, even for constructive social change—is seen as engendering a process of hate, the disregard of human values, a vicious circle of reprisal and repression that is carried over into the future and vitiates the new system that replaces the old. In situations of brutal repression, violent opposition might become a historical necessity. The society trapped in such historical conditions, however, will have to bear the inescapable cost of the violent solutions it seeks and finds. The systems that emerge will necessarily be flawed by the violent processes that gave birth to them, and that violence will be carried into the structures and institutions that are newly created and the social and political relations governed by them.

This brief discussion of the traditional ideology and value systems relating to violence in society contains sharply contradictory elements with respect to both the conception of man and society and the methodologies for dealing with violence. These contradictory elements are part of the traditional vision of reality. In such a vision the coexistence and interpenetration of secular and transcendental values manifest themselves in seeming inconsistencies, and at any given moment one set of values

may have sway over the other. In such a paradigm there is realistic
acceptance of the imperfection of the secular order, the lay life; but there
is no room for cynicism, as the temporal order is also the ceaseless
striving for the perfection of the spiritual order. The historical process
itself, in its broad cycle of good and evil, has no well-defined regularities,
no easily predictable pathways. The process consists of the moral de-
generation and regeneration of society, the rise and fall of human effort,
and the choices made in the search for spiritual deliverance.

Our analysis of violence in the process of development would therefore have to be set in a framework in which traditional norms and indigenous value systems relating to good government and the relations between
ruler and ruled are continuously interacting with emerging modern value
systems relating to the sources of power and popular participation. The
process is one of movement from the traditional ideal of righteous authoritarian rule in a predominantly religious society, to the modern ideal
of an equitable participatory social order in a predominantly secular society. It is a transition fraught with a potential for violence that can easily
deflect the developing society from its course toward the equitable participatory goal. It is a transition in which contending social groups are
driven to the use of force either to gain or to defend what they perceive
as their rights or as worth preserving. On the one hand, the emerging
order with its secular value system often cuts itself adrift from the traditional spiritual base and freely admits ideologies of violent change,
which result in a disruptive uprooting of its past. On the other hand, the
profound spiritual core of the traditional value system is almost inextricably bound to the existing structures of inequality. It cannot be easily
liberated from them to serve as a new basis for a radical nonviolent social
transformation, where spiritual values inform the struggle to remove inequality and oppression.

Here, however, simple conclusions are dangerous. Militant religious
movements are notorious for the intensity of violence they can release.
Militant Buddhism in Sri Lanka played a major role in creating conditions
that led to outbreaks of communal violence. At the same time, it would
be wrong to assume that the aggressive power drive of the militant
Buddhist movement was the only force at work. The more positive influences of Buddhist ideology had their pervasive impact on policy and
action. They reinforced the motivations that promoted the social-welfare
programs and the concern for alleviation of poverty. We would see later
that in moments of violent crisis the appeals made by the religious leaders
to the Buddhist conscience of the country and the activity of citizen
groups to preserve the moral foundations of society were not futile ges-
tures in a society where religion was a driving force. In the process of
development, therefore, religion can be as much a generator of violence

as it can be a spiritualizing, healing, and integrating agent in the midst of the violent, disruptive forces of change. Where the profoundly religious element in a society joins forces for structural change, the prospect of containing violence and evolving humane, nonviolent methodologies of change might be stronger than in an entirely secular, nonreligious framework.

Manifestations of Violence in Sri Lanka

The Political and Socioeconomic Setting

The generalizations that have been made in the preceding section need to be considered in relation to the specific historical evolution of a given society in order to gain some understanding of the propensity to violence in that society. The hypothesis was advanced earlier that this propensity was related to structures of inequality and systems that do not provide for dissent and negotiated resolution of conflict. Therefore, in examining the types of violence that have occurred in Sri Lanka and the system that has been evolved for the management of violence, we need to have an overview of the pattern of socioeconomic and political developments during the last three decades.[15] In the case of Sri Lanka, the conditions that either intensify or minimize the propensity for violence will themselves depend on the manner in which the social relations between the elites and the masses have evolved in the traditional precolonial polity as well as the structures that were developed during the period of colonial rule.

Developments in Sri Lanka in the period of British colonial rule and the constitutional changes introduced in the period preceding independence were vitally important in molding the system for conflict resolution. First, a Western-educated intelligentsia had grown that had absorbed Western democratic values and was eager to establish a Western-type governmental framework. Second, the British rulers had introduced universal adult franchise in the early part of the 1930s, along with a measure of self-government. The developments within British society itself, the concepts of the welfare state, and the growth of a socialist tradition with its critique of existing institutions were all exerting their influence on Britain's relations with its colonies. The Donoughmore Commission on constitutional reform in Sri Lanka, which issued its report in the late 1920s, hoped that a combination of adult franchise and a fair measure of responsible government would create the conditions in which the local elites would become increasingly responsive to the basic needs of the majority of the population.[16] It could be said that to a considerable extent these expectations were fulfilled. In the 1930s, after the new constitution came into force, the competitive political system that gradually evolved began acquiring the capacity to articulate the urgent demands of the electorate. The elected representatives were able to bring pressure on the executive for larger allocations of resources for the provision of social services to the constituencies they represented.

By the time Sri Lanka achieved independence, the government programs that were to become the main components of the social-welfare policies in the period after independence had already commenced. There was a steady expansion of the government health services. Educational facilities were developed to provide for a rapidly increasing rate of participation of children in the school system. In 1945 the government decided to provide universal free education up to the university level. A food-distribution system with subsidized food rations was introduced during World War II to serve the entire population. Substantial investments were being made to increase food production to meet domestic needs, particularly rice, the staple food of the population. Economic policies that emphasized the diversification of the agricultural sector and self-sufficiency in rice had a strong rural bias and were aimed at raising the productivity and income of the small farmer.

The country was therefore already poised before independence to promote two of the principal preconditions for conflict resolution—a socioeconomic base for ameliorating poverty and reducing inequality, and a competitive political system with a relatively literate electorate that provided a framework for bargaining by contending social groups. During the 1950s and 1960s the main elements of the social-welfare package that had evolved in the period immediately preceding independence were elaborated and developed into a comprehensive program. The system of mass free education led to the establishment of educational facilities spanning the entire island. The dispersion of schools was generally planned to make educational facilities at the primary level available within a radius of about two and a half miles. The number of schools increased from 5,945 in the mid-1940s to approximately 9,500 in 1979; the total school enrollment rose from 944,000 to 3.14 million; and participation of the school-age population in the school system rose from 57 percent in 1946 to approximately 80 percent in the late 1970s. The literacy rate had risen from approximately 57 percent to about 85 percent during the same period. With the steady expansion of health facilities, the crude death rate had dropped from 19.8 in 1946 to 12.4 in 1950; by the late 1970s it had further declined to 7.0. Similarly, infant mortality, which had fallen from 141 in 1946 to 82 in 1950, dropped to 37 by 1978. Maternal mortality continued to decline steadily, from 15.5 in 1946 to 0.8 in 1968. Life expectancy had risen from 46 to approximately 68 in the mid-1970s. At a relatively low level of per capita income, Sri Lanka's performance on selected indicators of physical well-being was already approaching that of developed countries.[17]

Government policies assured a nationwide distribution of essential foodstuffs at prices either subsidized or with a minimum markup. This was achieved through a trading system that relied on state imports and wholesale marketing, as well as on a scheme of retail distribution through a widely dispersed network of cooperative stores. The bundle of goods distributed through this system included rice, dhal, dried fish, and powdered and tinned milk, helping to maintain minimum nutritional levels for the large majority of the population. Even during periods of acute foreign-exchange scarcity, priority was assigned to supplies of the essential food items. It was a system that maintained a fairly stable structure of prices over the 1950s and 1960s. The consumer price index rose only 12 points during the entire period 1952–1965.[18] Government expenditure on health, education, housing, and food subsidies rose from about 5 percent of gross domestic product in the beginning of the 1950s to 12.4 percent in the mid-1960s. The core welfare program outlined earlier was supported by several other poverty-oriented programs. These included a nationwide village-expansion program that provided state land and subsidized housing to disadvantaged rural families and a program of agricultural settlements that transferred population from the densely inhabited southwest and central regions of the country to the sparsely populated north-central and eastern parts. Income distribution had moved progressively toward greater equality, with the lowest 40 percent increasing their share from 14.5 percent of the total income in 1953 to approximately 19 percent in 1973.[19]

Despite intermittent threats to the political system, democratic institutions and processes steadily strengthened themselves during this period. If we measure the political mobilization of the people and their participation in the political system by the proportion of the electorate that voted in elections, we observe that the rate of participation increased steadily from 61 percent in 1947 to 77 percent in 1960, 85 percent in 1970, and 86.7 percent in 1977.[20] The shifts of power that took place during the last three decades occurred in a manner that preserved the continuity of the system even while it underwent important structural adaptations. Power shifted periodically from left-oriented governments that took forward the process of strengthening the state sector and initiating structural changes, to the more conservative policymakers who gave more attention to the management of the economy, the promotion of private enterprise, and economic growth. The periods 1956–1964 and 1970–1977 represent the swing of the political pendulum to the left-oriented parties, and the periods 1948–1956, 1960–1965, and the ongoing tenure of power since 1977 represent the movement to the right. These oscillations did not result in sharp discontinuities leading to radical changes in the sociopolitical institutions or to the virtual liquidation of socioeconomic groups. On the other hand, within the short span of thirty years the country witnessed a unique sequence of political changes in which all parts of the political spectrum reached the centers of government power. All the major political parties that competed for power in the early 1950s, from the United National Party to the Marxist parties, at one time or another shared in the task of government and directly contributed to the changes in the system.[21] The system therefore had to digest a wide range of ideological approaches and make room for their coexistence. This also meant that the main political parties were ready to accept the principal rules of the prevailing political system and to attempt to work within it. From one point of view, the oscillations might be considered a serious drawback of the system. It would be argued that they prevented the pursuit of given development policies over a sufficiently long period to yield results. On the other hand, the oscillations reflected a system that was flexible enough to stop the advance along a particular path and enable society to change direction toward other development goals. This would be in the nature of a system that is open and seeks to respond to a diversity of needs. In the long term this particular process seems to have created conditions in which a healthy structure of countervailing power could grow and in which a democratic, equitable development style could endure. Therefore, in a relatively early phase of development, Sri Lanka had already begun to evolve toward a social democracy with representative institutions, free elections, a strong component of social welfare, and a growing public sector in a mixed economy.

Before concluding this overview, it is relevant to point out some of the major social and economic imbalances that grew out of the pattern of development described here. First, although the levels of social well-being that Sri Lanka had achieved were exceptional for a developing country starting at a low level of per capita income, the performance of the economy was less satisfactory. At the end of the 1970s, per capita incomes were still in the region of U.S. $230, and Sri Lanka remained among the poorest thirty-six low-income countries, according to the World Bank classification.[22] The rates of economic growth that Sri Lanka was able to maintain during the 1950s and 1960s cannot be regarded in themselves as poor. The annual average rate of about 4.5 percent growth during this period was only marginally below international targets. It became evident, however, in the mid-1960s that the process of development, with its emphasis on social well-being, had itself generated a new set of problems that seemed to demand faster economic expansion and higher rates of growth for their solution. An increasing imbalance had emerged between human capital formation, on the one hand, and physical capital formation on the other. The economy was not expanding fast enough in those sectors that could have absorbed the increasing cohorts of school leavers that the free education system was releasing into the work force. This resulted in a dramatic increase in the rate of unemployment in the early 1970s, one of the highest for developing countries, which was creating explosive social tensions.[23]

In order to understand this situation, it is necessary to examine the demographic changes that have taken place in Sri Lanka. Population had grown at an annual rate of 2.5 percent between 1958 and 1971. The work force had grown at approximately 2.1 percent. The economy, on the other hand, had been able to generate new employment only at an average annual rate of 1.1 percent. Between 1963 and 1971 the total work force increased by approximately one million additional participants, almost all of whom were new entrants to the work force in the age group 15–29. This addition to the work force represented an increase of approximately 29 percent over an eight-year period, or an annual rate of growth of 3.2 percent. The total number who succeeded in finding employment during this period was in the region of 430,000. The result was a massive backlog of unemployment, which grew to an estimated 24 percent in 1973—that is, over one million unemployed, most of them in the 15–29 age group. These conditions had their inevitable consequences in social tensions and the widespread outbreak of violence in 1971.

Second, the development processes during this period were also exerting undue pressure on the political institutions. In a situation of scarce resources, the political system became the principal means of access to and control of these resources, and the political parties the main benefactors. In this context political affiliation became an important criterion for the distribution of benefits and rewards. The successive changes of government and the oscillations of power to which we have referred have something to do with the manner in which each ruling party managed this process. The favors shown to political supporters and the open discrimination against political opponents intensified the antagonisms between competing political parties that manifested themselves in open violence immediately after changes of government.

A third outcome of the pattern of socioeconomic and political change that is relevant to our discussion is the impact of these changes on ethnic relations in Sri Lanka. As we would see later, the processes of democratization by themselves contributed to a heightening of ethnic conflict. The social-welfare program that had been successful in reaching almost all ethnic groups and the different strata of the population (with the exception of the estate Tamil community), was operating differently for different ethnic groups when it came to their prospects for upward social mobility through the system. In the case of the Sinhala majority, the free-education system combined with other social welfare programs was improving the opportunities for advancement for almost all social strata. In the case of the Tamil minority, the benefits of free education were being severely curtailed by the discriminatory policies affecting entry to higher education and recruitment to the public sector. Thus the very processes that were promoting conflict resolution in certain major areas were generating and intensifying conflict in the field of ethnic relations.

Economic Conflict and Potential for Violence

Within this setting, let us first examine the potential for violence in the conflict of socioeconomic groupings and classes in the Sri Lankan context. As we would see later, the public-security legislation that was formulated in the 1940s was prompted primarily by fear of worker unrest. At that time the main threat of violence against the system was perceived in the politicization of the urban working class. Unionization itself was not always viewed with favor by the employers. Working-class agitation and strikes occasionally led to violence and the use of force. The organization of the working class in trade unions, however, proceeded in a relatively peaceful manner from the 1920s on.[24] What was viewed with apprehension, however, was the mobilization of the working class under the leadership of the Marxist political parties.

In the initial phase immediately before and after independence, the Marxist parties presented themselves as revolutionary parties in orthodox Marxist terms. They characterized the parliamentary institutions as bourgeois instruments for the perpetuation of the rule of the propertied classes, explained their participation in parliamentary politics as essentially devoted to exposing the falsity and ineffectiveness of parliamentary institutions, and advocated a revolutionary transformation of society. The most widespread manifestation of mass discontent and unrest during this period was the *hartal* in 1953—a general stoppage of work in protest against the removal of the rice subsidy. This mass agitation was spearheaded by the left parties. The hartal, as a mode of social action, came into prominence in the nonviolent strategy advocated by Gandhi in the Indian liberation struggle. When it was adopted by Marxist revolutionary parties in Sri Lanka, however, the nonviolent character of the mass demonstration and the discipline within the nonviolent framework did not receive the same emphasis and commitment. The hartal resulted in several incidents of violence. An emergency had to be declared, and the army had to be employed to bring the situation under control. According to government reports, nine persons were killed during the disturbances.[25]

Several factors, however, led to significant changes of perspective until both the organized working class and the political parties that led it progressively reshaped their strategies to work within the parliamentary system. First, the working class itself began to enjoy the fruits of trade-union strength and to perceive its capacity for maneuvering and exercising power within the system. A system of progressive industrial relations steadily evolved, and over a period the security of workers and the processes of collective bargaining were established on a firm institutional and juridical base. As early as 1929 a collective-bargaining process was initiated when the Employers' Federation of Ceylon entered into an agreement with the All Ceylon Trade Union Congress. In the early 1930s government enacted legislation to provide for the settlement of industrial disputes through commissions and conciliation boards. This was followed by several pieces of legislation that were partly responses to agitation by the left parties and the trade unions. These included laws providing for workmen's compensation, maternity benefits, and minimum wages for various categories of labor. After the election of a left-oriented government in 1956, more substantial gains were secured by the working class. These included the amendment of the Industrial Disputes Act in 1957, which provided for the establishment of labor tribunals, and a national scheme for termination benefits for workers through an Employees' Provident Fund.[26]

Second, the political parties themselves began to strengthen their parliamentary power base and to see prospects of sharing power within the system to initiate change in the direction of a socialist society. In the general election in 1947 the Lanka Sama Samajana Party (LSSP) and the Communist party together obtained 15.5 percent of the total number of votes. In 1952 they had increased their share to 20.5 percent. The general trend was therefore away from revolutionary political action and toward the organization and exercise of trade-union power within the system. Underlying these developments was another important feature of the left movement in Sri Lanka that favored these trends. The major left party was Trotskyist. The Communist party, which owed allegiance to an ideological center outside the country, was in the minority. To some extent this gave the left movement a genuinely indigenous character and insulated it from external influences that could have otherwise permitted superpower rivalries to act more directly on the internal politics of the country, exacerbating its tensions.

These developments, however, do not mean that the trade-union movement has acquired an independent and secure position of power in the system. First, its power has fluctuated with the changes of government, its position being relatively strong when left-oriented governments have been in power, and weak with right governments. Second, although the politicization of the movement and its affiliation to parties has been a source of its power, it has also led to its fragmentation, seriously undermining its solidarity. In each government there has been a significant section of the trade-union movement that owed allegiance to the ruling party and therefore was reluctant to make common cause with the trade-union movement as a whole in any agitation against the government. Third, a core of political opposition to and distrust of a free trade-union movement persists. Lack of worker discipline is blamed on the trade-union movement. The movement is seen as having acquired power and resorted to modes of action that impede economic growth and are injurious to the community as a whole. It is also seen as having prevented the growth of a work ethic that is consistent with development.

Government action in July 1980 to deal with worker demands and a widespread strike illustrates the vulnerability of the movement.[27] An emergency was promulgated to declare the strike illegal on the grounds that it was politically motivated and a threat to public security. There was mass firing of workers in the public service who struck. The government flatly refused to enter into any negotiations with unions. Political conflicts and factionalism in the trade-union movement have led to violence that has been used adroitly by government to suppress trade-union agitation. Outbreaks of violence between anti- and progovernment factions have begun to assume an ugly form, obstructing legitimate forms of trade-union activity. No serious and systematic effort has been made by the authorities to protect the legitimate expression of protest and opposition. The recent history of the trade-union movement indicates that despite the growth of the countervailing power of the trade unions in the political and economic life of the country, the political system still cannot easily accommodate itself to opposition and protest. The intrinsic character of the system remains authoritarian. Each party that assumes office seeks an unchallenged exercise of power. It cannot easily contemplate the legitimate sharing and transfer of power.

In contrast to the developments in the urban working class, a surprising phenomenon is the absence of class-centered organization and agitation in the rural sector, particularly among the peasantry and rural labor. This could be partly explained by the strong rural bias that the electoral process gave to national politics. The mass of the voters were in the rural sector, and any political party seeking power had to have a political agenda that gave priority to rural needs. Hence the emphasis on social-welfare programs, distribution of state land and agricultural settlements, and heavily subsidized package programs in support of peasant agriculture. The competitive political structure, with several parties seeking to strengthen their rural power base, provided the rural population with a certain amount of bargaining power and ready access to elected representatives. In the pattern of land ownership in the peasant economy, concentration was not high, and structures of exploitation by a landowning class living on rental incomes had not grown to the same extent as in most other developing countries. Within the rural sector itself there was a gradation of incomes that prevented a sharp polarization of rich and poor. In this context the Marxist parties were incapable of developing an appropriate peasant agenda that would have provided a base for a revolutionary peasant-worker alliance. Many of the radical initiatives taken, such as the Paddy Lands Act,[28] and later the Land Reform,[29] were not prompted by any peasant agitation. They were engineered as reforms within the constitution and were carried out in a relatively peaceful and orderly manner without any violent class conflict. They failed to trigger any organized peasant movement. Even a more conservative form of peasant mobilization, such as farmer organizations for protecting and advancing the farming interests, failed to emerge. The cultivation committees, which provided an opportunity for radical peasant mobilization, did not develop into rallying points.[30] Class relations within the rural sector and the relationships of the peasantry and the power-holding elites continued on the basis of state benevolence and peasant dependence, creating conditions that kept rural society relatively free of the processes of sharp polarization and violent class conflict.

Ethnic Conflict and Violence in Sri Lanka

While the relations between socioeconomic groups were moving steadily away from confrontation and struggle into the social-democratic framework of collective bargaining and negotiated solutions, ethnic relations in the country moved in the opposite direction. The distribution of the population by ethnic groups is given in table 5–1. At the time the country became independent, the local elites that had risen to positions of power and influence under the colonial regime comprised a small Westernized English-speaking minority that was multiethnic and multireligious in its composition. They had imbibed part of the value systems and the social ethos of the Western industrial societies and were strongly influenced by the ideologies and sociopolitical institutions that had evolved in these societies. It was an ethos that had succeeded to some extent in reducing and moderating ethnic antagonisms. It showed the capacity to accommodate the concept of a pluralistic multiethnic society. With universal adult franchise and the democratic processes that were thereby set in motion, the electorate rapidly expanded far beyond the small Western-

148

Table 5–1
The Population of Sri Lanka by Ethnic Group

Ethnic Groups	1881 Number (000s)	Percentage	1946 Number (000s)	Percentage	1971 Number (000s)	Percentage
1. Sinhalese	1,847	66.9	4,620	69.4	9,431	72.0
Low country	—		2,902	43.6	5,426	42.2
Kandyans	—		1,718	25.8	3,705	29.8
2. Tamils	687	24.9	1,514	22.7	2,599	20.5
Ceylon Tamils			724	11.0	1,424	11.2
Indian Tamils			780	11.7	1,175	9.3
3. Moors	185	6.7	410	6.1	853	6.7
Ceylon			374	5.6	828	6.5
Indian			36	0.5	28	0.2
4. Burghers and Eurasians	18	0.6	42	0.6	45	0.4
5. Malays	9	0.3	23	0.3	43	0.3
6. Others (Veddahs, Europeans, etc.)	14	0.6	47	0.7	—	0.1

Source: Michael Roberts, *Collective Identities, Nationalisms and Protest in Modern Sri Lanka* (Colombo: Marga, 1979), table I, p. 97.

Note: There is regional distribution of certain minorities; the Tamils predominate in the north and the northeast. Enclaves of hill-country Tamils are also present in the central provinces. As the most explosive issue is the confrontation between the Sinhalese and the Sri Lanka Tamils of the north and east, the study will concentrate primarily on this conflict.

educated elite, and progressively larger layers of the population began to enter the political life of the country. As the base of political participation widened, ethnic identities began to be more sharply defined and accentuated, and ethnic interests became articulated in more assertive forms.

The transfer of political power to the local population brought two issues to the forefront. The first concerned the dominant role played by the English-educated local elites. The new social forces that were emerging saw the Western-educated elite as an alien by-product of the colonial system. They sought to broaden the access to privileges that up to now had been largely confined to the English-educated minority. At the same time they attempted to define a national identity in opposition to the Western-oriented ethos.[31] One aspect of decolonization was seen as a renewal of the country's religiocultural tradition. The second issue concerned the relative positions and the sharing of power among the various ethnic groups within the new political dispensation. Both these issues assumed a strong ethnic character as competing political parties began to mobilize mass support. The demands of the Sinhala Buddhist majority became the dominant factor in the changed situation. The initial effort on the part of the United National Party immediately after independence to maintain a multiethnic posture soon succumbed to the mass pressures generated by the opposing political groups.[32] Almost all political parties that were controlled by the Sinhala community hastened to adopt an agenda that satisfied the Sinhala Buddhist aspirations. Even the Marxist left, which was holding out for equal status for the Sinhala and Tamil languages, finally abandoned this position.[33]

Within the Sinhala community itself the appeal of this agenda lay not only in its capacity to create a new sense of solidarity based on racial sentiments but also in its egalitarian bias. It downgraded the English-educated elite and provided the Sinhala-educated majority with opportunities for rapid upward social mobility. What may have had an equity-oriented outcome for the Sinhala majority, however, assumed a highly discriminating character for the minorities. The group consciousness that evolved as a result of the nationalist movement, albeit a progressive mobilization against colonialism, could not develop into multiracial nationalism. Instead it became an exclusively Sinhala expression of historical rights and values. Therefore, in serving the purpose of mass mobilization, it also created strong barriers to a pluralistic solution of ethnic conflict in Sri Lanka. As the Sinhala majority began to assert the right to a paramount role in shaping the national identity, the Tamil community perceived these developments as a complete rejection of the concept of a pluralistic society that gave equal opportunity for all Sri Lankan citizens. The other minorities in the country—the Muslim community and the Burgher community, who were descendants of the Portuguese and the Dutch—made their own responses to the situation. The latter migrated in large numbers to Australia. The former, a small, widely dispersed group, showed a willingness to accommodate themselves to the changes and to bargain within the new framework. Relations between the Sinhala and Tamil communities, however, moved inexorably on a course of confrontation. As the positions of the Sinhala majority hardened, the support of the Tamil community shifted from leaders who had advocated collaboration with the majority community within the existing political system,[34] to those who agitated for a federal form of government,[35] and eventually to a political front that demanded separation.[36]

Although it was the political process released after independence that brought the Sinhala-Tamil conflict to the surface and intensified it, its origins lie in much more deep-seated divisions and antagonisms. The real dilemma concerning the relations between the two communities lies in the mutually conflicting historical perceptions they have of their own and each other's identities. These perceptions conditioned the expectations of each other and set the parameters within which they defined their rights as ethnic groups and their relative roles in the national policy. The typical perception of the communal problem by the Sinhala majority has been based on the concept of a historical polity in which Sri Lanka is projected as the homeland of the Sinhala people and the Sinhala language, and the special sanctuary of the Buddhist religion. It is often claimed that the Sinhala race was founded in the fifth century B.C. by an exiled prince, Vijaya, who was of Aryan descent. The notion that the Sinhala people were Aryans is constantly employed to differentiate between the Dravidian Tamils and the Sinhala majority and has formed the basis of most of the racist writings of the 1920s and 1930s.

The history of the Sinhala race is perceived as a constant struggle to protect the integrity of this homeland and its culture against external force. The major chronicles of the ancient Sinhala historians depict the early period as one of intermittent warfare with invaders from South India, who continuously threatened the foundations of Sinhala society from the second century B.C.[37] During the period of European expansion, the task was to enable the Sinhala Buddhist identity and culture to survive in the midst of the overwhelming pressures of the colonial system. These perceptions often tend to give the Sinhala majority a self-image of a small vulnerable community. When tensions between the Sinhala and Tamil communities mount, the aggressive and militant Sinhala elements are quick to revive the racial memory that projects the Tamil community as descendants of the historical enemies and as part of the large Tamil population in South India. Students of the communal problem in Sri Lanka have often observed that in this context the Sinhala community, despite its far superior demographic weight, tends to develop a minority psychology, with a mixture of defensiveness and aggression, in its relations with the Tamil community.[38]

The second component of the Sinhala national identity that affects perceptions of the communal problem is the belief that the Sinhalese are the defenders of the Sasana, the Buddhist faith. Very early in Sinhala ideology, two beliefs played a central role—first, the belief that Sri Lanka was consecrated by the Buddha himself, who visited the country, and second, that the relics of the Buddha were symbols of Sinhala kingship and that their possession gave power and legitimacy to the reigning monarch. The relics symbolized the concept of the Sinhala Buddhist monarchy and gave credence to the belief that the King was a future Buddha or Bodhisatva.[39] During colonial rule, however, Buddhism lost its prestige, along with its political and economic power. Therefore, nineteenth- and twentieth-century nationalism saw a period of Buddhist revivalism that was more assertive than the Buddhism of the precolonial era in that it had to play the principal role in reconstructing and restoring an ethnic identity that was threatening to disintegrate.[40]

The third component of the Sinhala identity that in recent years has assumed great importance in ethnic relations is the Sinhala language as the unique expression of the Sinhala culture. This element of ethnic identity, along with the claim of Aryan descent, united Sinhala Buddhists with Sinhala Christians. Although Sinhala became the language of expression for nationalist leaders, the assertion of Sinhala language rights emerged as a crucial issue in the nationalist movement in its struggle with colonialism and its conflict with the English-educated elite. With universal free education and the national languages as the media of instruction, a whole new generation proficient only in Sinhala and Tamil, and with little or no knowledge of English, was beginning to enter the work force. The pressure to change the language of administration from English to Sinhala began to gather momentum in the early 1950s. The militant groups among the Sinhala community perceived the measures advocated to give a Sinhala Buddhist orientation to the entire national polity as an effort to correct the imbalances that were created during the colonial period. They saw the colonial period as having seriously discriminated against the Sinhala Buddhist majority. They therefore rationalized the pro-Sinhala bias in the policies that were being advocated as a necessary redress of historical wrongs. In their view this would bring about a readjustment and a fairer distribution of power, which would reflect more equitably the balance of communities in the country as a whole.[41]

This entire political and social agenda was viewed by the Tamil community as a complete denial of the concept of a plural society. Combined with the decision to make Sinhala the only official language of the country, several other measures that had already been taken increased the apprehensions of the Tamil community. One such measure was the disenfranchisement of the Tamil population, which had settled as plantation labor during the colonial period.[42] Another was the rapid expansion of new agricultural settlements close to the areas that were regarded as the traditional homeland of the Tamils. In the first phase after independence, the Tamil community saw itself in the role of a national minority within a plural society, which would have enabled the Tamils to preserve their distinct cultural identity and to enjoy full equality of opportunity for participation in the national system. The community divided their political allegiance between a set of leaders who advocated cooperation with the Sinhala majority in a system that guaranteed parity of status to the minorities, and another set of leaders who advocated greater autonomy for the Tamil minority within a federal political system. Up to 1956 the former had the larger following in the community and provided it with political leadership. In the face of a steady erosion of the Tamil political base, preventing an effective challenge to the policies of the

Sinhala majority, Tamil perceptions of their identity began to change. The concept of the Tamil community as a national minority operating in a pluralistic society was rapidly transformed into the concept and ideology of a separate historical polity with a territorial base and distinctive manifestations of race, religion, and language.[43] In the changing context the Federal Party soon gained the leadership of the Tamil community.

Tamil perceptions of their history are greatly at variance with the Sinhalese perception of their historical development. In a battle of historians some Tamil scholars, pointing to early inscriptions, maintain that the Tamils came to Sri Lanka before Vijaya, thus engaging in a never-ending, often fruitless debate over who has territorial title to the northern region.[44] The battle of historians has in many ways only reinforced the conflicting perceptions of the two communities. Nevertheless, there is a consensus among historians that from the seventh century on there was a constant Tamil presence in Sri Lanka, and that from approximately 1215 A.D. until the Portuguese conquest in 1621 an independent Tamil kingdom existed in the north of the island. To the Sinhala historian the Tamil kingdom is a peripheral kingdom that emerged during the period of national dissension and chaos. Sinhala perceptions of history are built around the great Sinhala dynasties that unified the Sinhala kingdom. The intervening periods of history are seen as times of disintegration and decline. To the Ceylon Tamil, however, the period during which the northern kingdom flourished is the golden age of Sri Lankan Tamil culture. Though unrelated to the political process, growing fascination with aspects of this kingdom has resulted in new historical research, especially in the last decade, which has reinforced the perceived historical right to a homeland in the northern region.[45] These mutually conflicting perceptions have contributed to the breakdown in understanding and communication between the two communites.

At the root of ethnic conflict there would always be the stereotypical image that a traditional ethnic group or culture would have of the alien or the intruder. These stereotypes have certainly colored the ethnic relationships between the majority community and the minorities in the country. There is no doubt that during the period of colonial rule the Sinhala Buddhist majority saw the rest of the community as a favored minority. This applied to both the non-Sinhala ethnic groups and the non-Buddhist Sinhala minority. Within this, of course, the Tamil minority was singled out for more antagonistic reactions. The Tamil stereotype in the Sinhala mind was that of a community that did not identify itself with the nation as a whole and remained a close group with strong affiliations that they carried into the public service as well as other sectors of public life. This was particularly pronounced when it came to such questions as recruitment to the public service, where the Sinhala majority constantly alleged that recruitment by Tamil superiors had strong racial biases toward members of their own community. The Sinhala majority always tended to regard the Tamil leadership as communalistic and as not showing adequate capacity to transcend specific minority issues and respond to broad national goals. The representations made by the minorities, particularly the Tamil minority, to the Donoughmore and Soulbury commissions were seen as efforts by the minorities to prevent the majority from achieving independent nationhood.[46] These representations soured relationships at the very inception of the newly independent state and aroused mistrust and suspicion with regard to the political motivations of the Tamil leadership. The Tamil community, on the other hand, saw the Sinhala community as preventing the industrious and enterprising groups among the minorities from enjoying equality of opportunity and engaging in fair competition. By contrast to the industrious Tamils, the Sinhalese were perceived as indolent and less willing to engage in hard work; what was perceived by the Sinhala majority as an effort to redress historical wrongs became in the eyes of the Tamil minority an effort to rig the system and create structures of discrimination against an industrious minority. The Sinhala majority saw their effort to define their central role as one of asserting the position of primus inter pares. The Tamil minority, on the other hand, saw it only as an assertion of primacy and a denial of parity.

For all these reasons, the responses to ethnic issues and the search for solutions could not be contained within the parliamentary framework and the political process of orderly opposition and negotiation between the political leadership of the two communities. The responses involved popular passions; and, particularly in the case of the majority community, militant groups resorted to violent action outside this framework. The problems of violence that have emerged within the ethnic situation and the forms that the violence has taken have been diverse and highly complex. We can broadly distinguish three manifestations of violence arising out of ethnic conflict—first, outright mob violence; second, individual acts of violence by political groups that can be characterized as terrorist; and third, the violence used by police and army officers, including both the excessive use of force in maintaining law and order and retaliatory acts of indiscipline and violence. These three forms of violence have more or less followed each other in sequence, creating a chain of action and reaction that has embroiled Sri Lankan society in a vicious circle of violence from which it has become increasingly difficult for both the majority and the minority communities to disentangle themselves and move toward negotiated solutions.

Widespread mob violence occurred in 1958, 1977, and 1981. This resulted in large-scale looting, arson, murder, and rape, and caused great hardship and suffering to the members of the Tamil community who resided in regions in which the Sinhalese were in the majority. The 1958 violence was directed mainly against the indigenous (Ceylon Tamil) community. In 1977 and 1981 the violence included the Tamil residents in the plantations in the central region of the country. In 1958 the main cause of the communal riots was the controversy surrounding the enactment of the Sinhala Only Act and the abrogation of a pact between the leaders of the two major political parties representing the two communities.[47]

As civil disorder and rioting spread, the government reluctantly enacted emergency powers. Emergency was declared five days after the initial rioting began, although a curfew had been in operation during this period. The armed services were given broad powers to arrest and detain; to shoot curfew violators; and to give protection, shelter, and food to refugees. In addition, the government proscribed and arrested members of the Tamil Federal party and placed members of the Sinhala extremist groups under house arrest. Press censorship was also imposed with regard to any incident, as the press had contributed to the situation through circulation of false rumors. The fact that the government took five days to declare emergency, as well as the extension of that emergency for ten months after the riots had abated, has been severely criticized. The neutral role that the armed forces played during the riots in 1958, however, stemmed the tide of violence once emergency was declared and the army was placed in control.

The communal violence in 1977 followed soon after the 1977 general elections, which had an aftermath of violence, directed first at the losing political parties. The violence soon became communal, accentuated by the speeches of separatists and the demands of the Tamil opposition, which had won an overwhelming victory in the north and the east. There were several significant new elements in the outbreaks of violence in 1977 and 1981. First, they were nationwide, with the Sinhala Christian areas that had been uninvolved in 1958 taking part in the rioting. Second, the victims included the Tamil plantation workers, against whom no serious violence was directed during the 1958 riots. In 1977 the plantation workers had entered the national political arena, making common cause with the indigenous Tamil community and joining the Tamil United Left Front. They constituted a critical minority vote in certain electorates, and rival political parties saw their vote as having been decisive in the 1977 elections. Therefore, they attracted the antagonism of various political groups. Third, the immediate cause was the tension and hostility between the armed forces—especially the police stationed in the north—and the youth of that region. In 1977 the armed forces, especially the police, had also undergone some significant changes. They were affected by the

causes that led to communal violence. Communal biases and ethnic loyalties appeared to have eroded the neutrality in the armed and police
forces that in 1958 had been the major factor in bringing the violence
speedily under control. In 1977 the newly elected government, which
had campaigned strongly against the emergency rule of the previous
government, appeared to be constrained by the policies it had advocated
before coming into power.[48] The government refrained from declaring
an emergency; only a curfew was declared. For all these reasons, the
violence was widespread.

The political violence and terrorism that emerged in the north during
the 1970s could to some extent be perceived as the ethnic counterpart of
the violence that manifested itself in the insurgency in 1971. The riots
of 1958, the atrocities committed, and the violent uprooting of Tamil
families from their residences in the Sinhala areas left behind deep wounds
and bitter memories that were not easily healed or erased. The free-
education system had widened the participation of the school population
in the educational system for all communities. The policies in regard to
higher education, however, as well as the Sinhala-only policies, had
discriminated severely against the Tamil-educated youths.[49] All these
factors combined to create a hard core of militant Tamil youth who
rejected the existing system in its entirety and linked the cry of separatism
to a larger radical ideology. These elements seemed to favor the use of
extraparliamentary violent methods to achieve their goals. The strategy
they adopted included large-scale robberies, which were apparently intended to collect arms for an underground movement; assassination of
those leaders of the Tamil community who showed a desire to collaborate
with the majority community; and acts of violence against the police and
armed forces, including several killings. As this group became active,
security operations in the northern regions were intensified. This in turn
led to a deepening of the tension between the police and the people in
the northern Tamil-speaking areas, which hardened into an identification
of the police as an army of occupation. The government responded initially by proscribing a movement described as Tigers for the Liberation
of Eelam, which claimed responsibility for most of the incidents. A
seemingly draconian piece of legislation entitled the Prevention of Terrorism Act was introduced.[50] In July 1977 the government declared an
emergency in the north and sent an army brigadier to bring the crisis
under control within a period of three months. By early 1981, however,
political violence had begun anew. On 24 May the leading government
candidate for election of the newly established District Development
Council was killed, and on 31 May four policemen providing security
for the Development Council elections in the north were shot. Two of
them subsequently died.

The emergence of militancy in the north, coupled with terrorist acts, characteristically led to increased repression and acts of violence by the armed services in the north. The acts of violence directed against the police evoked reactions from the police force that tended to undermine discipline and erode police neutrality in situations of ethnic conflict. On 31 May, 1 June, and 2 June, after the shooting of the four policemen, about 250 members of the police force stationed in the north went on a rampage. There was widespread arson and looting by the police, including the burning of a public library.[51]

One part of the majority's political strategy has been to use the threat of mass communal violence to intimidate the minorities and contain their demands. The posture of politicians in power as well as that of leading opposition politicians has thus often become an incitement to communal violence or at least to tolerance of it. In this manner communal violence has become a part of the political armory. The more sensitive of the Sinhala politicians would present this as a dilemma. They would say that the propensity to mass violence on the ethnic issue is unavoidable. They would argue that they could maintain themselves in power and moderate the mood of the masses if they set themselves in open opposition to that mood. The separatist cry on the part of the minorities is now presented by the Sinhala majority as the main cause for communal violence. On the other hand, in the first phase of their struggle, the leadership of the Tamil minority organized themselves for nonviolent opposition. They employed instruments such as satyagraha, fasts and hartals (total stoppage of public activity), and civil disobedience in an attempt to adapt Gandhian political methods to the Sri Lankan situation. The indiscriminate mob violence that was unleashed in retaliation by the Sinhala majority, however, called into question the effectiveness of these methods in dealing with widespread ethnic conflict. To have the desired moral and political impact, nonviolent opposition required a level of mass participation and a total commitment and discipline that were difficult to achieve.

The strategy of the militant elements in the Tamil minority has been to move increasingly toward violence, both abroad and at home. The pattern of this violence, however, needs to be distinguished from other expressions of communal violence. It has been confined mainly to the northern region and has been directed primarily against those members of the minority community who are identified as collaborators and against the security forces in the north. At first the Tamil political leadership did not publicly condemn individual acts of violence, although they maintained that they were a democratic party committed to nonviolent agitation. This has been partly attributed to the fact that at first the leadership sought the support of these militant elements. Some Tamils may have even felt that the violent acts on the part of these militant groups would strengthen the bargaining power of the community.

More recently, both Sinhala and Tamil political leaders have had to take more unequivocal positions and explicitly disassociate themselves from incidents of violence in the south and the north, respectively. The pronouncements of the United National party (UNP) leaders, including the expulsion of a UNP politician,[52] on the one hand, and the condemnation of Tamil extremists by the Tamil United Liberation Front (TULF), on the other, represent the effort to reach consensus on the basic values and to evolve a moral framework that should discipline the political process in this area. One promising development was the decision of the TULF to participate in the new system of decentralization introduced by the government, which held out a prospect for greater autonomy to the Tamil regions. This offers a potentially effective means of defusing ethnic conflict. Combined with these developments, more specific initiatives were taken by the UNP and the TULF to commence negotiations on the main issues leading to the conflicts between the two communities. By the end of 1981 relations between the communities were showing signs of moving away from confrontation toward negotiated solutions.

The management and control of ethnic violence, unlike other forms of violence, have posed a special set of problems to the state. Violence arising out of ethnic conflict has a tendency to permeate all aspects of social life, to activate aggressive groups in almost all strata of society, and to penetrate even the machinery of the state that has the responsibility to control and prevent violence. At one extreme, the eruptions of ethnic violence in Sri Lanka have invariably unleashed the criminal elements of the underworld, who use the ethnic issue as a cover for looting and other acts against the Tamil community. Even the terrorist violence in the north soon began to deteriorate into organized crime directed against the community. On the other hand, law-abiding citizens have succumbed to the irrationality of ethnic loyalties and have acquiesced or even participated in acts of violence. Ethnic loyalties have divided the bureaucracy, the educational institutions, the trade unions, and even the security forces into antagonistic camps. Although interracial inequalities and socioeconomic differentiation between communities undoubtedly contribute to ethnic conflict, the violence that is implicit in the structure of ethnic relations appears to have its source in the conflicts of a more primal and irrational character that have been discussed earlier.

It is important to note here that the national strategies identified earlier as having reduced or contained structural violence in Sri Lankan society were implemented on a countrywide basis without ethnic discrimination. This applies to the social-welfare programs that helped eliminate the worst manifestations of poverty and inequality.[53] The only exception was the estate Tamil population, who were in an especially disadvantaged position because of the issue of citizenship. The indicators of well-being for the Tamil population, with the exception of the estate sector, showed the same improvement as for the rest of the country. In fact, the indicators for the northern region—the Jaffna District—were among the highest for the country.[54] These average indicators for the community as a whole, however, concealed the effect of discriminatory policies that acted with increasing severity on the higher social strata and were inhibiting the processes of upward social mobility that operated more freely in the Sinhala community.

In the multiethnic context, vertical inequalities among social groups and classes transform themselves and appear primarily as horizontal inequalities of an interethnic character. The comparative conditions of the ethnic groups and their elites receive primary attention. There is then an irrepressible tendency to attribute the prevailing disparities to ethnic relationships and to the discriminatory structures governing them. In this sense the potential for violence in ethnic conflict is different from the forms of structural violence discussed earlier. The national strategies, the conflict-resolving mechanisms, and the framework for negotiated solutions that normally reduce the potential for violence are therefore not entirely adequate for situations that are complicated by ethnic conflict. It is relevant to recall at this point the expectations that the members of the Soulbury Commission voiced in 1945 regarding the prospects for the solution of communal problems in Sri Lanka. They expressed the view that with the establishment of the parliamentary system and the formation of political parties based on socioeconomic groupings, the communal issues themselves would recede into the background. They argued that "there are definite indications of the growth of a left-wing movement more disposed to concentrate on social and economic than communal issues."[55] By the mid-1950s, however, communalism had made inroads into the left movement and created serious dissension and disunity within it.

The problems of ethnic conflict, as we saw, are further compounded where they arise out of mutually antagonistic and competing group identities and become transformed into nationality problems. The instruments deployed to contain violence are inadequate, as they tend to shift the balance of political arrangements further in favor of the majority. They thereby make the state even more vulnerable to challenges to its legitimacy from the minorities. The challenge of political violence arising out of ethnic conflict therefore poses problems for the evolution of our sociopolitical institutions that are qualitatively different from those that would confront an ethnically more homogeneous society. It calls for political institutions that provide space for affirmation of corporate identity and self-expression of different ethnic groups, while initiating processes of nonviolent conflict resolution directed toward their underlying grievances. It is for these reasons that in the Sri Lankan context, a decentralized polity appears to have offered the most promising option. The current policies for decentralization of the political and administrative systems have begun to provide a basis for the resolution of some of the most urgent ethnic problems.

In the long run, the resolution of conflict in ethnic situations can come only through a total readjustment in both vertical and horizontal relations between all social strata of both communities. Although a framework for the negotiation of solutions at the political level is all important, these must be supported by a reorientation of attitudes and values of each of the communities as a whole in their relations with each other. There must be a new morality that governs ethnic relations to which not only the political leadership, but also the intelligentsia and opinion leaders at all levels in both communities need to contribute. It must be a morality that would effectively eradicate deep-seated antagonisms and the stereotypes through which the communities have heretofore responded to each other. This highlights the need for more broad-based citizen involvement in the effort to resolve communal conflict and promote intercommunal harmony. One significant positive element has been the formation of citizen groups during periods of communal violence that have actively attempted to protect persons and property against ethnic violence. A centralized strategy for the suppression of disorder by itself cannot be wholly successful against ethnic violence because of the particular characteristics mentioned earlier. A special set of relations between the citizens, on the one hand, and the security forces and the state, on the other, becomes necessary to cope with the problems.

The Violence of Reaction and Revolution

The discussion on ethnic relations provides an appropriate entry to the efforts that were made by both the right and the left extremes to engineer a radical change in the system. The first attempt at a coup came two years after the first outbreak of communal violence. It could be broadly characterized as an attempt to reverse the trend that had begun in 1956 with the ascendancy of Sinhala Buddhist nationalism. It would be an oversimplification to see the attempted coup as merely an effort to restore and preserve the pre-1956 power structure. The composition of the group that planned the coup gives some clue to its underlying social and political motivations. The group was drawn from the bureaucracy, the police, and the armed forces. It included Sinhalese, Tamils, and Burghers, Christians and Hindus. One of the members was a Buddhist and son-in-law of a prominent Buddhist leader. He withdrew on the eve of the date fixed for the coup, however, and gave evidence for the state. The coup was therefore organized by an intercommunal group who saw that the era of stability, order, and communal accommodation sustained by the value system of a Western-educated elite was coming to a catastrophic end; a new communalistically aggressive elite, and along with it a new culture, was sweeping them out of power. The approach of the group behind the coup was that of a nonpolitical bureaucratic elite. They felt that the breakdown they saw was the outcome of mismanagement by politicians who had unleashed the communal passions of the masses for their own short-term goals of achieving and retaining power. They evidently desired the restoration of what they perceived as elements of the old order managed by the Western-educated elite.[56] Such a restoration could only have occurred with intervention from outside the democratic process, which was inevitably transferring power to the Sinhala Buddhist majority. The conditions following communal violence were favorable to the mobilization of this group and the organization of the coup. The campaign to control violence and suppress political agitation by the minority led to a long period of emergency rule in which there was a military buildup with close coordination of the administration, the police, and the armed forces. It gave senior personnel in these services the opportunity to work together to exchange views on the developments that were taking place and, in the process, support each other in their critical responses to the events around them. The day before the coup leaders were to put their plan into action, information reached the government. The leaders and others directly involved in the attempt were arrested, and the coup was aborted without any loss of life.

The coup attempt in 1966 seemed to have originated in a group that was in some ways the opposite of the group that tried to engineer the 1962 coup. The facts about this coup are somewhat obscure. The coup attempt appears to have been carried out by those who saw the return of the UNP to power in 1965 as a serious threat to the gains resulting from the changes that were made after 1956. In this sense it was an extremist response on behalf of the new Sinhala Buddhist elite and its mix of socialism and Sinhala Buddhist culture.

The full story of both coups has yet to be written. It is not clear whether any of the political parties or leading personalities in these parties were either directly or indirectly implicated in these events. Although there is no evidence that any widespread violence or liquidation of political leaders had been contemplated by the groups behind these attempts, there was obvious readiness to use force in the event of resistance. Those suspected of both coups were given the benefit of normal legal processes and were eventually released. They have been able to resume normal civilian life. The way in which the coup attempts were handled by the state and the treatment the suspects received revealed a system that was by and large committed to the observance of the due processes of the law.

The biggest challenge to the system was the armed insurrection of 1971. Any detailed analysis of the causes of the insurrection is beyond the scope of this study and would require independent treatment.[57] What is relevant, however, is the fact that, as in the case of ethnic violence and the attempts at coups, the political and social developments in the country produced a disadvantaged or dissident group that became convinced that the system as it operated could not offer its members any relief. The main contributory factor was the unprecedented growth of unemployment among the young educated population during the 1960s. We saw earlier that although the economy grew at an annual average of approximately 4.5 percent during the 1950s and 1960s, the work force grew at approximately 2.1 percent between 1958 and 1971, whereas employment grew at only 1.1 percent. The rate of unemployment among the population in the age group 15–30 rose to intolerably high levels, easily the highest in Asia. As against this, high expectations had been generated by the spread of free education from primary to tertiary levels. School leavers came into the labor market in increasing numbers, seeking employment in the organized sector; but the economy was able to create appropriate employment opportunities for only a small fraction of these job seekers.

Neither the social-welfare program nor the political system could cope with the pressures generated by the young population entering the work force. The social-welfare programs and the agricultural-settlement policy were geared to meet the needs and expectations of an older generation, developing out of a low-income rural economy relatively satisfied with the pattern of economic activity available to it. Although the social-welfare programs helped to mitigate the burden of unemployment that fell on households, they were totally inadequate to deal with the young generation who were seeking new income-earning opportunities at a higher level of education. The competitive political system only served to exacerbate the problem. Access to scarce employment opportunities became a matter of political patronage, which could be extended only to a few political supporters. Consequently, a massive unemployed work force had grown in the 1960s with no early prospect of participating in productive social activity. In such a situation, where succeeding cohorts of school leavers have no access to the existing system, the emergence of a movement for the violent overthrow of the system is not a surprising outcome. Although the insurgents included a considerable number of persons already employed, the large majority of the following were recruited from among the unemployed.

Several aspects of the insurgent movement relate to the issues of violence and development. First is the complexity of the development process itself insofar as it produces a breeding ground for violence. The equity-oriented pattern of development in Sri Lanka was not successful in avoiding the intense violence of the insurrection. The violence itself seems to have had its roots in the pattern of development that stressed social welfare and did not accord the needed priority to growth and employment creation. This has to be considered in relation to what was stated earlier about the pattern of development and the balance between different clusters of development goals. Second, the methodology of violence adopted by the insurrection was itself unique. It aimed at a one-night revolution. It expected to be able to overthrow the government by capturing the police stations and the army headquarters in raids conducted simultaneously in one night. The movement could conceive of such a strategy as being feasible only because of the low military presence in Sri Lanka and the relatively ill-equipped apparatus for internal security.[58] These conditions themselves were the outcome of a social order that did not feel the need for an elaborate system of internal security or defense. The politicians whose power was based on mass support were not overly anxious to build up a powerful security apparatus that could itself become a threat to civilian rule. The insurgent movement therefore caught the security forces in an alarming state of unpreparedness and succeeded in taking over several regions for a few days, with relatively simple equipment. Although there were atrocities on both sides and a high death toll among the insurgents, the number of casualties and the destruction of human life and property were not anywhere on the scale that might have been expected if the two parties had been matched at a high level of armed combat with more sophisticated weaponry.

Third, the insurrection was not a mass movement; it was essentially conspiratorial in character, carried out by trained cadres.[59] The movement therefore did not engender widespread mass violence, expropriation, and destruction of life and property. The violence was regulated and to that extent limited largely to the violence of combat. In the areas that the insurgents managed, reports indicated that civil law and order were effectively maintained. Fourth, the government response to the insurrection was somewhat contradictory and equivocal in nature. There was no doubt that many politicians in power had links with the insurgent movement and that many insurgent groups had supported politicians in power during the general election that had been held in the preceding year. In using the army and the police to bring the situation under control, political leaders appeared to be sensitive to the danger of military excesses and atrocities and the effect these might have on their own popular support. They were ready to court-martial and bring to trial officers who were guilty of excesses. On the other hand, they had to act so as to give full support to the security forces in speedily crushing the insurrection. They could not afford the cardinal error of undermining the morale of the police and army. Finally, the amnesty offered to insurgents and those involved in the movement, and the procedures devised for bringing the leaders to trial, show a degree of moderation that is rare in a developing country. They need to be examined as products of a sociopolitical process and a value system that promoted moderation in such crises. It is important to note that the leaders were not given capital punishment and were finally released, and that many of them have now returned to active politics, ready to work within the parliamentary democratic system. In fact, in all three cases of efforts to overthrow the system, the leading participants have returned to performing different legitimate roles within the system.

Postelection Violence

We now come to the violence that has occurred during and after parliamentary general elections. Elections have always been marred by a few acts of violence, even before independence when they were not fought on organized party lines. Acts of thuggery and intimidation were not uncommon in localities where a candidate commanded strong support. In the mid-1960s and 1970s, however, the pattern of electoral violence changed and assumed a form of systematic organized political revenge. The 1965 general elections were followed by a few outbreaks of this type, but in 1970 and 1977 the violence had spread to most parts of the country and had escalated in intensity. The violence often led to grave crimes, including looting, arson, destruction of property, and even rape and murder.

The nature of the violence and the way in which it seemed to be accepted by the political leadership point to some grave deformity in the political system. The violence is not what would normally have been expected, such as spontaneous clashes between rival factions at the height of an electoral contest; it is more or less premeditated violence directed at the defeated party. It is the pent-up violence of a faction that had accumulated resentment and bitterness over a long period when it was out of power and, during that period, was at the receiving end of acts of political vindictiveness and arbitrary exercise of power by its opponents. In some ways this violence shares the character of violence which follows on the revolutionary overthrow of a regime. The large political majorities that sweep the preceding government out of power contribute to the popular mood. The representational system based on simple majorities in each electorate exaggerates the extent of this majority and reinforces the sense of power. There is a temporary suspension of the system of law and order of the previous regime, a period of bloodletting and release of mass violence, when old scores are settled and past wrongs avenged. The value system that goes with this violence, the underlying political consciousness and attitudes, run counter to the values that are needed to sustain a democratic process. First, the opposition is not accepted as part of the system. At each change of government the party in power acts as though it operates a system that cannot and should not tolerate an opposition. Second, the indignation that accumulates is the reaction to a government that is not prepared to treat the opposition with fairness and equity and that uses any means, fair or foul, to incapacitate the opposition so that it cannot be a serious contender for power.

When the internal discipline in each party is based on these attitudes, such outbreaks of violence as have occurred are not surprising. On the other hand, the fact that the violence has been limited to what has occurred is partly due to the larger nonpolitical value system that sustains the network of social relations and is able to mitigate the factionalism and conflict fanned by partisan politics. These actions of the parties in power reflect the inability to internalize the democratic disciplines fully, to cultivate a political consciousness based on a limited tenure of power, and to recognize the crucial importance of the availability of an alternative government for a democratic society. Such a consciousness and acceptance require a genuinely democratic approach to power where the power holders can retire from power with grace and play the role of a constructive opposition with a sense of fulfillment. Some politicians and ideologues argue that the problem of political violence springs from a more fundamental source that is rooted within a multiparty system. They perceive the multiparty system, with its inherent propensity for party conflict, as alien to the indigenous traditions and political consciousness of the Sri Lankan society. They regard the party system as leading to an artificial mobilization of people on partisan lines. The alternative they advocate is a nonparty representative system of a consensual character. Some aspects of this critique no doubt deserve serious consideration, but no total operable alternative has been presented. A discussion of these issues need not detain us here.

What is surprising in Sri Lanka is that undemocratic attitudes toward the opposition persist in a context in which governments have been defeated so frequently and parties have had to move from power to the opposition so often. It would seem that each political party would have seen the alterations of power and opposition that it would have to accept for its own role and contributed to the creation of a genuinely democratic tradition that institutionalizes the opposition. Yet the parliamentary tradition has not succeeded in building up a tradition that accepts the opposition as an essential part of the system, to be afforded the opportunity to function effectively and with dignity. Political parties in power would always argue that the opposition acts in a way that is an obstruction to good government and only seeks to discredit the government and remove it from power by every means available. Then the vicious circle leading to victimization of the opposition and obstruction of the government can be broken only by a unilateral policy of profound statesmanship by one party when it assumes power, which sets the system in a truly democratic framework.

There are as yet no signs of statesmanlike generosity capable of changing the character of the system. Neither of the governments that came to power in 1970 and 1977 addressed itself seriously to the problem of postelection violence. Both governments appointed one-man commissions to investigate and report on the incidents.[60] The reports themselves, however, received little attention. The same public official was appointed to both commissions by the authorities. There was no systematic effort to compensate the victims or activate impartial legal processes against the offenders, who were almost invariably supporters of the winning party. No conscious attempt was made to establish the political norms and institute the necessary safeguards to prevent the recurrence of such violence in the future. The Special Presidential Commission that has been investigating the misdeeds of the previous government raises a number of complex issues about political accountability on the one hand, and the government's relations with the political opposition on the other. On the findings of the Presidential Commission, Parliament has imposed civic disabilities on the leader of the major opposition party. The overwhelming parliamentary majority of the government party enables it to give constitutional validity to its actions and a finality to its decisions that effectively shuts out appeal and closes all access to redress within the system. The situation that then arises, considered purely in its political aspects, leads inevitably to a confrontation of major political parties. It is the type of action that reinforces the processes that accentuate party conflict, reinforce the politics of revenge, and bring in their train all the problems belonging to a stage of political development that might be described as an immature democracy.

A Comment on External Linkages and Violence

So far we have considered the problems of violence as being entirely internal to any given nation or society. Such an approach would be

unrealistic, ignoring the fact that a developing society is linked economically and politically to an international structure of power and an increasingly integrated international system. The conflicts and rivalries
within this structure are transmitted in a variety of forms to the internal
political and socioeconomic processes in a developing society. The character and intensity of this penetration vary according to the importance
of a country or region to the strategies of the superpowers. The config-
urations of power in the two main power blocks in the global system—
the North American and Western European capitalist bloc, and the Eastern European communist bloc—are often reflected in social conflicts and
political alignments within the developing countries. The alliances of
local elites with either of these power blocs influence the pattern of
internal conflicts and, in extreme situations, determine the extent of open
violence and combat. Within this situation political parties subject to
strong ideological direction from major foreign powers, on the one hand,
and to the presence of foreign investment and transnational corporate
enterprise on the other, will play a role in the internal power balance.
Sri Lanka was relatively fortunate in that both politically and economically, the trends during the three decades after independence did not lead
to any such major intrusion. We already commented on the character
that the left assumed as a result of the Trotskyist party. On the economic
front, up to 1977 the mix of policies that have been adopted has progressively reduced the degree of foreign ownership and control of the
national economy.

In this context, the ideology of nonalignment and the effort to create
the political space for the autonomous development of developing countries, free from the pressures of global superpower rivalry, become vitally
important for the issues considered in this study. Sri Lanka's commitment
to nonalignment and the capacity it has shown to steer its foreign relations
and external linkages within the framework of nonalignment has been an
important factor in its management of the problems of violence and
development. In the case of the 1971 insurrection, Sri Lanka was able
to obtain support and military assistance from all the political blocs—
United States, Western Europe, the USSR, China—to bring the situation
under control.[61] This response from the international community was
partly the result of the country's nonaligned policy. External connections
have been alleged in the case of the insurrection and later in the case of
terrorism in the north of Sri Lanka. By and large, however, as already
noted in the case of the working-class movement, the political environment that Sri Lanka evolved was not receptive to the entry of external
influence in a manner that would have linked Sri Lanka more closely to

the conflicts in the international power structure. This contributed to the unique set of conditions that moderated the internal forces of conflict and violence in Sri Lanka.

The Instruments Used to Contain Violence

The experience of Sri Lanka has demonstrated that despite sociopolitical institutions that have incorporated many of the democratic mechanisms for conflict resolution and despite a relatively equitable structure of distribution, which has reduced the potential for intense social conflict, the violence and instability implicit in the processes of rapid change and development have erupted in various forms. The real dilemma that has faced successive governments is that of devising the mechanisms and the state apparatus to cope effectively with these outbreaks while still maintaining essentially intact the democratic structure and the framework of civil rights. On the one hand, governments had to equip themselves to deal with extraordinary situations. On the other hand, the extraordinary machinery that was needed had to be so designed that although it was effective for crisis management, it would also contain built-in safeguards to ensure a speedy return to normal government. It must be emphasized, however, that the instrument itself becomes effective and valid only within the framework of goals and strategies that have succeeded in minimizing structural violence. The controlled use of extraordinary machinery for the management of violence that is described here becomes feasible only within a larger socioeconomic and political framework that has succeeded both in establishing viable democratic institutions and in promoting structural changes that benefit the majority of the population. The system that evolved in Sri Lanka was able to show significant progress in both these directions. Therefore, the instrumentality for crisis management that evolved in Sri Lanka within this larger national system deserves careful examination.

We may now turn to some of the instruments employed to contain the outbreaks of violence. The most important of those instruments is the Public Securities Ordinance enacted in 1947, which empowered the government to declare a state of emergency and enact regulations that have the force of primary law.[62]

The Public Security Ordinance was enacted on the eve of the colonial period, in the context of a general strike sponsored by the Communist party, which affected commerce, the tea and rubber plantations, and essential services. The government perceived the strike as an attempt by its political adversaries to disrupt and paralyze the economy and the delivery of essential services.[63] The government contended that it needed to be armed with the necessary powers to ensure the distribution of food and the maintenance of public transportation. The ordinance was rationalized as an emergency measure to enable the state to contain extraordinary threats to public order and the economy.[64]

The legislation was resisted strenuously by opposition groups. They contended that it was intended to vest the executive with arbitrary authority to override the legitimate expressions of trade-union rights. They criticized the authoritarian and undemocratic character of the law, which clothed the state in judicial immunity with respect to acts committed during an emergency.[65]

The ordinance, which was modeled on parallel legislation in other British colonies, empowered the governor in his discretion to proclaim a state of emergency in the event of mutiny, riot, civil commotion, or threat to the supply of essential supplies and services.[66] Neither the proclamation of a state of emergency nor any emergency regulation could be challenged in a court of law.[67]

Subsequent amendments were effected to the Public Security Ordinance to mitigate some of the rigors of an emergency. The duration of an emergency was limited to one month, but extension was possible.[68] To provide for continuing parliamentary control and scrutiny, provision was made to summon Parliament when it was prorogued.[69] Further, machinery was established for administrative review of detentions effected during an emergency. At the same time, provision was made to enable the government to deploy the armed forces, impose a curfew, and take related measures to maintain security in any specific area without proclaiming a state of national emergency.[70]

The sweep of emergency regulations enacted during the emergencies that have been declared during the 1970s and early 1980s has been such that they have resulted in comprehensive restrictions on political freedom and individual liberties. These restrictions have taken the form of prohibitions against meetings, processions, and publications.[71] Newspapers have been proscribed, printing presses sealed, and the transmission of information abroad curtailed.[72] Freedom of movement has been curtailed by the imposition of a general curfew or by restricting individuals to their residences, from leaving the country, or from engaging in business and associating with others.[73] Also authorized were arrest without a warrant by a wide category of public officers, and preventive detention at any place designated by the inspector-general of police.[74]

Prison regulations relating to humane conditions of imprisonment were suspended. Widespread powers of search and seizure have been conferred with respect to vehicles and vessels. The substantive penal law was amended to create new offenses, such as conspiracy to overthrow the government, and to impose death sentences or mandatory prison sentences for offenses that would ordinarily have led to lesser sentences. Freedom of expression was curtailed by requiring prior police permission for the distribution of handbills and leaflets. Police officers' power of investigation of persons, including access to persons in custody, was strengthened.

The prerogative writs and related judicial remedies for the review of administrative action were suspended with respect to acts done during an emergency.[75] Wide powers of selective enforcement and prosecution were vested in the attorney-general, who also enjoyed the discretion to determine the court in which proceedings would be instituted. Rules against the admission of confessions were relaxed.

Emergency regulations were also enacted to suspend the local-government electoral process. Specific political parties were proscribed, political rallies curtailed, and newspapers sealed. Local-authority elections were suspended, and a parliamentary by-election was postponed for more than two years.[76]

These regulations were also employed to effect certain social measures that were unconnected with the emergency. Additional allowances were paid to plantation workers, and minimum wages were provided to textile workers. Similar regulations were enacted with respect to cultivation of food crops, encroachment on state land, and animal trespass.[77]

The declaration of a state of emergency and the exercise of emergency powers became matters of intense political controversy. The critics argued that an emergency was no longer a temporary measure to meet extraordinary threats to the stability of the state. Emergency rule has been arbitrarily extended long after the conditions that resulted in the crisis had significantly altered. Although the extensions of emergencies had been justified on the ground that new conditions of instability had arisen, the courts had been reluctant to look into these conditions. Once an emergency was declared, it soon became a permanent feature of the machinery of the government. It was also argued that emergency powers were frequently employed against groups that were not the source of the immediate violent challenge to authority. Thus a state of emergency and the enlargement of police and bureaucratic authority had a chilling effect on the expression of political dissent. Opposition leaders and trade-union officials feared restrictions on their freedom of movement, the publication of party newspapers, and the mobilization of party and trade-union members. The exclusion of judicial review had increased the threat of wrongful arrest, arbitrary acquisition of property, and requisition of movables of political opponents. Emergency powers, critics argued, posed a continuing threat to the effective functioning of democratic institutions.[78]

Particular concern was expressed about the suspension of fundamental freedoms and the prerogative writs. The argument was that certain basic human rights, such as freedom from torture and the right to due process of law, should remain inviolate even during public emergencies.

Others have defended emergency powers as a necessary safety valve in a growing democracy. Despite emergency powers, peaceful transfer of power from one party to another has been possible. The integrity of universal adult franchise had been sustained for five decades. These achievements, proponents argue, would not have been possible without the Public Security Ordinance and the ability to check violent threats to the stability of the state. Popular support for the constitutional framework is founded on the belief that the state needs to be armed with adequate instruments to contain coup d'etats and other challenges to constitutional authority.

The new government that was installed in power in 1977 viewed its electoral success partly as a popular denunciation of the use of emergency powers by its predecessor. Accordingly, the new government instituted certain fundamental changes in the instruments used to contain violence.

First, the proclamation of the state of emergency has to be approved by Parliament within fourteen days.[79] Second, the right to periodic extension of emergency from month to month was modified. Under the present constitution the emergency would automatically lapse within a period of three months unless two-thirds of the majority agreed to the extension of the emergency.[80] Although the present government has the requisite majority, no future government is likely to do so after the system of proportional representation comes into effect.

Third, the chapter on fundamental rights also recognized that certain fundamental freedoms could not be restricted by emergency regulations. These related to freedom of thought, conscience, and religion, and the prohibition against a person being subjected to torture or to degrading, cruel, and unusual punishment.[81] The restriction of these rights could be challenged by recourse to the Supreme Court.[82] The constitution thereby recognized that no exigencies of national emergency could justify the erosion of certain core human values.

While noting these developments toward the restriction of emergency power, it is necessary also to point to trends in the opposite direction. First, certain provisions originally that could be invoked only during an emergency have become part of the regular statutes. Under the Essential Services Law, the government, without an emergency, may issue an order limiting the rights to strike and related trade-union action in certain specified services.[83] The Proscription of Liberation Tigers Law and the

Prevention of Terrorism Laws armed the security apparatus with extraordinary powers relating to investigation, detention, and prosecution of members of organizations engaged in political violence.[84]

Both measures have been criticized for having clothed the state with authoritarian powers during periods when no emergency was operative. The second category of laws raises the state's dilemma in dealing with those who reject the values of constitutionalism and question the legitimacy of the state. Can the protective arm of the state relating to fundamental freedom and fair trial be extended to those who reject its basic postulates? Several civil-rights groups have emphasized the duty of the state to respect human rights even in dealing with those committed to its violent overthrow.[85] During the insurgency and in dealing with groups committed to destabilization of the state by force, however, special measures for investigation and trial have been introduced.

Some continue to criticize the use of emergency powers and urge the repeal of the chapter on public security. They argue that the manifestations of violence can be managed by a more professional police and military force without the attendant restrictions on freedom of expression and political freedom. They also emphasize the need for greater safeguards during arrest, interrogation, and detention. They would like to institutionalize consultation with the opposition prior to the proclamation of a state of emergency, as well as an enlarged role for the judiciary in scrutinizing emergency actions.

The political processes that have evolved since independence have progressively accorded importance to democratic freedoms and fundamental rights. Two of the most significant achievements have been the continuity of universal adult franchise and the effective emergence of a multiparty system. The growth of institutions of representational democracy has been noted as one of the factors that has minimized the propensity for violence. The social and political tensions that were the sources of structural violence were submitted to the process of bargaining and accommodation within the parliamentary arena. Social-welfare and equity-oriented policies surfaced out of this process. The growth of the political parties as the principal actors in the process of decision making, however, had important implications for the organization and expression of dissent. The political parties effectively appropriated dissent and inhibited the evolution of autonomous trade unions, student unions, and the like outside their sphere of influence and direction. The expression of dissent outside the parliamentary framework, even through nonviolent agitation, was viewed with disfavor and sometimes curtailed. The parliamentary form was soon regarded as the only legitimate mode of political discourse and agitation. The decision of the revolutionary Marxist groups that participated in the insurrection of 1971 to organize themselves as a parliamentary party is a remarkable submission to this political reality. If the system is to strengthen further its capacity to minimize the propensity for violence, however, it needs to provide space for full and unfettered expression of dissent. It needs to legitimize the nonviolent expression and resolution of dissent outside the framework of political parties and parliamentary processes.

Notes

1. Theories of conflict have attempted to explain all social deviance in terms of the underlying social conflicts between groups with opposing interests; see, for example, R. Serge Denisoff and Charles H. McCaghy, eds., *Deviance, Conflict and Criminality* (Chicago, 1973). Such an explanation would have little room for human values that have supposedly universal validity and therefore should apply to all conflicting groups in their behavior toward each other. See also Hans Toch, *Violent Men* (Penguin, 1972), and *Terrorist Mind* (New York: Bobbs-Merrill, 1974).

2. The rationale for revolutionary violence is given in Karl Marx's memorable statement: "Force is the midwife of every old society pregnant with a new one." *Capital,* vol. 1 (Moscow: Progress Publishers, 1977), p. 706. V.I. Lenin's *State and Revolution* is perhaps the most cogent exposition of the supposed necessity for revolutionary violence.

3. See Johann Galtung, *The True Worlds—a Transnational Perspective* (New York: Free Press, 1980), pp. 67–68: "The major distinction . . . is between person to person violence and structure to person violence. . . . Structural violence just happens without any specific actor behind it . . . the violence is built into the structure, usually derived from some fundamental inequity. . . ."

4. *Soft* as applied to states is a term Gunnar Myrdal uses in his *Asian Drama* (Middlesex, England: Penguin, 1968), pp. 66–67. They are states that are weak in so-called social discipline.

5. See Kautilya, *Arthasastra,* 1.4.9.

6. Homer H. Dubbs, *The Works of Hsuntze* (trans.) (London, 1928), p. 301.

7. Heinrich Zimmer, *Philosophies of India* (New York: Meridian, 1956), pp. 128–139.

8. "A king who oppresses his people will forfeit his life and his kingdom." Kewal Motwani, *Manu Dharma Sastra* (Madras, 1958),

p. 139. Traditional Chinese thought laid equal emphasis on the obligations of the king to the people. Mencius, for example, upheld the view that a ruler who fails to promote the welfare of the people should be removed.

9. The Chou who overthrew the Shang dynasty justified their action along these lines.

10. Zimmer, *Philosophies of India,* pp. 120–121.

11. According to Buddhist tradition, King Vessantara was the Buddha in one of his previous incarnations. Having made an absolute vow of chastity, Vessantara gave away all his earthly possessions and finally gave away his children. See E.B. Cowell, "Vessantara Jathakaya," in *Jathaka Stories,* vol. 5–6 (London: Pali Text Society, 1973), pp. 246–305.

12. *Mahavamsa,* chap. 25, pp. 106–111.

13. Ibid., chap. 36, pp. 93–97.

14. "Passive resistance is a method of securing rights by personal suffering; it is the reverse of resistance by force." M.K. Gandhi, *Hind Swaraj or Indian Home Rule* (Ahmedabad: Navajivan Publishing House, 1962), p. 79.

15. See Marga Institute, *Welfare and Growth,* Marga Publication, 1974; Godfrey Gunatilleke, "Participatory Development and Dependence," *Marga Quarterly Journal* 5, no. 3 (1978), special issue.

16. Donoughmore Commission, *Report of the Special Commission on the Ceylon Constitution—Colombo* (H. Ross, Government Printer, 1928), pp. 83–89.

17. "Trade-offs in Sri Lanka," in *World Development Report.* World Bank, 1980, p. 59; John Sewell and Staff of Overseas Development Council, *The United States and World Development Agenda,* 1977, p. 162.

18. See *Annual Report—Central Bank of Sri Lanka,* 1973, table 54.

19. Gunatilleke, "Participatory Development," p. 125; Lal Jayawardena, "Country Experiences, Sri Lanka," in *Redistribution with Growth,* ed. Chenery Hollis et al., p. 278.

20. Reports of the Commissioner of Elections, Colombo; G.P.S.H. De Silva, *A Statistical Survey of Elections to the Legislatures of Sri Lanka, 1911–1977* (Marga Institute, 1979).

21. Gunatilleke, "Participatory Development," p. 79.

22. World Bank, *World Development Report, 1981,* p. 134.

23. *Socio-Economic Survey, 1969/70,* Department of Census and Statistics, 1973; *Census of Population, Sri Lanka, 1971: General Report,* Department of Census and Statistics, 1978, pp. 150–152; *Consumer Finance Survey 1973,* Central Bank.

24. For a comprehensive account of the labor movement and growth of trade unions during the period 1880–1933, see Kumari Jayawardena, *The Rise of Labour Movement in Ceylon* (Durham, N.C.: Duke University Press, 1972).

25. See "The Public Emergency," in *Parliamentary Debates* 15 (1953):534–614.

26. U. Kariyawasam, *Industrial Relations and the Political Process in Sri Lanka*, Research Series no. 66, International Institute for Labour Studies, 1981.

27. Centre for Society and Religion, *Strike, July 1980*, in Dossier no. 77, 1981.

28. *Paddy Lands Act*, no. 1, 1958.

29. *Land Reform Act of 1972* and *Land Reform (Amendment) Act of 1975*.

30. For an analysis of cultivation committees in operation, see Wilbert Gooneratne et al., *The Role of Cultivation Committees in Agricultural Planning at Village Level*, Agrarian Research and Training Institute, Occasional Publication, Series no. 3, Colombo, February 1973.

31. C.R. Hensman et al., "The Role of Western Educated Elites," Community pamphlet, Colombo; All Ceylon Buddhist Congress, *Betrayal of Buddhism* (Balangoda: Dharmajiva Press); D.C. Wijewardene, *The Revolt in the Temple* (Colombo: Sinha Publications, 1953).

32. Eighth Annual Conference, United National Party, January 1956. The main resolution at this conference was that "Sinhalese alone should be made the state language of Ceylon."

33. In 1963 the United Front, consisting of the Lanka Sama Samaja party, the Communist party, and the Mahajana Eksath Perumana, fell in line with the SLFP language policy. In 1965 the LSSP, in their joint election campaign with the SLFP, accepted the existing Sinhala-only legislation.

34. The Tamil Congress, led by G.G. Ponnambalam.

35. The Federal party, led by S.J.V. Chelvanayagam.

36. The Federal party's 1960 election manifesto explicitly rejected the call for a Tamil separate state. In 1970 they again condemned policies that would result in a division of the country. In the mid-1960s, however, Federal party parliamentarians were already becoming increasingly skeptical of the possibility of achieving their demands within the framework of a united nation. (1964 Hansard, vol. 56, col. 255–256). The final decision to struggle for a separate Tamil state was taken in 1975, after the formation of the Tamil United Liberation Front. See Dr. Neelan Tiruchelvam, "The Making and Unmaking of Constitutions," *Ceylon Journal of Historical and Social Studies* 7, no. 2 (1977).

37. *Mahavamsa*, chap. XXI. The first Tamil conquest referred to in

the chronicle is that of Sena and Guttika, "sons of a freighter who conquered King Suratissa at the Head of a great army and reigned for twenty-two years, justly."

38. "The Sinhalese are the minority in Dravidastan. We are carrying on a struggle for our national existence against the Dravidastan majority. . . ." D.P.R. Gunawardene, in Parliament, 3 September 1962, Hansard, vol. 48, col. 1315. See also Rt. Rev. C.C. Wickremasinghe and Ven. Dr. Ratnasara Thero Hewanpola, "Sinhala Tamil Conflict in Sri Lanka" in *Logos,* vol. 16, no. 2, August 1977.

39. Gananath Obeysekera, "Vicissitudes of the Sinhala Buddhist Identities through Time and Change," in *Collective Identities, Nationalism, and Protest in Modern Sri Lanka,* ed. M. Roberts (Colombo: Marga, 1979), pp. 279–313.

40. See Anagarika Dharmapala, *Collection of Speeches, Essays, Letters* (Colombo: Government Press, 1965).

41. All Ceylon Buddhist Congress.

42. Ceylon Citizenship Acts of 1948 and 1949.

43. From the beginning the Federal party insisted that the "Tamil speaking people in Ceylon constitute a nation distinct from that of the Sinhalese," according to three principal criteria—"a separate historical past," "a linguistic entity," and "a territorial habitation." *The Case for a Federal Constitution for Ceylon,* Resolutions passed at the First National Convention of the Federal party, 1951.

44. Rev. Kanagaratnam, *Tamils and Cultural Pluralism in Ancient Sri Lanka* (Colombo: Ananda Press, 1976).

45. S. Pathmanathan, *The Jaffna Kingdom* (Colombo: Rajendra Press, 1978).

46. Donoughmore Commission, ibid.; Soulbury Commission, *Report of the Commission on Constitutional Reform, 1945* (London: His Majesty's Stationery Office), chaps. 8 and 13. Regarding proposals made by the All-Ceylon Tamil Congress, the commission commented, "Any attempt by artificial means to convert a majority into a minority is not only inequitable, but doomed to failure" (p. 70).

47. *Bandaranaike-Chelvanayagam Pact, 1957.* The joint statements made in Parliament by the prime minister and Mr. Chelvanayagam, leader of the Federal party, on 26 July 1957, contain the text. The pact included the recognition of Tamil as a language of the national minority, its use in the north and east, and the establishment of regional councils with powers over specified subjects.

48. *Parliamentary Debates,* vol. 6, no. 7.

49. C.R. De Silva, "The Politics of University Admissions Policy in Sri Lanka, 1970–1978," *Sri Lanka Journal of Social Sciences* (1978).

50. *Prevention of Terrorism Act: Emergency '79,* Published by the Movement for Interracial Justice and Equality, 1980.

51. See *Violence in Jaffna, June 1981: Incidents in 1981,* Centre for Society and Religion, Dossier 80, 1981.

52. Refer to the termination of membership in Parliament of Dr. Neville Fernando, M.P., in *Parliamentary Debates,* vol. 19, no. 1, December 1981, pp. 36–234.

53. See Godfrey Gunatilleke, "Some Socio-economic Aspects of Communal Problems," *Logos* 16, no. 2 (August 1977).

54. Marga Institute, "Needs of Children," Mimeo., 1980. See also H.D. Sumanasekera, "Measuring the Regional Variation of the Quality of Life in Sri Lanka," *Sri Lanka Journal of Agrarian Studies* 2, no. 1.

55. Soulbury Commission, *Report,* p. 72.

56. *Parliamentary Debates,* vol. 46, 13–14 February, col. 1120–1543.

57. A.C. Alles, *Insurgency, 1971* (Colombo: Apothecaries, 1976). Among the other analytical writings on the insurrection, see C.R. Hensman, "Rural Revolution in Ceylon," *Venture* 23, no. 6; Gananath Obeysekera, "Some Comments on the Social Backgrounds of the April 1971 Insurgency in Sri Lanka," *Journal of Asian Studies* (May 1974); and Wiswa Warnapala, "The April Revolt in Ceylon," *Asian Survey* 12, no. 3 (March 1972).

58. See text of broadcast to the nation by Sirimavo Bandaranaike, prime minister, 24 April 1971. *Parliamentary Debates,* vol. 94, 4.5 (1971). "What was deliberately done over the years was to minimise expenditure on defence. . . ." (p. 563).

59. Criminal Justice Commission proceedings, reported in *Ceylon Daily News,* 13–14 June; *Judgment of the Criminal Justice Commission* (Insurgency), Inquiry no. 1, Department of Government Printing (1976).

60. The report on the incidents in 1970 was published as a sessional paper after the present government came into power. *Sessional Paper III of 1977.* The report on the 1977 incidents has not been published. The 1970 report listed approximately 1,000 valid complaints. About 50 percent of these had been reported to the police, out of which only seventy-six cases had been taken to court. The total loss suffered by the victims had been estimated at Rs.3.6 million.

61. Bandaranaike, broadcast.

62. Ordinance no. 25 of 1947, which came into effect on 16 June 1957.

63. See D.S. Senanayake, Debates of the State Council of Ceylon, 10 June 1947; see also Memorandum by the chief secretary on trade

unionism among public servants in Ceylon, *Sessional Paper no. 6 of 1947*. The strike was perceived as having "a political as distinct from a purely industrial object."

64. See A. Mahadeva, Debates of the State Council of Ceylon, 10 June 1947.

65. See Debates of the State Council of Ceylon, 10 June 1947.

66. See Ordinance no. 25 of 1947, sec. 2.

67. See Ordinance no. 25 of 1947, secs. 3, 8.

68. See Public Security Ordinance (as amended by sections of Act no. 22 of 1949), sec. 2(2).

69. See Public Security Ordinance (as amended by section 2 of Act no. 22 of 1949), sec. 2(3).

70. See Public Security Ordinance, part III.

71. See generally, on the restrictions imposed by emergency regulations, *The Peoples' Rights: Documents of the Civil Rights Movement of Sri Lanka, 1971–1978* (Colombo: CRM, 1979), pp. 7–21; See also Suriya Wickremasinghe, *Some Aspects of Emergency Regulations,* vols. 1, 11, Bar Association of Sri Lanka Newsletter (1979).

72. See *The Peoples' Rights,* p. 9, on the emergency regulations relating to press ownership.

73. See ibid., p. 1, on the restrictions on freedom of expression and association of trade unions, political parties, and other organizations.

74. See ibid., pp. 11–15, on prosecutions, detentions, and the rights of persons in custody.

75. See ibid, p. 111, on the need for judicial review of emergency regulations.

76. See Wickremasinghe, *Emergency.* See also *The Peoples' Rights,* p. 73, which lists twenty-six local bodies whose term of office was extended by emergency regulations and whose elections were postponed. The Kankesanthurai by-election was also postponed for about two years.

77. See *The Peoples' Rights,* p. 72, which pointed out that although the objectives of some of these regulations are laudable, the ordinary democratic process had been bypassed.

78. See ibid., p. 99, wherein the civil-rights movement calls various political parties preparing for the 1977 general elections to make a firm commitment to human rights by, inter alia, undertaking a serious review of the whole question of the exercise of emergency powers. See also ibid., p. 110, where the civil-rights movement in a representation to the Select Committee on the Reforms of the Constitution lists some of the negative features of the Public Securities Ordinance and the exercise of emergency power.

79. See Article 155(6) of the Constitution of the Democratic Socialist Republic of Sri Lanka.

80. See Article 155(8) of the Constitution.

81. See Articles 10 and 11 of the Constitution, which are not subject to Section 15, which recognizes certain restrictions on fundamental rights that may be prescribed by law in the interest of national security. Section 15(7) states that *law* for these purposes includes emergency regulations.

82. See Articles 17 and 126 of the Constitution; but the enforcement of the article relating to freedom from torture has proved problematic for various procedural and evidentiary reasons.

83. The Essential Services Law.

84. The civil-rights movement, referring to the former law, protested that "This law brings into the ordinary law of the land measures normally used only in emergency situations, namely the power to ban organisations, detention without trial or charge at Ministerial discretion and censorship." See *The Peoples' Rights,* p. 119.

85. "We consider . . . that a democratic government even where its own existence is imperilled, has certain obligations which it must respect in resorting to emergency powers. . . ." See *The Peoples' Rights,* p. 112.

6

Technocratic Authoritarianism and the Dilemmas of Dependent Development

Alexander R. Magno

The dependence of numerous postcolonial societies on the capitalist centers matured into the crisis of poverty. This crisis has in turn generated political pressures taking the character of demands for change and development. These demands may be categorized in a general way as either liberal or radical socialist. To differentiate roughly, the liberal demand may be summed up into a demand to alter the political structure in some way to make it more responsive to the needs of development. The radical socialist, on the other hand, demands a revolutionary anti-imperialist break as a precondition for progress.

This chapter is a preliminary attempt to organize conceptually a description and explanation of the Philippine experience with the technocratic response to the crises of backwardness perceived and understood basically from a liberal standpoint. It will try to integrate in this description and explanation the roots of the dilemmas of development experienced by Philippine society in the ideological standpoint and political practice of the authoritarian regime that has been in place for close to a decade now.

This chapter will, at the onset, work on the premises of a standpoint critical of the trade-off explanation that sees authoritarianism as the contemporary need and political precondition for the achievement of progress. An explanation that requires the tentative surrender of freedom for a bowl of rice invariably tends to see the problem of backwardness as one that is resolved by the development of things rather than of people: in concrete terms, legitimizing the suppression of liberty as politically requisite for the growth of industry.

The notion of the state consolidating its political hegemony and repressive hold in the developing societies is a favorite theme among U.S. political scientists, who see it as an essential condition for a take-off toward the stage of full development.[1] (The state in developed societies must be seen in terms of the role imputed to it by the conditions of underdevelopment. This has to be emphasized since the dominant mode of political analysis, the bourgeois-technocratic in particular, has so far treated the problem of the overdeveloped Third World state within the ideological frame of so-called developing societies.) This theory of the polity, which not only apologizes for dictatorship but in fact proposes it, is clearly an adjunct to a specific ideological understanding of development: that which conceives of development in the underdeveloping (in their words, *developing*) societies in terms of emulating the historical experience of the industrial-capitalist societies of the west. This understanding of development works on the premise that the underdeveloped societies will progress only through closer integration with the developed ones, a premise that inevitably proposes the strategy of export-oriented, foreign-investment-led development supported by the funding institutions of the capitalist centers, which in turn require the type of so-called political stability for which dictatorships are most convenient.[2] This economic view is further enhanced by the theories of free markets and open trade that have been the guide calls for the capitalist penetration of the postcolonial societies and are essentially premised on theoretical derivatives of the classical trickle-down theory of the road to prosperity.

Martial Law, 1972

The declaration of martial law by President Ferdinand E. Marcos on 21 September 1972, and the subsequent inauguration of the so-called New Society, ushered in a new era in the development of the Philippine political system and, more important, the social mode of Philippine society.[3] The restructuring of state power along more authoritarian lines meant a qualitative change in the relationship between the institutions of power and the character of the neocolonial structure. The decisiveness of the shift from one political form to another cannot be underestimated. The seizure of the state apparatus by a faction committed to a definite vision of the Philippines had a compelling impact on Philippine society.

Several lines of interpretation have been advanced. The period that set the conditions for an authoritarian political force—conditions that were in turn negated by the emergence of such a force—is too complex to be categorized neatly. Politicians opposed to the Marcos faction see the imposition of dictatorial rule simply as a maneuver by the president to keep himself in power and thus protect his vested interests in the presidency beyond the limits set by the then-operative Constitution of the Republic.[4] Sections of the left saw it as a split in the ruling classes arising out of the crisis wrought by the imperialist stranglehold over the Philippine economy. Still others saw it as a consolidation of ruling-class forces in the face of a growing revolutionary and popular anti-imperialist mass movement.[5]

These various views are not necessarily mutually exclusive; rather, they are differences of emphasis on the most decisive factor in determining the nature and character of authoritarianism in the Philippines. This clarification applies to the regime's own explanation for its existence.

The declaration of martial law must be viewed in its economic, social, and political context; any attempt to reduce this phenomenon into simplified categories tends to overlook the intricate texture of the historical fabric into which this specific occurrence is woven. It cannot, in fact, even be reduced to the struggle between old and new social forces; for, as the regime of authoritarianism has unfolded itself over the last nine years, it has both preserved old relations and fostered new ones without clear-cut distinctions. Even among progressive and Marxist intellectuals in the Philippines, for instance, the question of whether the regime and its clientele of transnational corporations have transformed the Philippine countryside or merely disposed the process of semifeudalism remains unsettled.[6]

What is quite clear is that on the eve of the imposition of martial law, Marcos and his faction had begun to be politically isolated. There was rising discontent toward the latter part of the 1960s arising from popular perceptions of economic stagnation aggravated by corruption and inefficiency in government. There was consensus on the need for dramatic social change. This consensus was embodied in the decision to call a constitutional convention that would redefine the national vision of independence and progress, as well as restructure the governmental instrument for realizing that vision. Although there was consensus on the need for dramatic social change, however, there was bitter division on the nature, character, and orientation of the process of change itself. The formal political institutions (such as Congress and the political parties) were divided between those who saw the Marcos government as the main component of the establishment that had to be changed, and those who saw the government as the leading agent of change. The latter line was argued by no less a person than Marcos himself, in *Today's Revolution: Democracy,* which foreshadowed the imposition of martial rule a year after its issue.[7]

Economist Alejandro Lichauco relates the political confrontations and divisions during this period to the raging debates involving economic decontrol and the floating of the peso's value in the international markets.[8] In the latter part of the 1950s, then-president Garcia imposed strict controls on imports and pegged the peso to a defined rate with the dollar. These policies were geared toward encouraging national industrialization, import substitution, and the protection of national enterprises from foreign competition. Macapagal, succeeding Garcia, campaigned on a platform of decontrol and a renunciation of protectionism; he contended that they were the roots of backwardness. Marcos, succeeding Macapagal in 1965, pursued basically the same policies geared toward economic decontrol and free trade, an orientation that drew opposition from both nationalist economists and local industrialists.

At the beginning of Marcos's second term in 1969, his government devalued the peso and coidentified more closely with the International Monetary Fund (IMF)–World Bank's strategy for export-oriented development spearheaded by foreign investments. This economic posture stood at odds not only with the opposition in Congress, but also with a significantly popular nationalist faction in the constitutional convention. This faction had begun formulating provisions in the new constitution characterized primarily by economic nationalism.

Against a backdrop of worsening economic conditions, opposition to the Marcos government began to polarize around the rallying cry of economic nationalism and a renunciation of what were perceived to be unequal trade treaties forced on the Philippines by the United States. A significant mass movement of intellectuals, professionals, and businessmen developed around the ideals of the late Senator Claro M. Recto and the Democratic Alliance of the late 1940s, which he headed and which opposed the ratification of the trade treaties between the United States and the Philippines. This nationalist mass movement, the Movement for the Advancement of Nationalism (MAN), was headed by Senator Lorenzo Tanada. From its ranks were to develop the leaders of more militant and radical movements.[9]

The intensifying nationalist tendency in the Congress and the constitutional convention was given a boost by the sensational Supreme Court decision on the celebrated Quasha case. The Court ruled that U.S. nationals, even under the provisions of the parity-rights treaty, do not have the right to own private land. Since 1946, following an opinion of the Department of Justice, it had been understood that the Parity Ordinance gave Americans national treatment insofar as ownership of private land was concerned. The Court ruled that this was not so, and that, therefore, land acquired by U.S. citizens constituted illegal ownership. This ruling gave the opposition to Marcos new ammunition, and Congress immediately demanded for the escheat of these lands.[10]

The collision course followed by the proimperialist policies of the Marcos government on the one hand and the nationalist tide, which involved not only statesmen and intellectuals but also workers, businessmen, students, and peasants, came to a head by the onset of the 1970s. The president's State of the Nations Speech opening the Congress on 26 January 1970 drew a massive demonstration outside the congressional building that ended in a bloody confrontation involving students and workers, the military, and the police force. Henceforth the streets of Manila were the principal theater of confrontation between progressives, nationalists, and radicals on the one hand, and what they perceived as the symbol of the neocolonial establishment—the Marcos government—on the other.

The politics of polarization had intensified in the two years preceding the imposition of martial rule. In August 1971 unknown persons lobbed grenades at the political rally of the opposition Liberal party in the heart of Manila, seriously injuring the leading opposition personalities and killing several opposition supporters. The event was quickly followed by the suspension of the writ of habeas corpus. Intensification of student and worker protest in the cities, coupled with increasingly frequent skirmishes between government troops and guerillas in the countryside, helped set the stage for the eventual declaration of martial law.

Two significant forces were also developing at this time in a manner that foreshadowed their militant and prominent roles in the regime of authoritarianism. The Catholic Church, an extremely powerful influence in a predominantly Catholic society, had become increasingly sensitive and responsive to the crisis of poverty afflicting its flock in the years succeeding Vatican II.[11] Church groups had become involved with groups such as the Federation of Free Workers and the Federation of Free Farmers. Catholic and Protestant youth and student groups had become increasingly involved in community organizations of the militant student movement. Sections of the clergy became increasingly integrated into the national democratic movement that was now gathering momentum.

The second force that was to be of great significance was the Communist party of the Philippines. Reconstituted in 1968 by young and disenchanted members of the old Partido Komunistang Pilipinas, the CPP and its military arm, the New People's Army (NPA), brought new vigor to the armed revolutionary struggle that had been simmering for decades in the countrysides. Today the party, through the National Democratic Front (NDF), is undoubtedly the best-organized and best-armed political force outside that of the authoritarian regime. Throughout the years of martial law and despite the capture of a significant number of its leaders, it has expanded its mass base and dramatically advanced its armed revolutionary struggle by exploiting the strategic premises of a protracted war and by surrounding the cities from the countrysides. It is considered today to be one of the leading national-liberation movements in Asia and has emerged as the focal point of political forces opposed to the Marcos regime and its export-oriented strategy of development.[12]

The development of authoritarian processes in the Philippines, culminating in the martial-law regime and the expansion of the military establishment on which it depends, are inextricably linked with a specific view of development that this regime shares with the transnational corporations in the Philippines, the international banks, and the IMF–World Bank. The Philippine government now owes nearly $14 billion to these financial institutions.

A study of the political situation persisting in 1972, including the social bases of Philippine authoritarianism, is found in ''Authoritarianism and the Philippine Social Mode,'' in *Feudalism and Capitalism in the Philippines: Trends and Implications,* edited by Renato Constantino. The collection will soon be published by the Foundation for Nationalist Studies, Manila. In this essay the author develops the framework of the relative autonomy of the state and explores the hypothesis that Philippine authoritarianism emerged principally from a political crisis and not immediately from a structural breakdown in the social mode.

The specific act of declaring martial law was, for Marcos, a political necessity in the face of mounting opposition and increasing isolation in electoral and party politics. The act therefore was governed by subjective considerations. The fact that the regime has functioned objectively in favor of the neocolonial forces, however, arises out of a larger context in which imperialism is dominant. Martial law may, however, be related to an ideology of development with its distinct approach to the processes of social change. For a consideration of the latter, we must move from political economy to the problems of ideology and political culture.

Liberalism and Dictatorship

The development of authoritarianism in the Philippines has been not merely a political process but also an ideological one, cementing the transformation in actual relations and providing the legitimation of new forces and new structures. From the point of view of its architects, the imposition of martial rule constituted the only valid response to deteriorating conditions that threatened the very existence of the republic.[13]

The self-descriptive language employed by the regime resembles that used by similar strongman regimes in various other underdeveloping societies. Likewise, the development of a technocracy educated in the economism of Western schools and the consolidation of political power based on military control has become characteristic of those societies in the periphery that have been penetrated by monopoly capital. Though professing allegiance to the concepts of national security and national development, these regimes have pursued a more or less uniform line of development sympathetic to the demands of corporate imperialism. More significantly, these regimes have a shared antagonism toward national-liberation movements demanding a revolutionary break from imperialism.

Though opposed by the majority of political movements and trade unions, Marcos declared martial rule and thereby became dependent on the military apparatus and an expanding cadre of primarily U.S.-educated technocrats. This combination of military force and a technocratic elite is not uncommon in many emergent regimes in the neocolonies that have combined the iron fist with the promise of progress. It is a phenomenon that may be aptly categorized as *repressive developmentalism*.[14]

These regimes have been described as neofascist because of the primacy of the military in the affairs of state and the ideological tendencies of the technocracy to view social problems of backwardness as problems of efficiency, control, and management. The crisis of rising antagonisms aroused by underdevelopment is simply regarded as a failure of management. These technocrats tend to support the law-and-order line of authoritarian self-justification on the grounds that it is the requisite political framework for development. Although this may be viewed (especially by Marxists) as a rather naive understanding of social and historical processes, it is often translated to fit into entrenched and well-developed ideological systems and is thus presented as a supposedly rational view.

The similarities between the authoritarian process in the Philippines and those of the other neocolonial societies do not, however, diminish its uniqueness as a national experience rooted in specifically Filipino dimensions of history, culture, and political economy. Many of the trained managers and planners who formed the political core of the martial-law regime were the very ones who were spokesmen for the popular demand for a resolution of the crisis of stagnation. They had experienced that crisis as simply one of political immobilization and thus welcomed the inauguration of authoritarian processes with its self-described tentative nature and progressive character. They supported the orientation of the regime toward monopoly capital and its resultant neocolonial industrialization primarily because of their opposition to what they termed the inefficiency of precapitalist forms of production and their approval of controlled social transformation.

Three factors have inhibited the military from a more active state role than it now plays:

1. the lack of a tradition of political involvement in the military;
2. the fragmentation of the military itself, principally between professionals and integrees;[15]
3. an overriding loyalty to the person of Marcos.

It must be emphasized that this technocratic ethos that has risen to prominence during the regime of martial law is neither a fundamental ideological deviation nor, as technocrats are wont to claim, nonideological. This so-called ethos represents, instead, a distillation of classical bourgeois-liberal understanding of politics—from nebulous pluralist theory to the more cogent statism of authoritarian self-justification.

Even before the Marcos years, supposedly enlightened economists and businessmen were beginning to clamor against the high cost of politics, while demanding a stable political order that would provide a healthy climate for capital. The main instrument for achieving this would be the state—more specifically, the state as it is understood in the liberal view, as being essentially classless and the embodiment of the objective interest of the whole community.

In his inaugural address on 30 December 1965, for instance, President Marcos declared, "The Government must act as guardian of the law's majesty, the source of justice to the weak and solace to the underprivileged, a ready friend and protector of the common man and a sensitive instrument for his advancement not his captivity." Contained here is the essential bourgeois-liberal view of the state as guarantor of the general good and a sensitive instrument of society as a whole. This is a restatement of the neutral-arbiter conception of the state that is the basis of the bourgeois-liberal theory of pluralist democracy. In 1971, in *Today's Revolution: Democracy,* Marcos restated the same view when he noted that "revolution and democracy are inseparable. The work heralded what would later be referred to as the revolution of the poor: martial law. In 1977 the point would be reasserted in the very definite conditions of dictatorship: "There is no force in our society capable of protecting the poor other than the government."

The theory of a popular revolution emanating from above, in the institutions of state authority, is the central theme of the regime's effort at self-justification. This ideological theme rests almost entirely on the assumption of the nonideological nature of the state, or at least the conscious rejection of "isms." The state is "popular" because it is the embodiment of the general interest—although the general interest in the last analysis, may not, in the Rousseauan sense, be perceptible by all, or in the Hobbesian sense be a common interest made evident by necessity. In this sense the Aristotelian notion of constitutionalism, the underlying mean unaffected by the whole range of passions that is merely presumed in liberalism, becomes the expressed and cogent logic of self-justification in authoritarianism.

Utilization of the social-contract framework for rationalizing the authoritarian state is explicit rather than implicit. The state is to be understood as a natural mechanism for social regulation, and therefore as an inherent component of society. Although the myth of the social contract has been debunked as anthropologically baseless, the ideological attitude deriving from this naturalist theory of the state continues to be pervasive, especially as it is preserved in bourgeois legalism. A refinement of the social-contract framework in the discourses of the president is formulated thus:

> When we establish government we establish what is known as the social contract. All the people enter into such a contract. He agrees that there shall be a central authority which shall administer his rights, his properties and his relations with his fellow human beings. And in this agreement he agrees that the central authority will be the government. He delegates to the government certain of his rights and his rights are therefore embodied not in the Bill of Rights alone but in the entire Constitution.[16]

The scope of the social contract, as understood here, is more than just a procedural surrender of rights and acceptance of authority as in the classic formulations. It includes also the *administration* of the individual's relations with other men. In layman's terms, this portends regimentation, or what in the cold language of technocrats is called social engineering, guided by the one-dimensional and universal Reason of science.

The liberal ideological premises thus mentioned set the tone for the specific reconstruction of the bourgeois world view into the compelling argument for the authoritarian rule of the state—an authoritarianism centered around a person who is an extension of the state. Without the framework for social-class analysis, liberalism eventually distills into a classless view of the state and politics. The state then exists for nothing more than the authoritative allocation of values. At least ideally it stands above politics.

Along with the rhetoric on the end of ideology, the pure reason of science is held aloft for uncritical reverence of the almost mystical premise of an absolute Reason. A political authority acting in the name of this scientific Reason is therefore unquestionable and unchallengeable. Superimposed on the social-contract framework, this scientific delusion reduces the problem of political oppositions into a problem merely of opposition to the state. Since the State is held to be the objectification of the general will or its categorical equivalent, then opposition to the state is historically, rationally, and politically invalid. Thus the antipolitics or apolitical attitude and ethic of technocrats is subsumed into the ideological fiber of authoritarianism—and their uncritical submission is assured, since it is contrary to the technocratic wit to think beyond the logic of positivism and the limitations of the workable.

The type of ideological distillation was evident at the onset of the martial-law regime. Although some have interpreted it merely as a paranoid reaction on the part of the chief executive, the view that every mode of opposition is antigovernment and therefore pitted against the public welfare is in fact a common view expressed by other authoritarian regimes.

In the *Politics of Transition,* which calls to mind the images of Rousseau's benevolent dictator battling "particular wills" to achieve civil society, the necessity for martial rule was thus presented by Marcos:

> On the eve of the proclamation of martial law, our nation was in a state of siege. There were many who held dim hopes that our democratic political system could still survive.
>
> A searching analysis of the situation which the nation faced revealed seven sources of threats to the Republic. These divided into the traditionalists and the Maoists; second, the rightists who sought power by means of a coup d'etat; third, the Muslim secessionist movement in Mindanao and Sulu; fourth, the private brokers in Philippine society at the time; fifth, organized crime, which had taken advantage of the situation to entrench itself; sixth, the oligarchy which sought by all means to maintain the status quo and effectively stymied government efforts at economic, social and political reform; and seventh, the foreign interventionists, evidence of whose funding of anti-government groups in the country were confirmed through banks in Hongkong, Japan and the United States.[17]

Several important assumptions are laid down in this statement and the structure of arguments deriving from it. Principally, the crisis confronting Philippine society is viewed merely as a crisis of the political order rather than a crisis of underdevelopment. Therefore, it must require only a political solution by the existing political authority. None of the competing groups are regarded as being involved in the national resolution of the crisis; they are all particular wills. Even if these groups were admitted to be "an accumulation of response to the ills of society, which were rooted in social and economic imbalance and inequities," they were categorized primarily as antigovernment and thus regarded as problems rather than alternative solutions. The martial-law regime, conversely, is more than an alternative solution; it is *the* solution objectified. The regime represents the necessary political precondition for Philippine society to realize itself. In Rousseauan terms, it is the transitory condition marked by the systematic eradication of all particular wills that is at once the process of self-realization, a condition where:

> the political authority must therefore educate itself and our people to an awareness of our national identity. . . . A consciousness of our history as our people's continuing struggle for human freedom must inform the programs and projects of all government agencies and instrumentalities. Our national identity can only be as enriched by our present concern for the future. Our national experience must command

our vision of the future and sustain the ethic of work and unity among our institutions and among our people.[18]

The basic line of confrontation is therefore understood as that which divides the government and all opposed to it; the government being the objective embodiment of the nation and all others mere subjectivities. The essence of the so-called democratic revolution—the declared objective of the martial law regime—is merely to make government work.

The view that government is the neutral arbiter of conflicting forces necessarily assumes its adherence to some unalterable and rational objective. This view would thus perceive social forces in opposition as constituting aberrations from the norm, and therefore as mere disturbances. Social conflict must then be eradicated rather than resolved, and a state without politics is thus required. The martial-law regime specifically presents itself as the embodiment of the interest-of-the-whole, whose realization is retarded by partisan contests.

Here is the crucial link that unites the bourgeois-liberal view of the state with that of the fascist. Underdevelopment does not exist from this ideological standpoint in the same way that exploitation does not exist in the theoretical construction of the world, in bourgeois economics. What does exist is the political cancer that eats up the polity and inhibits it from responding effectively to the crisis; it is this political cancer that is itself the crisis, and the effective political order is not merely opposed to the crisis but also constitutes its resolution. This conceptual sleight-of-hand, using the inherent world view of nineteenth-century theoretical systems, is made to appear as a sophisticated and novel political process for the emulation of all developing societies.

The Democratic Revolution

President Marcos and his regime have tried consistently to present the regime as the revolutionary solution to a social crisis—the appropriation of this revolutionary characteristic being regarded as crucial for credibility. It had to retain the constitutionality required to sustain its legitimacy, however, especially in the eyes of the old forces on which it relied for support. The combination of constitutionality and a revolutionary claim is essential because the regime had to appeal to the broadest sections of a decidedly polarized society. Since the regime has not been equipped with a historical, long-range program of revolutionary social overhaul, it must rest on the one hand on its constitutional claims. Since it must substantially restructure the mechanisms of law and governmental process to eliminate opposition, centralize power, and assure its own political survival, as well as to convince the people that it is intent on resolving the crisis of political immobilization that had developed in the years preceding the declaration of martial law, it needs the rhetoric of revolution—more so as it transforms the precapitalist sections of the economy and integrates them into a new, more advanced mode of dependence and domination.

The reconciliation of these two aspects still finds fertile ground in bourgeois-liberal political theory and hospitable quarters in the bourgeois legalism of the old republic. The democratic revolution is the ideological expression of the regime's distinctive feature: that on the one hand it transforms old relations and advances them from semifeudalism, and on the other hand integrates the society more closely into the neocolonial mold, thus fortifying the old structures of class rule even while it liquidates precapitalist class forms.

The formulation of this so-called democratic revolution also serves more immediate political functions. One such function is to draw revolutionary legitimacy away from those who compete politically with the regime. This is accomplished by denying the validity of revolutionary movements outside the state apparatus. In order to invalidate revolutionary movements, especially those of an anti-imperialist character, the regime must appropriate revolutionary legitimacy for itself by monopolizing the revolutionary transformation of society, denying the revolutionary validity of those opposed to the state. Marcos thus argues:

> The process of radical change, although constitutional, is a convulsive one. The force of law is no less violent for being legal. Violence must be controlled in a revolution by constitutional means, and only a strong democratic government can give any such assurance. And in this endeavour, the clearest and deepest consent of the people is imperative.[19]

Since the state is value free according to the ideological premises of liberalism, only a revolution launched by the state can possibly represent the general welfare. It is also the most convenient since it is presented as the alternative to a bloody upheaval, a prospect quite distasteful to the middle-class constituency that has been the immediate mass base for the authoritarian regime. The democratic revolution also represents the most rational human undertaking in an age of reason and science, as contrasted with the popularized caricature of a revolutionary barbaric past. This state-sponsored revolutionary undertaking is thus to be understood as an expression of the maturity achieved by modern human civilization.[20]

For the regime to claim a monopoly as the radicalizing force, it combines the national-security function with that of national development. This combination was made evident at the onset of the martial regime, which was ostensibly imposed to "save the Republic and form a new society."[21] The combination of the functions of national security and national development and their inseparability from the standpoint of the regime's doctrine, is expressed concretely in the unified technocratic and military bureaucracies, with the military enjoying an expanded role through involvement in the national-development effort and the technocracy relying on the centralized command and control structures of the military for the implementation of its plans. To better secure this monopoly, it is necessary to invalidate both the autonomous radicalizing capability of the masses and to argue their inability or incompetence at formulating or even understanding a comprehensive line of development beneficial to them. This leads logically to an elitist attitude granting a mandate to the technocracy, as well as to a subtly cultivated contempt for mass initiative, which validates the repressive role played by the military.

Bourgeois social science has consistently maintained that sporadic revolution is disruptive and patently dysfunctional. Only when revolution is redefined as a conscious, planned, and institutional process that does not result in breaks and discontinuities but occurs within the realm of expectancy and continuity of control is it acceptable—that is, within the framework of state control and initiative. This redefinition thus castrates revolution of spontaneity and popular initiative. We must be reminded:

> Recent memory also brings to mind the experience of China. Barely four decades ago, doubts were cast as to whether or not the semi-feudal, semi-colonial conditions in the mainland could lend to a restructuring of Chinese society. But the masses, though strictly speaking, did not originate the revolution, nevertheless they responded to the call and leadership of a revolutionary minority which, regardless of its purpose, succeeded in instituting a new social order.[22]

This represents the bourgeois attitude that the masses do not make as well as compose a revolutionary phenomenon in history and are thus either led down the path of a particular line of historical development or sit back and wait while history is made for them. Not only is this line of understanding contemptuous of the masses, but it also represents the narrow understanding of historical processes characteristic of bourgeois-liberal understanding. Contempt for the historical creativity of the masses is but the initial step toward the ideological rationalization for processes of domination and control exercised over the masses by a technocratic establishment backed by the organized violence of the military. Thus the view that the masses cannot be a fully conscious and determining historical force, even if it is their interest that is at stake:

> Through the years of political radicalism, the masses have been

undergoing a political education in mass democracy. It is doubtful, however, if their political education includes an appreciation of the *complexities* of modern nationhood. The agitators' job is done when they have demonstrated the causes of mass poverty and insinuated the remedy of revolution. The rest possibly is left to political partisanship, the method of which is the organization of discontent for winning elections. But unless free elections result in substantial social changes, dicontent will be organized to capture state power.

The constant *hammering* into the minds of the masses of the necessity for a new society must create an urgent demand for its realization. And unless the political authority is capable of creating that new society, it will be repudiated and the task entrusted to another. A society like ours dares not risk this, for the result may mean the end rather than the expansion of human liberty.

We cannot allow our political society to become the victim of unrealized aspirations. Having aroused the hopes of the masses for a new society, the political authority must embark on the task of creating it.[23]

This contemptuous view of the masses is the raison d'être for a technocratic establishment, planning for the masses rather than with them.

Isang Bansa, Isang Diwa

The core of the martial-law regime's effort at political integration and ideological incorporation is a sustained appeal to nationalism—specifically, a definition of nationalism that follows a line of least resistance. More precisely, it is a nationalism that does not have an anti-imperialist character, yet draws from the old bourgeois-democratic revolution of a century ago. The crude nationalism of the past century has, however, been distilled into a glorification of the nation-state, a *Weltanschauung* of sorts, to capture popular imagination and present a consequent classless view of politics that provides the ideological preconditions for a corporatist political order.

The main slogan of this corporatist-nationalist ideological line is *isang bansa, isang diwa* ("one nation, one spirit") which recalls Hegel's projection of the abstract nation into the concrete individual. The political images exuded by the regime convey its corporatist-nationalist appeal in more concrete forms. The glorification of the bourgeois-nationalist revolution of 1896 is meticulously propagated. The pursuit of a nationalist image extends to its foreign policy thrusts, as it seeks to develop an image of nonalignment, and resorts to occasional anti-American tirades designed for domestic consumption. The renaming of the smallest political unit from *barrio* to *baranggay* dates back to the pre-Hispanic communities. The president's own voluminous work on Philippine history,

Tadhana (Destiny) provides a reinterpretation of history that gives historical substance to the regime.[24] Technocrats and bureaucrats are clothed in the *barong tagalog* of the illustrado nationalists who agitated against the friars a century before.

This cultural nationalism—involving the reconstruction of monuments and the influencing of modern architectural design; its influences on fashion, its glorification and idealization of the Filipino, so distant from the daily lives of the masses that it is almost foreign—has one distinct advantage: it appeals to a value transcending conflict and class differentiations. In the modern day, nationalism is understood as a conservative and preservative force that builds rather than destroys.[25] The imputation of a national essence to the individual binds him to his nationality and therefore to the nation-state, which is the objective embodiment of the national spirit and the national destiny. The state thus presents itself as the clear view into the future from a vantage point unavailable to the individual. It denies the individual a separate view comparable in significance to that of the state, which has the benefit of the heritage of a society and a profound grasp of its collective historical effort. Therefore, to oppose the public-welfare state would be to oppose public welfare. To oppose the national-development state would constitute opposition to national development, and to oppose the national-security state would constitute a threat to national security. Thus political repression is not only validated, but even necessitated.

The cornerstone of the social ethics of authoritarianism is an absolutist view of man. The one-dimensionality of reason in Lockean thought, and the constancy of a human nature in the Hobbesian sense, form the essential premises of technocratic consciousness and the authoritarian preference for social control and social engineering. In an interview with *Time* (7 June 1976), for instance, Marcos thought man to be "a strange mixture of the good and the bad. But given the opportunity, the good will come out." Thus, logically, the state controls the bad aspects of man and determines from some imagined absolute reason the conditions whereby the good aspects of man are made to surface.

The one-dimensional reason in technocratic liberalism also expresses itself in the unidimensional understanding of social change that is in no way historically relative and is therefore absolute and nonpartisan. The process of change is understood as a completely conscious process, one for which technocrats may plan. Men as individuals must submit themselves to this singular reason and consequently to the plans detailed from above to achieve a condition of development that is known to the reason of state but not autonomously available to individual consciousness. From the standpoint of this singular reason, men must conform eventually not through coercion but by free option on the basis of innate rationality, as in the civil society of Rousseau after the period of the benevolent dictatorship. This kind of individual transformation ultimately makes the democratic revolution an internal revolution.[26] This is the theoretical essence of the call for national discipline as the alternative to long-term overt repression.

The technocrats are said to derive their mandate from some scientific reason, and they draw on this reason to brush aside all social issues and fundamental ideological differentiations impeding their resolution. Technology is regarded as providing the final solution to human and social problems. Also posited to this approach is the infallibility of a political apparatus laying claim to scientific reason. By posing technology as the liberating element, technocratic consciousness invalidates the question of social relations as the focus of any effort at social change. The social structure is not seen as tentative relations historically developed and transformed by human will, but rather as a phenomenon determined wholly by available technology and changed simply by technological alteration.

There should be no room, therefore, for subjective human impulses. The absolute reason of science provides man with a total understanding, an understanding liberated from history itself and determining history, no longer on the basis of the cognition of historical necessity but on the external logic of scientific technique. This technologism seeps into the world view of conventional social science, rendering it scientistic rather than genuinely scientific by confining every problem to one of technique and method and by making social control the overriding tendency in the social sciences.[27]

It should now be relatively simple to reconcile the ideological mold of advanced liberalism as it has transformed into a neoconservatism and the specific line of development pursued by such authoritarian regimes as that which prevails in the Philippines. This takes us full circle to the question of export-oriented, foreign-investment-led development after our attempt to illustrate the repressive ideology of underdevelopment as it is concretized in the authoritarian regime. Backwardness, according to the bourgeois-liberal social science exported by the advanced capitalist countries, is merely a transitory condition caused by a rapid infusion of modernizing *social* influences from the West and the lag emerging from the slow adaptability of the non-Western societies. The logical solution, then, is the establishment of strong political orders that would maintain the stability of these transitory societies and allow for rapid adaptability and transition from the backward cultural systems that served to bottleneck development. Development, as mentioned earlier, is taken to be synonymous with Westernization—or, to those sensitive to its ethnocentric implications, the creation of an efficient culture that would give full play to the society's creative potentials that remain unrealized because of the old values.[28]

The marital-law regime, governed by this view, sees itself as the initiator of development as it sets the political basis for transcending the condition of backwardness.[29] By taking backwardness to be a result of the political paralysis of society rather than of its neocolonial linkages, no inconsistency is seen between the new society and its nationalist guises on the one hand, and continued foreign intrusion on the other. Foreign capital is the harbinger of progress and thus of the good life for all—a line that echoes the development economists of the international funding institutions. Marcos himself puts it more succinctly:

> We place our hopes on investments, both domestic and foreign, to play the role of catalysts of growth. But at the same time, the main reliance is placed on our people themselves—on the capacity of a reawakened Filipino nation to overcome its own historical shortcomings.[30]

By working around the premise that foreign investments bring progress, apologists for the regime have argued that economic nationalism is not only impractical but also unpatriotic. On this general orientation, the technocratic cadre that form the governmental corps of the regime see their subservient role to the transnational corporations as one that is not fundamentally in conflict with their avowed nationalism.

Ethics and Ideology

In the context of the ideological culture that shrouds the authoritarian processes, a culture based on a preexisting and deeply rooted liberal consciousness among the Filipinos, the trade-off framework is a secondary, but not unimportant, ideological consideration. It reconciles the repressive character of the regime with the vision of prosperity that the regime sees as its future.

The most fundamental element, however, is the technocratic liberalism that the regime has popularized as ideology. This technocratic liberalism, which emphasizes the corporate ethic of national discipline as the foundation for progress. It has justified a culture of subservience and is embodied in numerous policies, from the ban on strikes to the regimentation of the educational system and the reorientation of education toward building the skilled labor forces required by neocolonial industrialization.[31] Another frequently cited informal policy has been that of self-censorship, especially among journalists—an informal policy that has not been difficult to enforce considering that the major instruments of mass media are either government owned or controlled by the people close to the leadership. The range of restrictive presidential decrees is exemplified by one that even penalizes rumor mongering.

Official thinking has been oriented explicitly toward seeing the problem of prosperity largely as one that will be resolved by the entry of technology and the anticipated industrialization that will come in its wake, rather than on the redistribution of the means of production. In what the regime calls an agricultural-modernization program, technocratic planners have invested heavily in rural electrification without in any way altering the economic state of the peasantry. They have expanded port facilities without building the social structures for self-sufficiency. They have sought to raise rural incomes by encouraging crop varieties heavily dependent on imported fertilizers, and this has contributed to the rising cost of agricultural production in an economy where wages are systematically depressed in the interest of maintaining the competitiveness of exports. A towering symbol of this obsession among technocrats for technology without the accompanying concern for social equity is the nuclear power plant now being built by Westinghouse at a cost of $1.9 billion, despite the objections of the antinuclear movement.[32]

The regime's human rights record is a testament not to the violence of a military unrestricted by an organized citizenry, but to the callousness of the technocratic consciousness that has become predominant during the regime of martial law.[33]

It is close to a decade since Marcos imposed martial law on the Filipino people, but the promise of national prosperity has become more distant than ever.[34] The iniquitous distribution of wealth has worsened rather than lessened, and much of the available local finances are controlled by close associates of the First Family. Official corruption has become so widespread that it even surprises Filipinos long used to dishonesty of civil servants. Marcos's own circle is in danger of splitting into antagonistic factions, and the stability of the regime itself is so threatened that the international financing institutions have become alarmed.[35] The armed revolutionary movement continues to strengthen and the radical opposition in the cities has risen to prominence, at a rate that surprises even the stalwarts of the open opposition.

Although definitive studies have yet to be completed, it is apparent that social relations have been substantially transformed, though not to the benefit of the larger sections of the population.[36] The decline of the agricultural elite has been marked as the regime has become increasingly insulated from their influence and has identified more closely with the urban corporate financial establishments.

The shortsightedness of the liberal-technocratic world view and its incapacity to understand and cope with the crisis of underdevelopment become all the more evident as Philippine society slides deeper and deeper into dependence and poverty, even after a decade of repressive developmentalist rule.

With the New Society regime suffering from a serious crisis of credibility and the alignment of political forces becoming increasingly polarized, Marcos decided to lift martial law in January 1981. In a plebiscite held in April of that year, however, a constitutional revision was made granting extraordinary powers to the office of the president, apart from the retention and incorporation of all decrees issued during the regime of martial law into the law of the land. Opponents of the regime denounced this process as a constitutionalization of dictatorship.

In an effort to shore up the credibility of the Marcos government, elections to the presidency were called for June. The leading open opposition groups, however, called for a boycott of this political exercise and thus endorsed the tactical line taken much earlier by the National Democratic Front (NDF). This move, which defied legal measures taken by the government to quash the boycott movement, has been interpreted as a qualitative progression toward radicalism in the ranks of the opposition.

Authoritarianism and the Economy

Since economic development stands as the principal raison d'être of the authoritarian regime, it is necessary to look more deeply into the performance of the Philippine economy over the last decade and substantiate the general statements made in the preceding section.

The activist role played by government resulted in profound changes in the national economic structure—changes whose magnitude was possible only because of state intervention in the economy. The investment-incentives policy and the expansion of the country's financial institutions have resulted in a visible degree of industrialization. The gross value added by the manufacturing sector has expanded consistently (in constant 1972 prices) from ₱13.388 billion in 1972 to ₱21.146 billion in 1979. The number of light-manufacturing establishments climbed dramatically, from 7,891 in 1970 to 66,936 in 1977, with the number of employees expanding from 278,585 to 1,480,404 during the same period. The number of heavy-manufacturing establishments increased from 2,605 in 1970 to 7,685 in 1977, with the number of workers employed increasing from 110,352 to 223,299 during the same period.[37] By 1977, after continuously accumulating balance-of-payments deficits, the Philippine economy achieved a surplus of $164 million. This, however, proved to be quite short lived, as a deficit of $54 million was registered the following year. This deficit ballooned to $570 million in 1979.[38]

At constant 1972 prices, the GNP expanded from a rate of 4.31 percent in 1970 to a peak of 9.64 percent in 1973, shortly after martial law was imposed along with the execution of the Foreign Investments Incentives Act and massive foreign borrowing to fund infrastructure and industrial projects outlined in the government's development program.[39] From 1977 on, however, the growth rate of the GNP suffered a sustained decline. In 1978 actual growth rate went down to 6.5 percent. This declined further, to 5.9 percent in 1979 and 4.7 percent in 1980.[40]

By mid-1981 the Central Bank rated the country's economic performance "satisfactory" (from "relatively good" the preceding year). This rating took into consideration the following:

1. The balance-of-payments deficit had increased by 22 percent, to $243 million.
2. The trade deficit had swelled 53 percent, to $1.29 billion.
3. Import payments had gone up 11 percent, to $3.6 billion, while export earnings had gone down 3.5 percent, to $2.3 billion.
4. Consumer prices had gone up 13.3 percent on the average.
5. Outstanding foreign debts rose to $13.77 billion (rising further, to about $15 billion, by the end of the year.[41]

To avert serious economic setbacks due to a ballooning of the balance-of-payments deficit, the Central Bank in 1980 undertook compensatory borrowings of $1 billion, more than double the previous year's $481 million.[42] The inflation rate climbed from 7.3 in 1978 to 16.5 and 17.8 in 1979 and 1980, respectively.[43] The purchasing power of the Philippine peso (pegged at 1972 prices) declined rapidly, from 0.4350 in March 1979 to 0.3515 in March 1980, and even further, to 0.3118, for the same month in 1981.[44]

Although some appreciable degree of industrialization has been in progress over the last decade, the real wages of common laborers, for instance, went down from ₱11.63 at the end of 1970 to ₱5.33 at the end of 1980.[45]

The entry of foreign investments and transnational corporations into the agricultural sector of the economy had a marked impact on the character of Philippine agriculture. From 1970 to 1980, total hectarage devoted to food crops increased by only 27.6 percent, whereas those devoted to commercial crops increased by 52.8 percent. Rice-crop production (rice is staple to the Filipino diet) during this period increased by only 12.5 percent, compared with coconut, which increased by 66.0 percent, and pineapple, which increased by 117.2 percent.[46] This factor has been a primary cause of the rise of food prices, which in turn has made the Philippines a society with one of the highest rates of malnutrition.

The figures quoted in this section provide strong support for the argument that the relatively significant growth of the Philippine economy in the few years after the imposition of martial rule was in the last analysis basically superficial, as it was largely achieved by foreign investments and massive national borrowings that accomplished little in terms of constructing a stable economic structure marked by social equity. The serious decline in growth and in the quality of life of the largest sections of the population over the last few years attests to the brittleness of the development line pursued by the authoritarian regime.

This is not the occasion, however, to generalize about foreign-investment-led and export-oriented economic growth. It will suffice to take the position that such a development line has, at least for the moment, benefited chiefly the transnational corporations and local financial centers, but not the broadest sections of Philippine society.

Reexamining the Dilemma

Projecting the future of Philippine society and the trend social development will pursue over the long term becomes more difficult as the authoritarian regime aggravates the dynamics of discontinuity without in turn setting the conditions for continuity.

The fragile social base for industrialization of a neocolonial type, sustained by external debt, dominated by the transnational corporations, and pursued with the repressive violence of an authoritarian state, raises numerous questions of appropriateness in the Philippine experience. In economic terms, the authoritarian regime's open-door policy toward the transnationals effectively weakened autonomous national economic processes. This has left the economy extremely susceptible to pressures and downturns in the international capitalist market. Whatever economic consolidation occurred during the last decade was founded almost wholly on the brittle basis of foreign aid and public debt. The large external debt incurred by the regime's planners and serviced by the whole economy has become more and more a heavy weight on any effort at national progress.

The regime's dependence on the technocrats and the military on the one hand, and on the institutions of monopoly capital on the other, effectively worked against the development of popular policies that would be fostered by, and would in turn foster, a broad political base of support. In all political exercises over the last decade, the regime relied on salaried supporters and mercenary enthusiasm: a political base that, as seen elsewhere, melts away as soon as the political leadership becomes unable to provide the material requirements of such groups. Carried by the logic of technocratic authoritarianism, the regime acted unilaterally and hierarchically throughout its tenure, and thus failed to construct the governmental structures of popular initiative and consensus, as well as a culture of spontaneous political mobilization. Such a base would facilitate the continuity of the political system after the cult personality has left the scene. Having virtually dissolved the traditional system of political-party mobilization that contributed vastly to legitimizing the old political order, the regime failed to develop a viable apparatus for the promotion of popular leaders and is thus left without a crucial second line necessary for continuing its political and developmental strategies.

By weakening the judiciary and failing to strengthen the new legislative machinery, the regime has unwittingly set the conditions for long-term instability. The recent intensification of factional contests centered on palace politics, the failure of the regime to dispel the popular culture of cynicism even after it had gone through the motions of "normalizing" and "democratizing" the political process, and the mushrooming of armed resistance groups other than the National Democratic Front and the Moro National Liberation Front all point to the long-term weakness of the regime and the line of development it embodies.

In sum, the Philippine case presents strong arguments against the validity of a development line that combines the economic orientation of dependence on the capitalist centers and authoritarian structures that result in increasing unpopularity. It is not a condition wholly attributable to the tendencies of the regime in power, as the logic of exploitative production relations becomes more determining in the last analysis. The Philippine experience at technocratic authoritarianism, on the other hand, presents a clear illustration of the limits of bourgeois-liberal ideology, in its nonideological form, to grasp and cope with the crisis of underdevelopment.

Notes

1. See, for instance, Samuel P. Huntington, *Political Order in Changing Societies* (New Haven: Yale University Press, 1968); Lucian W. Pye, *Aspects of Political Development* (New Delhi: Amerind 1972); W.W. Rostow, *Politics and the Stages of Growth* (London: Cambridge University Press, 1971).

2. An appropriate critical source book on this aspect as it specifically applies to the Philippine experience would be Walden Bello and

Severine Rivera, *The Logistics of Repression and Other Essays* (Washington, D.C.: Friends of the Filipine People, 1977).

3. The regime of martial law was referred to as the New Society. With the lifting of martial law on 17 January 1981, and after Marcos's "reelection" to the presidency, the New Republic was inaugurated in its place on 12 June 1981.

4. Reuben Canby, *The Counterfeit Revolution* (Manila, 1980). See also Felix Casalmo, *The Vision of a "New Society"* (Manila, 1979). A new constitution came into force and effect in 1973, and the term of office for Marcos in the old constitution should have ended in that same year.

5. Since the views of the Philippine left could not be published legally in the country, documents on the debates concerning the nature of martial law and the strategic perspective taken on the issue by the revolutionary movement are scarce. The official political line of the Communist party of the Philippines is expounded on in its underground organ, *Ang Bayan*. Abroad, the documents and publications of the Anti-Martial Law Coalition more or less adhere to the strategic views of the National Democratic Front.

6. Rigoberto Tiglao, "Non-Progress in the Periphery," and comments on the paper, *Diliman Review* (April–June 1979).

7. Ferdinand Marcos, *Today's Revolution: Democracy* (Manila: Marcos Foundation, 1971).

8. Alejandro Lichauco, *The Struggle against Underdevelopment in the Philippines* (Manila: Nationalist Resource Center, 1981).

9. MAN, *Ang Demokratikong Pilipinong Uhong* (Manila: Malaya Books, 1969).

10. Lichauco, *Struggle against Underdevelopment,* p. 51.

11. Rolando Yu and Mario Bolasco, *Church-State Relations in the Philippines* (Manila: St. Scholastica's Foundation, 1981).

12. The apprehension of U.S. foreign policymakers over the possible loss of a staunch ally in the Philippines is best expressed in Richard J. Kessler, "The Philippines: The Next Iran?" *Asian Affairs* 7, no. 3 (January–February 1980).

13. Ferdinand Marcos, *Notes on the New Society* (Manila: Marcos Foundation, 1973).

14. Herb Feith, "Repressive Developmentalist Regimes in Asia: Old Strengths, New Vulnerabilities," Monash University, paper previously presented at the New York Conference of the World Order Models Project, 1–4 June 1979.

15. For a detailed discussion of this, see Carolina Hernandez, "The Military in Philippine Politics," Ph.D. diss., State University of New York, 1979.

16. Ferdinand Marcos, "Liberty and Discipline," June 1973.

17. Idem, *Introduction to the Politics of Transition* (Manila: Marcos Foundation, 1979).

18. Idem, *Notes on the New Society II* (Manila: Marcos Foundation, 1976).

19. Idem, *The Democratic Revolution in the Philippines* (Manila: Marcos Foundation, 1977), p. 101.

20. Ibid., Preface to the 1st edition.

21. Idem, Presidential Proclamation 1081, 21 September 1972.

22. Idem, *An Ideology for Filipines* (Manila, 1980).

23. Idem, *Democratic Revolution*.

24. A whole series of this multivolume work has yet to be completed.

25. Marcos, *Ideology for Filipines*.

26. Idem, *Notes,* p. 215.

27. Jurgeon Habermas. *Legitimation Crises*, trans. Thomas Mc-Carthy (Boston: Beacon Press, 1978).

28. Rostow, *Politics*.

29. Marcos, "Business and Government," Speech, 23 November 1973.

30. Idem, Speech before the Asian Pacific Council of American Chambers, 23 October 1973.

31. Presidential Decree 823, 1975.

32. Citizen's Alliance for Consumer Protection, *CACP Journal* 1, no. 1 (April 1981).

33. Kilusan Para Sa Katarungan at Kapayapaan, *Iron Hand, Velvet Glove,* World Council of Churches, 1980.

34. Alejandro Lichauco, "Notes on the Economy and the Political Situation: The Struggle against Underdevelopment in the Philippines," paper based on a talk given on 16 February 1981 before the Clergy and Lay Workers of the Diocese of Imus, Cavite.

35. "Take Advantage of Splits within the Marcos Camp," Editorial, *Liberation*, published by the National Democratic Front, 5, no. 7 (October 1981):2. See also William Ascher, "Political and Administrative Bases for Economic Policy in the Philippines," excerpted in *Diliman Review* 29, no. 4 (July–August 1981).

36. *Mindanao Report: A Preliminary Study on the Economic Origins of Social Unrest,* AFRIM Resource Center, Davao City, July 1980, pp. 126–132.

37. *1981 Philippine Yearbook* (Manila: National Census and Statistics Office).

38. Ibid, table 23.19.

39. "GNP at Current and Constant Prices: 1970–1979," *1981 Philippine Yearbook.*

40. "Review of Economic Developments," *National Economic and Development Authority* (December 1980).

41. *IBON Facts and Figures,* no. 73, Manila, 30 August 1981.

42. *Business Day,* 14 January 1981.

43. "Current Labour Statistics," November 1980, Ministry of Labour and Employment, Manila.

44. *IBON Facts and Figures,* no. 67, Manila, 31 May 1981.

45. *Central Bank Statistical Bulletin, 1980,* Manila.

46. *Summary: Agricultural Land Civilization by Kind of Crops,* Bureau of Agricultural Economics, Manila, 1981.

7 Dilemmas in Developing Social-Security Programs for Korea

Sang Mok Suh

Economic development in Korea since the early 1960s has been characterized by a rapid growth in output and income. Although increased output and income are necessary conditions for improved welfare, they do not automatically provide an adequate standard of living for all segments of the population. Increased employment opportunities may help reduce the number of the absolutely poor; but the incomes of many families may be kept at unsatisfactorily low levels by the premature death of the breadwinner, old age, disability, sickness, or unemployment.

Since the enactment of the Social Security Act of 1935 in the United States, the term *social security* has been absorbed into the vocabulary of many countries, albeit with differing meanings. In the wider sense, social security encompasses everything that gives a feeling of greater security to the weaker groups in the society. More narrowly, social security is understood in terms of social-insurance schemes, designed mostly for employees. The International Labor Office (ILO) defines the major fields of social security as (1) social insurance; (2) family allowances; (3) public employees, military and civilian; (4) public-health services; (5) public assistance; and (6) war victims.

For the purposes of this chapter, social security is defined to include social insurance, public assistance, and social-welfare services. This is in fact the most commonly used definition of social security in Korea.

The objectives of this chapter are to review the existing social-security programs in the light of current socioeconomic conditions of the country and to identify potential dilemmas in developing full-fledged social-security programs for Korea.

Needs for Social Security

Social security has become a major element of the socioeconomic and public policy of a modern nation. A recent survey by the U.S. Social Security Administration shows that some type of social-insurance program was in effect in 129 countries in 1977, compared with 80 countries in 1958 and only 58 countries in 1949. This section reviews the existing socioeconomic conditions of Korea, which are conducive to the development of social-security programs.

Income Distribution

Korea is often cited as an example of a developing economy that has been able to maintain harmony between growth and equity. As a result of the initial, relatively equal distribution of human resources and material wealth, as well as the improved employment opportunities for unskilled labor, the rapid economic growth during the 1960s has not resulted in the deterioration of income distribution, as often observed in other developing economies. Table 7–1 shows that the size distribution of income among households actually improved during the period 1965–1970.

Korean income distribution, however, has deteriorated during the 1970s. The income share of the lowest 40 percent declined from 19.6 percent in 1970 to 15.5 percent in 1978. The income share of the highest 20 percent increased from 41.6 percent in 1970 to 46.7 percent in 1978. The Gini ratio increased from 0.332 in 1970 to 0.404 in 1978. The causes for such a deterioration in income distribution are manifold: (1) a shortage of highly educated and technically skilled workers has resulted in widening wage and salary differentials; (2) the emphasis on large-scale heavy and chemical industries has led to higher levels of business concentration; and (3) the rapid increase in real-estate prices has resulted in a widening inequality of wealth distribution and property income.

As the current trend in income distribution is likely to continue, the achievement of harmony between growth and equity emerges as a key socioeconomic policy objective. Hence income redistribution through the development of social-security programs is likely to be an attractive policy option.

Table 7–1
Size Distribution of Household Income

Year	Income Share (%)		Gini Concentration Ratio
	Lowest 40%	Highest 20%	
1965	12.2	41.8	0.344
1970	19.6	41.6	0.332
1978	15.5	46.7	0.404

Source: Korea Development Institute (KDI).

Poverty

In Korea the rapid economic growth of the past brought about a substantial decline in absolute poverty: the percentage of the absolute poor
declined from 41 percent in 1965 to 23 percent in 1970 and 12 percent
in 1978 (see table 7–2). The incidence of relative poverty (the relative
poverty line, defined as one-third of the mean household income in a
given year), however, has increased from 5 percent in 1970 to 14 percent
in 1978 because of the deterioration of overall income distribution during
this period.

As the overall level of living standards improves over time, alleviation of poverty is not only politically desirable, but also an economically
feasible policy objective. The development of social-security programs
can be an effective means of reducing both absolute and relative poverty.

Urbanization

Rapid industrialization in the past has resulted in the concentration of
the population in urban areas and a reduction in the average size of
families. The percentage of the urban population increased from 28.2
percent in 1965 to 43.1 percent in 1970 and 50.9 percent in 1975. During
1965–1975 average family size declined from 5.9 to 4.9 persons in urban
areas and from 6.2 to 5.6 persons in rural areas (see table 7–3).

The shift from rural to urban living has resulted in a trend toward
the nuclear family unit. The traditional cultural values attached to the
large, extended-family system, wherein the aged and the economically
inactive are taken care of by the young, economically active members
of the family, have gradually changed. The modern family in urbanized
Korea tends to be a small, parent-child-oriented family, with only weak
ties to grandparents and other relatives, unlike families in traditional rural
society. In this context the development of social-security programs initi-

Table 7–2
Incidence of Poverty
(In percentages)

Year	Absolute Poverty	Relative Poverty
1965	41	12
1970	23	5
1978	12	14

Source: KDI.

Table 7–3
Urban Population and Family Size

Year	Percentage of Urban Population	Average Family Size (Persons)	
		Urban Areas	Rural Areas
1965	28.2	5.9	6.2
1970	43.1	5.1	5.8
1975	50.9	4.9	5.6

Source: Bureau of Statistics (BOS), *Population Census.*

Table 7–4
Patterns of Employment

Year	Percentage of Workers in Primary Industries	Percentage of Wage and Salary Earners
1963	63.1	31.4
1973	50.0	37.8
1978	38.4	46.6

Source: BOS, *Employment Surveys.*

ated by the government can play a vital role for the welfare of the aged and the poor who can no longer rely on the support of their relatives.

Industrialization

Economic growth has brought about a rapid change in employment structures. The percentage of workers engaged in the primary industries such as agriculture and fishery declined from 63.1 percent in 1963 to 38.4 percent in 1978. Furthermore, industrialization has resulted in a growing number of wage and salary earners, as against the self-employed. The percentage of wage and salary earners increased from 31.4 percent in 1963 to 46.6 percent in 1978 (see table 7–4). Rapid industrialization and urbanization have increased the risks of accident and sickness. Industrial injuries and nonoccupational disabilities such as traffic accidents can cause prolonged unemployment and severe economic hardships for the families so affected. The development of social-security programs can relieve the hardships arising from accidental injuries and sickness, which are the inherent social risks of a highly industrialized and urbanized society.

Levels of Wages and Salaries

When the overall level of wages and salaries in the nation is low, it is difficult to introduce a meaningful social-security program, since financing such a program would be too much of a burden for the workers. Real wages in Korea have increased rapidly. In fact, during the period 1970–1978 the real wage increased by more than 200 percent (see table 7–5).

Population Structure

As life expectancy has increased and the birthrate has gradually declined, the age distribution of the population has changed, leaving Korean society with an increasing proportion of the very old and a declining proportion of the very young (see table 7–6). The role of the aged has changed rapidly in an industrialized urban society. Job opportunities diminish rapidly as the worker grows older; and not only are the aged handicapped in finding new employment, but many of the aged are required to retire. Consequently, there is a growing need to ensure social and economic security for the aged through the development of social-security programs.

Social-Security Programs in Korea

The social-security system in Korea is currently made up of (1) contributory social-insurance programs (medical insurance; pension

Table 7–5
Indexes of Wage Levels

Year	Nominal Wages	Real Wages
1975	258.1	126.7
1978	623.6	210.7

Source: Labour Office, *Wage Surveys.*
Note: 1970 = 100.0.

Table 7–6
Age Structure of Population

	1965	1975	1991[a]
Life expectancy at birth	62	68	74
Index of old population[b]	6.2	5.9	7.6
Index of young population[c]	81.7	66.6	43.8
Population over 60/Total Population (%)	5.2	5.6	7.8

[a]Projected by KDI.
[b](Population over 65)/(population 15–64) × 100.
[c](Population under 14)/(population 15–64) × 100.

programs for public servants, military personnel, and teachers; and industrial accident insurance); (2) noncontributory public-assistance programs for the poor; and (3) social-welfare services to the disadvantaged,
such as delinquent children and youth and the handicapped.

Social-Insurance Programs

Medical Insurance. The nation's medical-insurance program, initiated
in July 1977, covered workers and their dependents in firms employing
500 persons or more. In January 1979 coverage was extended to workers
and their dependents in firms employing 300 persons or more, as well
as to public servants and schoolteachers and their dependents. At present
about 21 percent of the population is covered by the medical insurance
(see table 7–7).

Insurance fees are set at 3–8 percent of a person's wage bill—on
the average 3.2 percent for employees and 3.8 percent for public servants
and teachers. Insurance fees are shared equally by insured persons and
their employers (the government in the case of public servants). The
insured are required to pay 20 percent of hospital expenses and 30 percent
of outpatient expenses.

The major problems with the present medical-insurance program are
as follows:

1. Employees of small firms are not covered under the present medical
    insurance, although their income levels are lower than those of large-
    firm employees, and thus their need for medical insurance is rela-
    tively greater. Furthermore, the self-employed, particularly in the
    agricultural sector, are not covered.
2. Since those covered under the present program are located mostly
    in urban areas, the introduction of the medical-insurance program
    has resulted in a sharp increase in the demand for medical services

Table 7–7
Persons Covered under Medical Insurance
(In thousands)

	1977	1978	1979
Employees	3,149	3,820	4,684
Employers	63	63	63
Public servants and teachers	—	—	3,041
Total	3,212	3,883	7,788
Percentage of the population	8.8	10.4	20.7

Source: Ministry of Health and Social Affairs (MHSA).

in urban areas. This will aggravate the present problem of concentration of medical facilities and personnel in urban areas.

3. Since medical-insurance associations are organized at the level of firms and organizations, the quality of medical services differs among associations; the medical-insurance program tends to play only a limited role in income redistribution and risk sharing.

4. Medical fees for the insured are controlled by the government and thus tend to be lower than those charged for other patients. There is no government subsidy to the medical-insurance scheme, however. Therefore, patients not covered by the insurance are in effect subsidizing those patients who are under the insurance.

Industrial-Accident Insurance. The industrial-accident insurance initiated in July 1964 is compulsory for all firms employing sixteen persons or more in the manufacturing, construction, and mining industries. At present about 23 percent of all workers are covered under this insurance. Although the work-related accident rate is declining over time, it remains relatively high compared with rates for more developed countries. The insurance rate, which has declined over time, on the average amounts to 1.13 percent of the workers' wage bill. Industrial-accident insurance is administered centrally by the Labor Office (see table 7–8).

The major problems associated with industrial-accident insurance are as follows:

1. Coverage needs to be extended to all industries and even to firms employing fifteen persons or less.

2. Although insurance fees have been declining over time, insurance payments have fallen far short of insurance receipts, resulting in a large accumulation of funds. By the end of 1980 the estimated accumulation of funds was 33 billion *won*.

3. Insurance benefits are too low to maintain a reasonable standard of living for the insured. Furthermore, there are too many lawsuits concerning insurance payments.

Table 7–8
Trends in Industrial-Accident Insurance

	1965	1970	1975	1979
Firms covered	289	5,588	21,369	55,763
Workers covered	161,150	779,053	1,836,209	3,607,595
Percentage of all workers	2.0	8.0	15.3	26.7
Work-related accident rate (%)	5.9	4.9	4.4	3.6

Source: Labor Office.

4.   The insurance rate is the same for all firms in a given industrial
     group. Firms with a good safety record are not given any conces-
     sions but are equated with those with a bad safety record.

Severance-Pay System. All firms employing sixteen workers or more are
legally required to make severance pay to the employee terminating his
employment, at the rate of at least one month's salary as remuneration
for each year of service. In many firms, the rate of severance pay increases progressively with the duration of service.
     The major problems with the severance-pay system are as follows:

1.   Accumulation of severance-pay obligation is becoming too heavy a
     burden on the finance of business firms. Severance-pay obligation
     amounts to more than 50 percent of the firm's estimated equity at
     47 percent of all firms.
2.   Since many firms do not put aside funds for severance pay as re-
     quired by law, the present system often becomes inoperative when
     a firm goes bankrupt.

Pension Program. The old-age, invalid, and death pension is available
to civil servants, military personnel, and schoolteachers, who constitute
about 2 percent of the population. The insurance rate is set at 11 percent
of the remuneration of the insured person, and contributions are shared
equally by insured persons and their employers. The pension program
was started in 1960 for civil servants, in 1963 for military personnel,
and in 1973 for schoolteachers. The major problems with the pension
program are as follows:

1.   The present coverage of pensions is too narrow and needs to be
     extended to wider population groups. The National Welfare Pension
     Program, covering all employed workers from 18 to 60 years of
     age, was legislated in 1973; but its implementation is still pending.
2.   The present pension programs are administered by three different
     public agencies, resulting in high overhead costs and an unequal
     distribution of benefits among different pension programs.

Public-Assistance Programs

Livelihood-Protection Program. The Livelihood Protection Act of 1961
is the legal basis for the present Livelihood Protection Program for the
Poor. Under this act the poor can be classified into two categories:
(1) those unable to work (over 65 years, under 18 years, mentally or

physically handicapped, and pregnant women); and (2) those able to work but deemed absolutely poor. Such people are those who either have no legal guardian or have a legal guardian who is not capable of supporting them; and persons whose income and wealth do not exceed the ceilings set by the government each year.

At present there are about 1.8 million persons under the Livelihood Protection Program, making up 4.9 percent of the population. Assistance is given in kind—for example, the distribution of cereals to those unable to work. This assistance amounted to 22 billion *won* in 1979. Cash assistance for fuel expenses is provided (amounting to 7.8 billion *won* in 1979) and middle-school tuition fees are waived (amounting to 3.9 billion *won* in 1979) to both categories of the poor (see table 7–9).

The areas in which further improvements need to be made are as follows:

1. The criteria for selecting those eligible for assistance need to be determined on a more objective basis. For example, the income ceiling needs to be made equal to the poverty line, which indicates the minimally acceptable living standard.
2. The level of assistance given is too low to maintain even the minimally acceptable living standard.
3. Once the poverty line is officially determined, the level of public assistance needs to be based on the difference between the poverty line and the estimated income of a household.
4. Assistance in kind needs to be limited to those cases where cash assistance is inappropriate (for example, health care and education).

Self-Help Work Program. The self-help work program is an important means of helping the poor who can work. Public expenditure for these programs was estimated at 34 billion *won* in 1979. Employment-creation effect was estimated at 11 million man-days in 1979. Current wage rates

Table 7–9
Persons under the Livelihood-Protection Program
(In thousands)

	Those Unable to Work				
	Those in Welfare Institutions	*Those in Private Homes*	*Those Able to Work*	*Total*	*Percentage of the Population*
1965	288	72	3,563	3,922	13.3
1970	306	63	2,116	2,486	7.9
1975	375	52	904	1,331	3.8
1979	282	47	1,500	1,829	4.9

Source: MHSA.

under the self-help work program are 2,500 *won* per day for a male and 2,000 *won* per day for a female worker. Typical employment under this program consists of road construction or improvement, cleaning of small rivers and streams, construction of rural irrigation facilities, and miscellaneous urban construction projects (see table 7–10).

The major problems with the self-help work program are as follows:

1. The average number of work days for eligible households under the self-help work program, estimated at twelve days in 1979, is so low that the present program cannot be a meaningful income supplement for those households.
2. The present self-help work program is by nature temporary, and it needs to be supplemented by programs designed to create more permanent employment opportunities for the poor. In this respect, emphasis needs to be given to programs designed to improve the employability of the poor who can work, through job-training and employment services.

Medical-Assistance Program. Along with the introduction of the medical-insurance program in 1977, the medical-assistance program was also formulated to cater to the poor who are protected under the Livelihood Protection Act. All medical services are free for the poor who are unable to work. The poor who are able to work pay 50 percent of hospital expenses but enjoy free outpatient services.

Major problems with the medical-assistance program are as follows:

1. Since medical-service fees under the medical-assistance program are set at 70 percent of those under the medical-insurance program, this often results in the poor receiving inferior medical services.
2. Since many of the poor cannot pay 50 percent of hospital costs, even hospital expenses need to be made free.

Table 7–10
Trends in the Self-Help Work Program

	Public Expenditures (Billions of Won)	Employment Generation (Thousands of Man-Days)	Average Work Days for Eligible Households
1974	151	15,504	34.7
1976	196	13,078	29.3
1978	150	6,104	12.3
1979	343	11,149	12.0

Source: MSHA.

Social-Welfare Services

There is a wide range of social-welfare institutions in Korea, as shown in table 7–11. About 94 percent of the social-welfare institutions are privately managed, and 67 percent of them are located in urban areas. Since these social-welfare institutions can finance only a small portion (9 percent in 1977) of their total financial expenses by themselves, they rely heavily on external sources for financing. Government (both central and local) subsidies amounted to 56 percent of total expenses in 1977; the rest was financed by private sources, both domestic and foreign.

The major problems with social-welfare institutions are as follows:

1. The present welfare-service facilities fall far short of the demand for them. For example, the homes for the aged accommodate only 35 percent of those who require such facilities; and the homes for mothers with children take care of only 1.4 percent of those who need such facilities.
2. The wage and salary level for the social-welfare-service worker is so low that many professional social workers are discouraged from working in this field for a long period. It is estimated that only 27 percent of those engaged in the social-welfare service are professionally qualified, and the turnover rate is as high as 26 percent per annum.
3. The social-welfare service relies too heavily on voluntary agencies. In order to extend the coverage of social-welfare services, the government should play a more active role in this field. Furthermore, the integrated delivery of basic welfare services at the community level is required.

Table 7–11
Social-Welfare Institutions

Types of Institutions	Number of Institutions	Number of Persons in Institutions
Aged	46	2,920
Handicapped	30	5,259
Child welfare	380	33,464
Job training for abandoned women	26	2,710
Home for mothers with children	35	3,888
Day nursery	611	41,632

Source: MHSA.

Dilemmas in Developing Social Security

Financing Social Security

As the development of social-security programs has been a relatively low priority with policymakers in Korea (compared with, for example, the development of export industries), the Korean economy spends a smaller proportion of its gross product on social-security programs than other countries with similar economic conditions. In 1974 the total expenditure on all the social-security programs in Korea amounted to only 0.68 percent of GDP, whereas the average ratio of social-security expenditures over GDP ranged from 1.2 percent in the countries with the lowest per capita incomes, to 16.2 percent in those countries with the highest (see tables 7–12 and 7–13).

   Social-security expenditures can be financed either by general government revenues or by contributions from insured persons and their employers. Public-assistance and social-welfare-service programs have to be financed by the former, whereas social-insurance programs can use both methods of financing. It is often administratively easier and finan-

Table 7–12
Social Security Expenditures in Korea
(In millions of won)

	1974	1978	1979
Social insurance	29,720	150,043	240,358
Public assistance	15,796	65,264	100,774
Welfare institutions	1,059	3,514	5,811
Total	46,575	218,821	346,943
Percentage of GDP (%)	0.68	1.07	1.17
Per capita GNP (1974 constant prices), U.S. $	523	746	794

Source: MHSA, EPB.

Table 7–13
Social-Security Expenditures in Other Countries

Per Capita Income Group ($)	Number of Countries	Ratio of Social-Security Expenditures to GDP
Under 500	12	1.2
500–1,000	11	2.6
1,000–2,000	10	6.4
2,000–5,000	17	9.6
Over 5,000	13	16.2
Total	63	7.6

Source: ILO, *The Cost of Social Security;* World Bank, *World Atlas.*

cially more feasible to formulate social-insurance programs based on contributions by employees in large-scale firms and their employers, as in the case of medical insurance to Korea. The beneficiaries of this type of social-insurance scheme, however, turn out to be the relatively richer members of society, so that the original objective—for social insurance to help the weaker segment of the population—is not met.

Developing social-security programs for the poor and the deprived usually involves greater expenditure by the government. Actual implementation of this type of action, however, often encounters many obstacles because the poor and the deprived do not carry much weight in the society.

Developing a comprehensive social-security scheme in Korea would involve a significant reallocation of the nation's financial resources toward the sector in need of social security. For example, the additional income transfers required to bring the income of all the poor families up to the poverty line (U.S.$135 per month in urban areas and $113 in rural areas for a family of five persons) is estimated at 1.1 percent of GNP and 7.0 percent of total government expenditures in 1978.

When the available financial resources are limited, it is crucial to define priorities among the alternative uses of resources. In Korea these decisions are particularly difficult to make because existing political conditions require that national defense should take priority over other needs. Moreover, economic growth is regarded as a prerequisite for improving the economic welfare of the population and thereby achieving social stability. Thus increases in social-security expenditures must be justified on the ground that the defense fund will not be depleted and that social-security expenditures are conducive to generating long-term social stability and economic growth.

Setting Priorities among Programs

Since social-security expenditures cannot be doubled or tripled overnight, it is important to define appropriate priorities among different social-security programs. At the early stages of the development of social-security programs, public assistance, for example, should receive priority over social insurance, which would benefit only a small fraction of the relatively advantaged section of the population. This has been the experience of England, which has the longest history of a social-security program. In the United States, however, public assistance received attention only after social insurance was fully developed. In Korea, social insurance is likely to receive a higher priority than public assistance because the former is more visible and its beneficiaries more vocal.

Among social-insurance programs, industrial-accident insurance is usually the first one to be implemented, as was the case in Korea. In 1977 there were 129 countries in the world that had some type of industrial-accident insurance. In 1977, 114 countries had some type of old-age, sickness, and survivor-benefit programs, although implementation of the national-welfare pension program is still pending in Korea. By 1977 some type of medical insurance was in effect in 72 countries, including Korea, and some form of family-allowance program in 65 countries, although Korea has not adopted such a program. Unemployment insurance also was available in 38 countries by 1977, but such a program is not available in Korea (see table 7–14).

It is commonly agreed that it was right to develop industrial-accident insurance at the first stage and medical insurance at the next.[1] However, there are divergent views on what should be done next in the field of social insurance. Labor unions and business groups take the view that unemployment insurance needs to be introduced immediately, particularly in view of the fact that the economy in recent months has not generated enough employment prospects. Researchers and professors concerned with the complexities of social security, however, argue that it is premature to introduce unemployment insurance now because there are no established public channels for job placement and training. They propose that the implementation of the national-welfare pension program and the extension of coverage under medical insurance take priority over the introduction of unemployment insurance.

One of the most controversial issues in social insurance is the question of what to do with the severance-pay scheme when either the national-welfare pension or unemployment insurance scheme is introduced. Labor unions believe that the severance-pay scheme should be kept intact and that other social-insurance programs should be introduced on an additional basis. Management groups, however, take the view that the

Table 7–14
Number of Countries with Social Insurance

Per Capita Income Group ($)	Pension Program	Medical Insurance	Industrial-Accident Insurance	Unemployment Insurance	Family Allowance
Under 500	34	13	48	2	16
500–1,000	18	12	19	1	6
1,000–2,000	24	19	24	9	14
2,000–5,000	21	14	21	10	15
Over 5,000	17	14	17	16	14
Total	114	72	129	38	65

Source: U.S. Social Security Administration, *Social Security Programs throughout the World.*

introduction of other social insurances on top of the severance-pay scheme will place too great a burden on the firm's finances and thus will not be acceptable to management. This has been the major reason for delaying the implementation of the national-welfare pension program, although the necessary legislation was completed in 1973. Some compromise between labor and management must be reached before a new social-insurance program can be introduced.

The question has been raised whether it is wise to introduce a new social-insurance program when the existing ones, particularly the medical-insurance scheme, have very limited coverage of the population. It has been suggested that priority should be given to extending the coverage of existing social insurance, rather than to introducing a new one with limited coverage. They argue that social insurance, with its coverage limited to employees of large firms, has an adverse impact on income distribution, which is contrary to the original purpose of social insurance. It can be argued, however, that it is very important to make a start because it takes a long time to develop a mature social-insurance program covering the entire population. In the meantime, public-assistance programs can take care of the urgent needs of the low-income group.

Administering Social Security

Administering social-security programs is not easy, particularly when coverage extends to a large segment of the population. Since a number of government agencies are now administering various social-security programs, formulating a comprehensive plan on social security and maintaining an appropriate balance among programs in terms of financing methods, benefit levels, and so on, is difficult. The desirability of forming a central public agency in charge of administering various social-security programs (a Social Security Administration) is an important issue that will have to be discussed and decided in the future. The advantages of having such a central agency would be reduction in administrative costs by economies of scale and consistency in planning and implementation. The possible disadvantage would be that such an agency might become too big and bureaucratic to be efficient (see table 7–15).

Some people argue that private insurance companies should be encouraged to manage various types of social insurance and that the government should minimize its direct involvement in administering insurance programs. If coverage of social insurance is limited to employees in large-scale firms and insurance contributions are not subsidized by the government, there is no reason that private insurance companies cannot administer insurance programs such as medical insurance and pension

Table 7–15
Social-Security Administration Agencies at Present

	Social-Security Programs
Ministry of Health and Social Affairs	Medical insurance, public assistance, social-welfare services
Labor Office	Industrial-accident insurance, severance-pay system
Ministry of Defense	Pension for military personnel
Ministry of Education	Pension for schoolteachers
General Affairs Administration	Pension for public servants
Veterans Relief Administration	Assistance for war victims

programs. If coverage is to be extended to those segments of the population who cannot bear the full cost of social insurance, however, some type of public intervention in the administration of social security becomes necessary. This would depend on the desirability of expanding the role of the government, relying on its efficiency and philosophical accommodation.

Social Security and Socioeconomic Development

It is arguable that social security forms a basic need of families in modern industrialized society and thus that social-security programs need to be developed, even at the expense of short-term economic growth. The majority view in Korea, however, is that social security should not be developed at the expense of economic growth. Since social security and economic growth pursue the common goal of improving the living conditions of the population, in the long run they should complement rather than compete with each other.

Mobilizing domestic savings is often regarded as a prerequisite for generating rapid economic growth. One school of thought, however, takes the view that social security implies redistribution of income from the rich, with a relatively higher marginal propensity to save, to the poor, with a lower marginal propensity to save, which results in the reduction of overall savings and economic growth rate. Another view is that the accumulation of financial reserves under social-security schemes designed to meet long-term risks represents deferred consumption and net additional capital accumulation. It is difficult to generalize the impact of social security on private savings because this would depend on the type of social-security program and the means of financing it.

Social security can be an important means of redistributing income from the rich to the poor when the entire population is covered by social-security programs. At the early stage of the development of social security programs, however, when social-insurance coverage is often still limited to public servants and employees of large firms, the income-redistribution effect of social security may not be as favorable as originally envisaged. The relatively worse off, who are not covered under social-insurance programs, may end up subsidizing the relatively better off, as in the case of the present medical-insurance program in Korea.

In an open economy such as that of Korea, where the private sector plays a vital role, the possible impact of social security on the competitiveness of business firms has an important bearing on policy decisions about social security. On the one hand, social security can be regarded as an extra labor cost to be borne by business firms. On the other hand, social security protects workers and their families from social risks and uncertainties arising from sickness, death, old age, and unemployment, and thus results in higher labor productivity and better management-labor relations.

It is also felt that the traditional values in Korea, such as the extended-family system wherein the old and the economically inactive were supported by the young and the economically active, need to be preserved, and that the introduction of Western-style social security should be delayed for as long as possible. These traditional values are being rapidly eroded, however; the real need for social security is increasing as the Korean economy becomes more industrialized and urban oriented. Under these circumstances, Korea may have no alternative to developing Western-style social-security programs, although the scope of such programs can be modified to meet prevailing Korean economic and social conditions.

Note

1. Medical insurance was initiated earlier than other social-insurance programs in Korea because the late President Park took the firm view that medical services are a basic need for the population.

Ethical Dilemmas Arising from Urban Development and Environmental Change: Singapore

Chia Lin Sien

In the foreword to the proceedings of a seminar on Modernization in Singapore: Impact on the Individual, held in 1972, Dr. Hernon has this to say:

> Since the end of World War II, Singapore has been the scene of more changes in every aspect of life whether personal, communal, political, industrial, economic and so on, with more far-reaching consequences than in any previous quarter century of her history. The pace of change has been such that not everyone has been able to "evolve" most effective adaptation for survival in "modern Singapore."[1]

In this regard Singapore's experience has been similar to that of other Southeast Asian nations that had to reconstruct their shattered economies after World War II. These countries also had to develop economically in order to cope with rapid population growth, rising unemployment, and an increasing tempo of urbanization, with their attendant problems of labor unrest and social turmoil.

An important element of the postwar experience is the rise of nationalism and the attainment of statehood of most Southeast Asian countries, including Singapore. Singapore achieved self-rule from the British colonial government in 1959 and in 1963 joined Malaysia in a short-lived union before separating to become an independent state in August 1965. Singapore has therefore been an independent sovereign nation for only a little over a decade and a half. For Singaporeans the idea of loyalty to their country is still relatively novel, and the quest for a Singaporean identity is a high priority.

I am grateful to Professor Wu Teh Yao, Mr. Chiew Seen Kong, and Dr. R.J. Warwick Neville for their critical comments on an earlier draft of this chapter. I also benefited immensely from discussions with the directors of the Marga Institute, Messrs. Chandra Soysa and Godfrey Gunatilleke, and Dr. Neelan Tiruchelvam, as well as from stimulating discussions during the Seminar on Ethical Dilemmas of Development in Singapore, jointly coordinated by Dr. V. Selvaratnam and myself, and held on 15 March 1980 at the Regional Institute of Higher Education and Development (RIHED) in Singapore.

The history of Singapore prior to World War II was not entirely tranquil. The British acquired the territory in 1819 and established a trading post to take advantage of the strategic position of the island, which is located at the eastern exit of the vital Straits of Malacca and Singapore. The subsequent development of the colony was tied to the era of Western colonial expansion in the region and the Far East. Singapore's economy thrived on entrepôt trade, channeling the region's primary produce to the Western metropolitan countries and in turn selling Western-manufactured products to the region. In the process the colony also developed a trading network within the region, and in many ways present-day Singapore continues to play the part of the regional entrepôt, together with that of a financial, insurance, and communications center.

The rapid economic expansion of nineteenth- and early twentieth-century Singapore was achieved in part through the influx of immigrant populations from China, the Indian subcontinent, and the surrounding territories. The population of Singapore was only 150—consisting of 120 Malays and 30 Chinese—at the time Stamford Raffles first stood on the shores of Singapore in 1819. By the year of the first census in 1871, the population had increased to just under 100,000. By 1948, soon after World War II, it had surpassed a million. The number reached 2 million just prior to the 1970 census, and at the 1980 census the population was determined to be 2.41 million.

Early Singapore society could best be described as a migrant community characterized by a predominance of males, with a tendency for the residents to remit their earnings to their home countries and eventually to return there in retirement. Not until the 1930s did the colonial government institute a series of tough immigration laws to restrict immigration, while allowing female immigrants with the view to stabilizing society in Singapore. Since then the sex ratio of the population has become increasingly normal, and the growth in population was due largely to natural increases, although movements of population between Singapore and Malaya continued to be unrestricted until after the separation of Singapore from the Malaysian union in 1965.

An important aspect of the immigrant population of Singapore is that it is also a plural one. By the 1871 census, the proportion of Chinese had reached approximately 56 percent, that of the Malay population was around 27 percent, Indians accounted for some 12 percent, and the remaining 5 percent were a mixture of other races including Eurasians and Europeans. Since that time the proportion of Chinese increased, to account for some 78 percent of the total population in 1947, whereas that of Malays showed a corresponding decline to about 14 percent. The proportion of Indians remained fairly stable throughout the interval. In the last two decades, however, there has been a reversal of trends between the Chinese and Malay populations, due largely to greater fertility among the latter, although more recently the differences in growth rates among the major races have been small.

Thus over a period of 160 years of Singapore's modern history, the social and economic conditions of the state have undergone rapid structural and qualitative changes. Singaporeans, therefore, are used to adapting to new situations as they arise. Although the postwar period has been identified as the period of greatest change, the period since the attainment of self-rule in 1959 must be regarded as the most crucial era in the evolution of modern Singapore. It is on this period that the present study focuses.

Developmental Goals and Constraints

When the present ruling party, the Peoples' Action party (PAP) took over the reins of government in 1959, one of its first tasks was to assess the country's economic and social needs and to plan for development. The State of Singapore Development Plan 1961–1964 was adopted. The plan identified a number of problems that faced the country, including a high population-growth rate coupled with rising unemployment and little prospect for the traditional entrepôt trade as a source of economic growth. Serious labor unrest in the 1950s also threatened social stability.

In order to find new sources of growth for the economy and to create employment opportunities, the plan delineated bold schemes to promote and diversify industries and to launch an ambitious program of public low-cost housing. The sequel to these and other development programs is well known and needs no elaboration.[2]

The successful economic program of Singapore should be viewed in the light of the country's limited physical base, without any natural resources to speak of, as well as the adverse circumstances that confronted Singapore during the 1960s.[3] Indonesia declared its policy of confrontation against the formation of Malaysia, including Singapore, and this resulted in severe economic setbacks for Singapore's economy. Confrontation ended after Singapore separated from Malaysia. The dislocation brought about by the separation, however, was costly and, for the peoples of the two territories, which have traditional social as well as economic ties, constituted a traumatic experience. This was followed by the withdrawal from Singapore of the British military base, which directly employed some 30,000–40,000 persons and contributed a substantial portion of the country's national income.

Despite the adverse conditions under which the nation emerged as an independent state, Singapore registered impressive growth rates, which saw double-digit annual figures throughout the second half of the 1960s and early 1970s. The per capita gross national product for Singaporeans came to S$7,167 in 1980, about three times higher than the 1970 figure. The momentum of growth generated during the period before the oil crisis in October 1973 was carried over, albeit at a reduced rate of growth; in 1980 the economy rebounded to register 10 percent growth, the first double-digit growth rate since the oil crisis.

Speaking of the role of government at a seminar on modernization in Singapore, Dr. Goh Keng Swee, Singapore's deputy prime minister, held that "so far as Singapore is concerned, we see the modernisation process in terms of creating increased material well-being for our citizens. This means more jobs, bigger incomes, better career prospects, better homes, in short a better life materially."[4] The emphasis on improving the material well-being of Singaporeans was indeed the preoccupation of the government throughout the 1960s, with calls for belt tightening in order to withstand externally derived adverse economic conditions. Since the latter part of the 1960s, however, the government has gone beyond merely acquiring material wealth and providing better homes for the population, and has put much effort into improving the physical environment through planning and environmental control. Much attention has also been paid to upgrading the republic's education system, health and other social services, and cultural activities. Indeed, the present concern is with the qualitative aspects of society as much as with the quantitative aspects of the economy.

Much attention has also been paid to forging a Singaporean identity out of a multiethnic, multicultural society. This has been done through such measures as abolishing monolingual schools; allocating Housing Development Board low-cost flats on a first-come, first-serve basis; and requiring compulsory national service for males on reaching the age of 18. Indeed, in looking at the plural society in Singapore, Chiew has concluded that "de-pluralization has taken place between 1959 and 1979 [and that it] is extensive, affecting many areas of social life—education, political culture, housing, and the economy."[5] Given the short period within which the process has taken place in the new environment, however, it must be regarded as at best the initial stage of a long evolutionary process. Whether the direction taken in the first few steps is the correct one can only be judged in time.

Environmental Change as a Source of Social Tension and Conflict

The physical changes in Singapore have been rapid and extensive, even to the casual observer. A substantial portion of the changes took place only over the last two decades. Part of the alteration of the environment has been due to the creation of satellite towns and the rebuilding of a considerable portion of the central area of the city. These changes have necessitated massive relocation of the population, thereby disrupting not only the spatial pattern of their social behavior but also their means of livelihood, community interactions, and social ties.

The physical transformation of the landscape of Singapore gives rise to a number of related ethical questions:

1. Have government agencies such as the Housing and Development Board (HDB), Urban Redevelopment Authority (URA), and Jurong Town Corporation (JTC) stifled the activities of private enterprise?
2. Have the design, arrangement, and location of the low-cost HDB flats contributed to the loss of traditional values of society?
3. Has the new built environment contributed toward molding a Singaporean identity?
4. Has congested high-rise living raised the level of anomie among the residents?
5. Have the new living conditions reduced or increased public participation in community affairs?
6. To what extent has the new built environment contributed toward a more cohesive, just, and moral society?

It must be noted, however, that although it is easy to pose these questions, the answers are by no means clear. They are not easily quantifiable, and the effects of the change may take some time to manifest themselves. There are also many other factors impinging on the situation. It is not possible to separate the contribution of the impact of the new environment from that of the greater degree of urbanization experienced by Singaporeans as a whole and the influence of the education system, mass media, the influx of over 2 million tourists per year and large numbers of foreign workers, and other sources. One can only note the indications and trends from the studies made with these questions in mind, as well as the discussions and opinions of other social observers.

The Extent of the Physical-Environmental Change

It is not the intention here to provide a detailed description of the physical transformation that Singapore has undergone over the past two decades, as there are accounts available elsewhere.[6] The following brief review is intended to highlight the major areas in which changes in the physical landscape have taken place, to give the reader a better appreciation of the impact of these transformations, which are still taking place.

Physical Planning

Physical planning is undertaken for the country as a whole by the Ministry of National Development. The ministry administers the Statutory Master Plan, the primary instrument controlling physical development, which was completed in 1955 and adopted in 1958. The Master Plan was drawn up by the Singapore Improvement Trust (SIT), a body created in 1927 to undertake the work of slum clearance and building public housing, mainly for those affected. The Master Plan divided the country into the central planning area, the urban planning area, and the rural planning area. A major objective of the plan was to decongest the city center and to decentralize the population by moving people into planned satellite towns. It also provided for industrial estates and public and recreational amenities. A green belt of open spaces was delineated to prevent urban sprawl. The plan was to be revised once every five years, although revisions were made only in 1965 and 1975.

It became evident that the Master Plan was static and therefore incapable of keeping up with the dynamic changes that are shaping the country's physical landscape. The government therefore established the State and City Planning Project, which was to undertake comprehensive as well as project-level planning of the future use and development of land and transportation. The project resulted in what is now known as the Comprehensive Long-range Concept Plan, or simply the Concept Plan, which was designed to provide guidelines for physical development.

Public Housing

The Housing and Development Board was established in 1960 and given wide statutory powers to clear slums, redevelop urban areas, undertake resettlement projects, acquire and own land, and build low-cost housing. The Land Acquisition Act of 1966 enabled the government to acquire land compulsorily as long as it was for the public benefit. Under the First Five-Year Building Program (1960–1965), the board completed some 54,000 units. In the Second Five-Year Building Program a total of some 66,000 units were built; in the Third Program some 113,000 units were constructed. In 1979, 27,000 units were completed, bringing the total of housing units constructed during 1976–1979 to about 118,000. As of 31 March 1980, 67 percent of the total population of Singapore was housed in Housing Development Board flats. Eventually, as much as 75–80 percent of the population may live in government-built housing units.[7]

The Housing and Development Board is also responsible for the planning and development of new towns and housing estates, as well as the provision of communal and social facilities within them. The earlier housing estates were located near the city center, utilizing available pockets of land within short transportation distances from the majority of workplaces. Newer housing estates and towns such as Toa Payoh, Ang Mo Kio, and Woodlands are located at some distance from the city. These are provided with access roads for carrying the appropriate volume of peak-hour traffic.

Industrial estates, of which the Jurong industrial town is the best known, came under the management of the Jurong Town Corporation. In the case of Jurong Town, housing was built by the corporation for low- and medium-income groups. Residential areas are located within the overall planning area of the township. Smaller industrial estates are built in the vicinity of housing estates and new towns in order to tap the pool of labor available.

It should also be mentioned that housing, mainly in the form of high-rise flats, is also built by other statutory bodies, such as the Port of Singapore Authority for their employees. In addition, the government has embarked on building projects to house government officers and middle-income earners as well.

Urban Redevelopment

The Central Area represents only 1.2 percent of the total land area of the main island but accommodates some 15–20 percent of the total population. Apart from the squatter areas that sprouted up immediately after the war, much of the housing stock was in poor physical condition and many blocks of buildings were housing as many as over 2,500 persons to the hectare. Fires in tenement houses and squatter settlements were frequent, and sanitary conditions were appalling. The Rent Control Act of 1947, which was introduced to prevent excessive rents, had the effect of discouraging landlords from improving and keeping up the houses. The narrow streets within the city central area were totally inadequate to serve the modern needs of high-volume and high-speed motor transportation. These were the conditions prevailing up to the 1950s.

Surveys conducted by U.N. teams of consultants in the early 1960s produced recommendations for a comprehensive urban-renewal program. As a result, the Urban Renewal Department was established within the

Housing and Development Board in 1964. The functions of this body were subsequently taken over by the Urban Redevelopment Authority, which became a statutory body in April 1974. The Central Area was divided into nineteen precincts; and the work of land acquisition, resettlement and relocation of business premises, and redevelopment of whole street blocks of buildings proceeded from the two extreme ends and progressively worked into the more difficult areas near the center. So far redevelopment has progressed apace. Sections of the Central Area have already been rebuilt, and residents have moved into the Crawford, Rochore, and Havelock Road areas. The comprehensive program of redevelopment provided not only flats for residential purposes but also commercial and shopping premises, public buildings, health and social amenities, and cultural and recreational facilities.[8]

Other Areas of Physical Development

Apart from the aforementioned major areas of physical development—public housing, urban redevelopment, and industrial estates—there have been considerable physical changes in the landscape of Singapore through the efforts of the Port of Singapore Authority in the area of port development and expansion; the construction and upgrading of the city's network of roads, overpasses or interchanges, pedestrian malls, and overhead bridges; the construction of a new international airport at Changi, which opened in December 1981; and, perhaps the most striking of all, the work of the Parks and Recreation Division of the Public Works Department in providing open spaces, parks, and tree planting.

The private sector was not to be outdone. Developers and private enterprises built skyscrapers, hotels, shopping complexes, high-rise apartments, housing estates, and condominiums. The result of two decades of feverish building construction by government and private agencies was a complete transformation of the physical and built environment of the republic. For the majority of Singaporeans, moving their homes and finding new and alternative employment have come to be regarded as commonplace. Adaptations to novel situations has become part of life in Singapore.

Ethical Issues Arising from Rapid Change

The vast changes in the physical environment described in the previous section are symptomatic of much more deep-seated social and cultural transformations, brought about primarily by the outstanding economic and political successes of the republic over the last two decades. These dynamic changes, which have by no means lost their momentum, have inevitably brought about tensions and conflicts for society as a whole and its component groups. The following sections examine the major ethical issues that have come to the fore in public debate and private discussions.

Breakdown of Traditional Values

There is considerable concern about the impact of urbanization, increasing affluence, and the continual influx of Western life-styles and values on Singaporean society, leading to what a sociologist, Dr. Riaz Hassan, calls the "transition syndrome," which he describes as being "a set of psychological and behavioural orientations, such as receptiveness to change, social mobility, economic rationality, achievement, materialism, individualism, acquisitiveness and above all an orientation which emphasizes change and progress as a highly desirable end."[9] This has led to the loss of traditional values and mores and the abandonment of customs and practices associated with them. Concern is expressed particularly with the breakdown of the extended-family system associated with the Chinese.[10] There is also the problem of the disappearance of the *kampong* (village) life-style of the indigenous Malaya. Urbanization in any case would have ensured that these changes would eventually have taken place in Singapore. The success of the HDB low-cost housing program, however, has hastened the pace of the transition.

The problem is in part the result of the design of the flats, which cater to the nuclear family. The success of the public-housing program stems from this, since there is already an existing trend toward the disintegration of the extended-family system as a result of other factors. During the 1960s the housing program was aimed at remedying the severe housing shortage as quickly as possible. Given the relatively limited resources available to the HDB at the initial stages, a large proportion of the housing units were of the one-, two-, and three-room type. Only toward the end of the 1960s and the 1970s were four- and five-room units built. The size limitations meant that it was no longer possible for more than a few members of the extended family to live together in one flat.

A related problem is the fact that in the 1970s the housing estates and new towns were located further away from the city so that the nuclear family units, once they are located in such towns as Ang Mo Kio, Clementi, or Woodlands, became physically well removed from their paternal homes. The system of allocation of flats on a first-come, first-served basis and ability to pay or purchase did not help to bring the components of the larger family within the same housing estate.

In recent years the government provided for joint applications and for exchanges of flats between different housing estates to enable related families to be located in the same housing block. Measures have now been taken to give priority to three-tiered families in the allocation of flats. This was done in recognition of the virtues of the extended family, wherein the aged are cared for, the young have retired members of the family to look after them in cases where both parents are working, and traditional value systems are passed on to the younger generation. A related move has been to allow income-tax relief in cases where retired parents are living with a taxpayer.

In Dr. Hassan's study of families in one- and two-room flats, he reports that after relocation these families tend to increase their reliance on immediate family members in the case of emergency—sudden but minor illness or injury, small loans, and advice on personal matters. The results indicate the decline of the role of neighbors with relocation, which is then compensated for by greater reliance on kinfolk. Another finding is that those with less than twelve years of residence in their former home are relatively more satisfied with their new environment than are those who lived in their previous residence for more than twelve years. This indicates that there is a sense of rootedness and community solidarity among communities that have lived together longer. Attempts should be made to establish an appropriate social infrastructure to accelerate the process of neighborhood and community development.[11] Here the government has not only developed community centers for each electoral district and established Citizens' Consultative Committees, but also has set up organizations for individual housing estates and even for individual housing blocks to increase community participation in the management of community affairs and to organize community activities. One HDB sociologist has suggested block relocation of entire squatter communities in order to preserve the community ties and milieu already established.[12] In earlier years this was actually done in the case of fire victims, as in the Bukit Ho Swee housing area.

The question of losing traditional values and thereby foregoing the cultural ballast necessary for maintaining societal stability has received some public attention (further discussed in a subsequent section). There is much interest in the Japanese model, wherein scientific and modern technology with economic achievements are integrated into a society that retains its traditional culture and way of life. The Japanese have seemingly been able to sustain a stable society despite rapid change. In Singapore the desire to preserve traditional cultural values and practices obviously conflicts with the policy of "from each his economic best, and to each his economic worth'' expressed by the prime minister, Lee Kuan Yew.[13] The principles of meritocracy encourage efficiency, diligence, individualism, public acclaim, and personal advancement. The recent emphasis on moral education in the schools and the second language are measures directed at inculcating traditional values in the young.

Social Justice and Equity

The ethical questions relating to justice and equity touch on many facets of life and society, but only those concerned with urban redevelopment and public housing will be discussed. Three separate areas will be examined. The first is the question of adequacy and fairness in compensating those affected by land acquisition and relocation; the second relates to distribution of benefits; and the third deals with the impact on the aged and the disadvantaged.

A 1968 survey of public-housing tenants revealed that 26 percent of the households living in public housing had been evicted by the government, and another 5.3 percent had been moved by private landlords for development.[14] Those evicted include squatters affected by slum clearance, residents and shopkeepers affected by urban renewal, and farmers whose land has been acquired. People whose premises have been acquired by the government are given varying sums of money based on a certain formula. Should their residence be affected, they are given the choice of a flat located in their preferred area. Shopkeepers and owners of industrial premises are similarly given a choice of preferred shopping complex and industrial estate or flatted factory, respectively. Shopkeepers and owners of industrial establishments are charged reduced rents that are progressively increased to market rates. In cases where there is more than one applicant for the same premises, allocation is made by balloting.

The findings of surveys conducted by HDB and Hassan have shown that, in general, involuntarily relocated residents consider their new environments an improvement over their previous housing conditions. There is generally more space, better ventilation, and better facilities than in their previous residence, although most were dissatisfied with higher rentals, and others complained of loss of job opportunities and goodwill of clients after relocation.[15]

Compensation for land acquired under the Land Acquisition Act is generally very modest. A recent case in which the present minister of defense unsuccessfully sought increased compensation for land so acquired demonstrates the effectiveness of this piece of legislation. An earlier case of demolition of a Chinese Buddhist temple by the HDB for developing a housing estate, against the appeals of the temple owners to preserve a historic building and a place of worship, points to a similar conflict of interests. In this case the question of adequate compensation was compounded by other issues relating to cultural heritage.

The Rent Control Act was enacted in 1947 to protect tenants occupying prewar houses from being exploited by landlords. The act adversely affected the interest of the landlord, since prewar rents were not commensurate with present-day rentals. Tenants have been able to take advantage of the central locations of such premises to run profitable businesses. In 1964 the government decontrolled an area (now known as the golden shoe because of its shape) to enable land owners to repossess their land for redevelopment. Compensation is based on twenty times the monthly rent, provided that land owners can demonstrate their intention to redevelop the land. For premises outside the decontrolled area, tenants continue to enjoy low rents at the expense of landlords. There are frequent appeals and letters to the press urging the government to do away with the act.

In order to evict squatters, who enjoy squatters' rights provided they have been occupying the land for over a certain number of years, land owners must negotiate with the squatters for a mutually agreeable sum of compensation, which can be substantial. Overall, there appears to be no consistent policy governing compensation for persons affected by land acquisition by private and public agencies.

As for the question of equitable distribution of benefits, Hassan has shown that public housing has benefited the lower-income groups more than the higher-income groups. Over the years, however, the income ceiling for households eligible for HDB housing has been raised. Eligibility has also been extended to single individuals; as a result, more than 95 percent of the total households in Singapore are eligible for public housing. In the 1970s HDB built a greater proportion of larger flats and flats for middle-income households, and some one-room flats were torn down for redevelopment. The policy is to increase the supply of housing units to meet the shift in demand toward the larger, more expensive units. Hassan shows that there is a significant group of the poorest segment of households who for various reasons cannot afford even the lowest rents offered. He calls for a reexamination of the policy on housing subsidy to take into account the needs of these poor households. Although the smaller flats are subsidized by a small amount, the larger flats are yielding a profit.[16] The government, however, has reiterated its policy of not providing subsidies and has allowed medical charges and bus fares to rise. It is unlikely that the amount of subsidy for HDB operations will increase.

The related question of providing special assistance to the aged and other disadvantaged persons has only recently begun to receive attention. As a result of the drastic reduction in the population growth rate of the country, from over 4.0 percent just after the war to about 1.3 percent per annum since 1977, the proportion of the old will increase significantly, with a corresponding increase in the demand for health and social facilities. The designs of public buildings, housing estates, and roads do not take into account the special needs of the old and the physically handicapped.

In the case of the young, much more has been achieved in terms of providing play facilities and access to primary schools, although highrise flats are intrinsically unsuitable for the needs of the young. Many children are physically confined to the flats by their parents for fear of their mixing with bad company and because of the problem of supervision. This disability can to some extent be remedied by better-designed housing estates and better organization for the young. For the newer housing estates, the ground floor is left empty to provide a sheltered area for play and other uses. Also in recent years the government, through the community centers, has begun kindergartens and day-care centers. The aim, however, is to help working mothers.

Ethnic Relations and the Singaporean Identity

In Singapore, as elsewhere in the region, ethnic, cultural, and religious cleavages tend to reinforce one another thereby rendering difficult the task of integrating the various communities and forging a Singaporean national identity. The problem can apparently be approached by urging each group to play down the incompatible aspects of their beliefs and customs and to emphasize those that promote common understanding. Tolerance, a greater degree of interaction, mutual cooperation at both the community and the individual levels, and avoidance of public discussion of sensitive issues are called for. The objective of creating a common identity, however, conflicts with the desire to promote traditional values and cultures. Thus the current emphasis on speaking Mandarin (as opposed to dialects) has been regarded by some as drawing the various ethnic groups away from each other.

The HDB policy of allocating flats on a first come, first served basis and not encouraging segregated blocks or even floors appears to have had the beneficial effect of fostering greater interaction, closer understanding, and cooperation among the different ethnic groups. Hassan concluded that on the whole living in public housing produced "favourable and relatively positive interethnic attitudes" and that "generally

each ethnic group had very favourable perceptions of the others . . .
interethnic relations were fairly harmonious.''[17]

Other contributing factors helping to cement the major component
ethnic groups include:

1. removing ethnic schools and introducing integrated schools where
    English-Mandarin, English-Malay, English-Tamil, and English-Ma-
    lay-Tamil are taught;
2. promoting multiethnic participation in uniform groups such as the
    Red Cross and Scouts, and organizing multiethnic sports;
3. replacing school textbooks published in Taiwan and Hong Kong
    with locally written texts based on syllabi provided by the Ministry
    of Education;
4. since 1966, introducing compulsory bilingualism in the schools,
    although only English is used as the language of instruction in the
    tertiary institutions;
5. adopting national symbols from 1960, such as the national anthem,
    national flag, and national day, and instituting the Yang Di-Pertuan
    Negara or president of the republic;
6. since 1957, fostering proportional representation of Chinese and
    Malay labor forces in the various economic sectors, although the
    class gap between the Chinese and Malay, as measured by mean
    education and monthly income, worsened (in favor of the Chinese)
    between 1957 and 1975.

The foregoing factors are listed by Chiew Seen Kong, who concludes
that ''de-pluralization has taken place between 1959 and 1979.''[18]

In addition to the factors contributing toward greater interethnic solidarity, one might include other factors, such as compulsory national
service for all males on reaching the age of 18, as important. The membership of Singapore in the Association of South East Asian Nations
(ASEAN) formed in 1967 has had the effect of emphasizing the sovereignty of the republic in the eyes of neighboring states as well as in the
eyes of its nationals and thereby promoting the image of the Singaporean
regardless of the ethnic origin of the particular individual concerned. One
should not dismiss the importance of the participation of the multiethnic
Singaporean team in the Singapore-Malaysia interstate annual football
competition, which has produced the proud Kallang roar—the roar of
approval and support for the national team heard at the Kallang stadium
during football matches—in focusing attention on the Singaporean image, although Singapore's participation was terminated after 1980.

In a separate study, Chiew undertook a sample survey in 1969–1970
on the question of the Singapore national identity and concluded that

after only ten years of self-government, the "levels of national identity in Singapore were very high for a new nation."[19] The creation of a national identity can only be achieved given a number of favorable factors under a conducive environment over an extended period of time. The underlying conducive circumstances are the ready acceptance of rapid change among Singaporeans nurtured in an environment of dynamic economic expansion and political and social stability. Only time will tell how deep-rooted and substantial is the national identity achieved thus far.

Problems of Keeping the Environment
Clean and Green

The common-property nature of the environment means that keeping the city streets and housing estates clean, minimizing pollution from industries and motor vehicles, and beautifying the landscape with plants constitute formidable tasks. Environmental protection requires proper physical planning, large financial outlay, and a high degree of discipline on the part of both government environmental agencies and private citizens. Without question, Singapore's experience in environment management has been a highly successful one, particularly since it has been achieved over such a short span of time.[20]

Earlier accounts in this chapter of the economic development of the republic suggested the generally favorable background to successful management of the environment. There have been ample financial, technical, and other resources within the country to undertake the task. The small size of the state, together with the absence of a high population-growth rate and large influx of the rural poor into the city, are also favorable factors. Even given these favorable conditions, however, there was no guarantee of success in creating such a pleasing result as can be seen today. One might even argue that the well-groomed look of the island republic has to some extent contributed to its economic achievements.

It was clear that environmental planning and city management could not have been left up to private bodies but required a major government role. The measures taken to clean up and beautify the nation's environment can be summarized as follows:

1. establishing an appropriate institutional framework and providing adequate financial and other resources;
2. formulating sound policies and ensuring that environmentally related plans and projects are carrried out efficiently;
3. adopting effective laws coupled with strict law enforcement;

4. implementing a program aimed at inculcating social consciousness in the public through the schools and a series of countrywide campaigns;
5. implementing massive public-housing and urban-renewal schemes that have effectively removed the slum and squatter areas and, in the process, cleaned up a large part of the city's environment.

The Singapore model in dealing with the environment is based on strong government initiative and direction. Despite the success so far, it is clear that the effort carried by public agencies must be sustained and is becoming increasingly expensive. Ultimately, the problem of maintaining a clean city is best tackled at the source: individuals, factory managers, and persons in responsible positions must exercise restraint so that a minimum of solid waste and other pollutants are discharged into the receiving environment. Encouraging individuals to act voluntarily according to their civic pride and social conscience, however, will take time and may require deliberate encouragement on the part of the government.

Currently, there is concern that the environment should not only be clinically clean but also needs the enlivening influence of tradition and culture that has sustained the development of Singapore's society. The Ministry of National Development is considering going beyond preserving individual buildings and historical monuments to whole blocks or areas of historically and culturally valuable buildings. This development is unfortunately a little late, though not too late, in view of the rapid pace of urban renewal now taking place. There appears to be a need for appropriate mechanisms to monitor and check the policies and activities of public agencies to ensure that their overenthusiasm does not cause irreparable damage to Singapore's heritage of built and natural environment. Much more sensitivity and awareness of the impact on people in implementing public projects need to be exercised to ensure social justice and equity for those affected.

Conclusions

The issues discussed in this chapter are not the blood-and-thunder sort encountered in some other Asian countries. Nevertheless, the fragility of the fledgling society and Singapore's open economy in the face of strong external pressures and influences impels us to examine these social issues with extreme care. The country's major objective—building a strong economy—has been achieved with signal success. Concern now shifts toward the question of fostering greater social stability and national cohesiveness. In this regard, Singapore's society is at a crucial phase of its evolution, and it is hoped that continued favorable domestic and external economic and political conditions will prevail so that this society can gain the strength and resilience to withstand future, and perhaps inevitable, shocks.

Singapore's economic success over the last two decades has resulted in its acquiring a set of social values that emphasize individual merit and self-advancement at the expense of traditional cultural values. Ideals aimed at strengthening the vital tissues of society as a whole are often incompatible with those based on meritocracy. The chapter has shown that the transformation of the built environment through government agencies has contributed in some ways to the breakdown of the traditional social and family structure, and with it some of the traditional mores and values. To the extent that the built environment is highly durable, its impact will be felt for a long time to come. This impact needs to be examined continually, and appropriate measures and responses should be implemented to minimize adverse impacts and correct undesirable consequences.

The current concern with fostering traditional Asian values expressed publicly by political leaders,[21] together with a series of measures—including the introduction of moral education in the schools, the emphasis on a second language, tax reliefs for caring for the aged, and so on— are well timed and necessary to building a cohesive and resilient society and to fostering a Singaporean national identity. A consistent policy capable of responding to the hard realities of the international marketplace, on the one hand, and the needs of a society based on cultural values that defend the weak and disadvantaged members, on the other, has yet to emerge and will probably take a long while to develop.

Notes

1. P.K. Hernon, "Foreword," in Tham Seong Chee, ed., *Modernization in Singapore: Impact on the Individual,* (Singapore: University Education Press, 1972), p. 5.

2. See, for instance, various chapters in You Poh Seng and Lim Chong Yah, eds., *The Singapore Economy* (Singapore: Eastern University Press, 1971).

3. The total land area of Singapore stands at 618 sq. km, with some 30 sq. km of land area added through reclamation.

4. Goh Keng Swee, "Modernisation in Singapore: Impact on the Individual," in Tham Seong Chee, ed., *Modernization in Singapore,* p. 19.

5. Chiew Seen Kong, "The Socio-cultural Framework of Politics in Singapore," in Jon S.T. Quah, Chan Heng Chee, and Seah Chee Meow, eds., *Government and Politics of Singapore* (Kuala Lumpur: Oxford University Press, 1981).

6. See, for instance, chapters in Stephen H.K. Yeh, ed., *Public Housing in Singapore* (Singapore: Singapore University Press, 1975); Ooi Jin Bee and Chiang Hai Ding, eds., *Modern Singapore* (Singapore: Singapore University Press, 1969); and Chia Lin Sien, "Planning and Environmental Management in Singapore," in Colin MacAndrews and Chia Lin Sien, eds., *Developing Economies and the Environment: The Southeast Asian Experience* (Singapore: McGraw-Hill, 1979), pp. 201–232.

7. For a detailed account of public housing in Singapore, see Teh Cheang Wan, "Public Housing in Singapore: An Overview," in Yeh, *Public Housing,* pp. 1–21; and Singapore, Housing and Development Board, *50,000 Up: Homes for the People* (Singapore, 1966).

8. For detailed accounts of the urban redevelopment of Singapore, see Chew Chee San, "Key Elements in the Urban Renewal of Singapore," *Singapore Institute of Planners* 2, no. 1 (1972): 37–46; Alan F.C. Choe, "Urban Renewal," in Ooi and Chiang, *Modern Singapore,* pp. 161–170.

9. Riaz Hassan, "Symptoms and Syndrome of the Developmental Process," in Riaz Hassan, ed., *Singapore: Society in Transition* (Kuala Lumpur: Oxford University Press, 1976), pp. 339–347. Quotation taken from Riaz Hassan, *Families in Flats* (Singapore: Singapore University Press, 1977), p. 14.

10. See, for instance, Peter S.J. Chen, "Changing Values and the Individual," in Chee, *Modernization in Singapore,* pp. 53–62. Note, however, that the extended-family system, where several generations of a family lived under the same roof and were subjected to the absolute authority of the patriach, was seldom strictly practiced by the immigrant Chinese in Singapore. The term is therefore interpreted in a fairly loose sense in the context of the republic.

11. Hassan, *Families in Flats,* p. 69.

12. Abdullah Tarmugi, "Some Problems of Relocation: The Squatter Settlement and the Central Area Case," *Berita Peranchang* 1, no. 1 (1970):31–34.

13. Quoted in Chen, "Changing Values."

14. Stephen H.K. Yeh and Statistics and Research Department, Housing and Development Board, *Homes for the People—A Study of Tenants' Views on Public Housing in Singapore* (Singapore: Government Printing Office, 1972), quoted in Hassan, *Families in Flats,* p. 10.

15. See Tan Tsu Haung, "Planning for Man and Society," in Chua

Peng Chye, ed., *Planning in Singapore* (Singapore: Chopmen Enterprise, 1973), pp. 45–53; Stephen H.K. Yeh and Tan Soo Lee, "Satisfaction with Living Conditions," in Yeh, ed., *Public Housing in Singapore* (Singapore: Singapore University Press for Housing and Development Board, 1975), pp. 214–39; Hassan, *Families in Flats,* p. 50 ff.

16. Hassan, *Families in Flats,* p. 9.

17. Ibid., p. 79.

18. Chiew Seen Kong, "Socio-cultural Framework."

19. Idem, "Singapore national identity," Unpublished M.Soc.Sci. thesis, University of Singapore, 1971.

20. For a detailed account, see Chia Lin Sien, "Environmental Pollution—the Search for a Solution in Singapore," in R.D. Hill and Jennifer M. Bray, eds., *Geography and the Environment in Southeast Asia* (Hong Kong: Hong Kong University Press, 1978), pp. 53–68; and idem, "Planning and Environment Management in Singapore," in Colin MacAndrews and Chia Lin Sien, eds., *Developing Economics and the Environment: The Southeast Asian Experience* (Singapore: McGraw-Hill, 1979), pp. 201–232.

21. See, for example, the prime minister Mr. Lee Kuan Yew's Chinese New Year message on "The Building Bricks of Society," delivered over television on 4 February 1981; and the speech by Mr. S. Dhanabalan, minister for foreign affairs, at the dinner of the Faculty of Arts and Social Science, National University of Singapore, on 3 January 1981.

9

Conclusion

Godfrey Gunatilleke and
Neelan Tiruchelvam

In this concluding chapter we intend to examine some of the central themes in the case studies that have been presented in order to relate them more explicitly to the ethical framework discussed in chapter 1. In that framework attention was drawn to elements in the development process that continually pose dilemmas to policymakers and the main actors contributing to that process. These included the instruments employed to engineer change and implement development policies; the strategies that these instruments serve; the clusters of development goals to which these strategies and instruments are directed; and finally the societal vision that shapes and animates these development goals and objectives.

We begin with the case study that is concerned with the last component—the one that generates the conflicts that overarch the development process as a whole. This is the case study of the management of the relationships between religion and development in Indonesian society (chapter 2). In his introductory comment, the author defines the scope of the chapter. He is not centrally concerned with the substantive issues arising out of the conflict of religious tradition and the modern value system. He goes directly to an evaluation of the institutional framework that Indonesia has installed to manage the diverse responses of religious elites to development and their relationship with the secular polity in Indonesia. Several significant assumptions are implicit in Wahid's approach to his subject. For instance, he does not spend time arguing the case for the role of religion in development, but begins with the assumption that religion is central to the entire social, economic, and political development of Indonesian society, and then proceeds to examine what this implies. For Wahid, the problem is one of adapting the religious foundations to carry the new superstructure of development.

In the conceptual framework within which Wahid formulates his issues, the intellectual assault of scientific materialism and empirical reasoning on the transcendental value system and beliefs does not seem to cause any serious concern. He does not envisage any serious threat to the religious foundations of Indonesian society from the materialist non-religious ideology that might emerge out of the process of modernization and social conflict. It is as though Wahid is speaking from a situation in which the majority of the modern generation is religious in outlook, unaffected by the disbelief and irreligiousness often unleased by the processes of modernization, and therefore deeply concerned with the problem of reconciling their transcendental values and beliefs with the demands made by the historical processes that are generating change in Indonesian society. In brief, there is an assumption in Wahid's chapter that Indonesian society as a whole is seeking an Islamic response to development.

Perhaps a decade ago an article discussing religion and its relationship to development on the postulates contained in Wahid's survey of the Indonesian situation would have been entirely out of place in a book on development issues. The recent revivalist manifestations of religion and its response to social change, however, particularly in the Islamic societies, compel us to pause and reflect on the way in which societies that have major religious traditions such as Islam as the base of their moral order approach the process of modernization. Wahid's assumptions are also partly derived from trends that have been recognized by other observers—trends that suggest that the younger generation in many of these societies is in search of new societal models and is disenchanted with the models that have come out of the experience of the industrialized societies, whether of the capitalist or the socialist type. The disenchantment may stem from both the major crisis of values and the societal imbalances that have manifested themselves in the consumer-capitalist systems of the West, as well as from the basic internal changes that have taken place in socialist societies like China, which had been regarded as an acceptable model.

The chapter gives us a comprehensive account of how various strands of religious ideology have responded to the problems of development. Several conclusions can be drawn from this survey. The need for a base in the dominant religious ideology appears to permeate all parts of the political system. Each group sees the need to make its own reinterpretation of the religious framework in order to derive the religious and moral sanction for the agenda it presents. In this sense religious ideology by itself does not appear to have any firm, clearly defined class base. At one extreme, some components of the traditional ideology will accept and defend the prevailing structure with its inequities. At the other extreme are groups that reinterpret the ideology to advocate far-reaching changes in the structure. To some extent these different ideological expressions correspond to the socioeconomic status and interests of the various groups, but such a conclusion is capable of different interpretations.

On the one hand, the Indonesian experience may be seen as reflecting the overriding need of all social groups to hold together the religious and secular dimensions in their responses to social conflict and change. It may therefore reflect a social consensus that religion and material well-being are both valid and necessary attributes of the development of Indonesian society. On the other hand, the historical materialist would argue that the ideological conflicts and religious heterogeneity in contemporary Indonesia are epiphenomena that reflect the more basic underlying social conflicts that are being accentuated in the process of development. These ideological struggles would therefore have no intrinsic validity in themselves and would be important only to the extent that they are capable of either legitimizing or undermining and attacking existing structures. The materialist might further argue that when the social conflicts in Indonesia reach a stage at which they require a radically new ideological expression in order to find their resolution, then the vast intricate debates and discussions on the minutiae of religious precepts that now preoccupy the religious elites and their following would be swept aside, and a more scientific and secular ideology would play the dominant role. In presenting such an argument, they would point to the experience of modern societies, whether socialist or capitalist, wherein religious ideology itself has become increasingly peripheral to social change and social organization.

Most modern writings on the role of religion in development adopt a functionalist or instrumentalist approach. They ask how religion promotes or retards technological change and the increase of material well-being, which are taken as the primary objectives. At the one extreme, religion is perceived as a major conservative force that consolidates all the personal and social attributes that stand in the way of modernization. At the other extreme are the apologists of religion, who, although they would not express themselves on the intrinsic validity of the religious paradigms, its system of meaning, or its interpretation of reality, would nevertheless concede that religion continues to have relevance as a major force for value formation. Within such a perspective the problem is finding the appropriate religious form for the necessary attributes of a modern society. The Protestant revolution and its role in the emergence and growth of capitalism would be seen as an example of how religion reconciled the new ethos needed for change with the inherited core of transcendental beliefs and goals—and in so doing created the necessary internal moral disciplines to facilitate and accelerate the processes of social change.

The historical materialist might be critical of such an approach and argue that the balance between religious ideology and scientific materialistic thinking has altered drastically since the time of the Protestant revolution and that contemporary history cannot reproduce the conditions that enabled religion to play a vital role as an agent of social transformation. Wahid's position is the opposite of the instrumental approach. He regards religion as providing the fundamental system of meaning within which development must take place. The problem, then, is not how religion should adapt to development, but how both should adapt to each other. This requires a twofold approach, a critique of both the conventional religious paradigms and the prevailing development models.

In the context described here, several dilemmas arise. If religious values are assigned a central place, what is the relationship of religion with the political processes and how will it permit the evolution and growth of modern participatory democratic systems? How is the religiousness of a society in accord with intellectual freedom, open inquiry, and dialogue? How do we separate the conservative forces in religion from its spiritual capacity and moral power to transform society and motivate structural change?

The Indonesian experience with religion and development provides some valuable insights into these issues. It is possible to identify four sets of problems relating to the process by which religion and development adapt themselves to each other. First, there are problems concerning the ideological reinterpretation of Islam to enable Indonesian society to go through the necessary technological and socioeconomic transformation—a task that is essentially intellectual. Second, but closely interlinked to the first set of problems, is the question of how religion can move more positively away from being a conservative force that legitimizes inequitable social structures, and become instead a major moral and social force for structural change through its core of religious values and its own vision of the desirable social order. This requires an appropriate mode of religiosocial action—the right praxis. Third, there is the task of providing a valid intellectual critique of the modern materialistic and scientistic paradigms of development by enhancing the intellectual capacity of the Islamic tradition to meet the challenge of these paradigms, to select their essential elements, and to reorganize them within the religious paradigm. Finally, the transition to a new religiocultural synthesis must itself be managed in a manner that controls the latent propensity for explosive conflict and violence that is present in religious conflict and that provides a framework of intellectual freedom, tolerance, and pluralistic dialogue. Wahid deals mainly with the first two sets of problems, together with the last set of problems concerning the management of the first two. He does not address himself directly to the third set of problems, which by implication he assumes would find their solution in the responses to the first two.

Of special interest in the Indonesian case is the way in which the political leadership, at the very commencement of independence, faced the issue of religion and secularization. It had to find a social instrument that would invest the new social agenda with the fundamental religious values of Indonesian society, but would do so in a way that did not restrict the political evolution and the socioeconomic development of Indonesia within theocratic structures. It had to find the appropriate accommodation between the secularizing elites and the traditional elites. While maintaining the religious center, it had also to create a framework of tolerance and religious plurality. The leadership was able to accomplish this through the state ideology of *panchasila,* around which it sought to provide religiocultural continuity to the development process and set moral limits to development. Although panchasila was expected to perform this role at the ideological level, the Ministry of Religious Affairs was established to give expression to the ideology and to provide the institutional framework in which the pluralistic religious dialogue could take place and could relate itself in a sustained manner to the processes of change.

The Indonesian experience, as analyzed by Wahid, illustrates the complexity of the task of managing religiopolitical relations and attempting to provide a religious foundation for the evolution of a modern society. The overarching framework has sought to create an appropriate balance between religion and the forces of secularization and to evolve mechanisms for conflict resolution. At one end, in its efforts to preserve the religious character of Indonesian society, Islam in Indonesia expresses itself essentially in defensive forms, in the return to the truth in Islamic scriptures, in an uncompromising fundamentalism. At the other end is the effort to separate the historical accretion from the *sacral* core of Islam, to confront the contradictions of poverty and inequality that have grown in the society for which Islam has provided the religious foundation, and to develop an Islamic strategy of structural change. The very process of moderating conflict, however, seems to preserve an ideological system in which the conservative forces continue to have the heavier weight.

On balance, Wahid's assessment of the management of the dialogue is strongly critical. He recognizes the positive aspects of panchasila and the institutional framework. He concedes that it is "a model of a moderating institution in a society troubled by deep cleavage in nearly every facet of its life, including the religious one." He sees the entire framework, however, as having been incapable of promoting a genuine search for solutions to the four sets of problems enumerated earlier. In its arbitrating role, it tried to hold the balance between competing religious advocacies, and in doing so created space for the growth of dissident groups and avoided exclusivity and religious intolerance. This process itself Wahid sees as being flawed by the underlying political manipulation of groups who needed such a balance for their own purposes. He sees the mediating role as confining the Ministry of Religious Affairs to the path of compromise and to "the middle ground that renders it ineffective." It has been unable to evolve the "dynamic and creative policies that can resolve the conflicts between religion and modernization." Panchasila itself becomes an ideological common denominator, a frame of reference for both the oppressors and the oppressed; it fails to provide the motive force for a social agenda of structural change and cultural renewal. He sees the challenge faced by the ministry as related to the fostering of a pluralistic religious conscience capable of sustaining a process of socioeconomic transformation. At the same time, Wahid is himself caught up in the dilemma. He is actually conscious of the problems that can arise if the mediating role "is entirely removed from the scene." He himself brings us to the point at which he pleads for "an overarching framework that, while containing conflict, provides for more constructive interaction," and leaves us there.

It is difficult at this stage to answer the question of whether the Islamic ideology, through its own internal struggle and adaptation, will be able to reinforce and accelerate the social transformation of Indonesia, or whether that transformation will find an ideological vehicle that is essentially secular and will therefore be inherently opposed to Islam. In dealing with this set of issues, Wahid's chapter does not throw much light on the role of the Communist party in Indonesian politics and its response to the religious ideology of Indonesia. The traumatic violence of the civil disorder, in which the Communist party was almost annihilated, raises certain basic issues. In these events it is difficult to separate the element of socioeconomic conflict between classes and social groups and the more deep-seated and fundamental antagonisms that were aroused by the threat to an entire religious ethos from an alien ideology with materialistic and non-Islamic roots. We have as yet little understanding of the way in which the deep personal insecurities and spiritual disturbances created by a threat to religious certitudes and religious systems of meaning aggregate into mass aggression and violence. The way in which the Communist mass movement had gathered strength between the 1950s and 1960s, however, suggests that the conflicts between the religious and nonreligious ideologies in Indonesian society may be more complex than set out in the chapter. At the same time, it would seem that even for the time being the effort to provide a new ideological base outside Islam for the forces of social change has not met with success and that in the present situation the major developmental conflicts are still striving for an Islamic expression.

Chapter 3, on the quest for equality in India, brings out some of the deepest tensions and conflicts in Indian society arising from the affirmation of equality in the Indian Constitution and its extension to millions of scheduled castes and tribes, which had been ritually excluded and historically deprived. Dias highlights the fact that the legal and political values underlying the constitutional order were in opposition to the practices and beliefs that sustained the prevailing social order, and that even at a symbolic level secular equality represented a radical departure from the past. More so, the instruments that were fashioned to advance these constitutional concepts of equality set in motion forces of change and reaction that almost undermined and endangered the fragile legal and political order installed since independence. The dilemmas in the quest for equality in India thus relate not merely to conflicting societal visions, but also to the choice of the instruments of change and the management of the processes of reordering social relations.

The chapter contrasts the approach of Gandhi and that of Ambedkar toward the betterment of the conditions of scheduled castes and tribes in India. It is a distinction with important implications for the conceptions of equality that sought to bind the emergent Indian polity. Gandhi's conception of equality was corporate, and in that sense it was more compatible with the values of the traditional social order. It recognized the validity of the division of labor and occupations along hereditary caste lines but accorded equal value and worth to each occupation. His conception of equality was one of status and not of occupation. Gandhi rejected the concept of impurity associated with cetain caste occupations and functions, as exemplified by the phenomenon of untouchability. He confronted the ethos of ritual exclusion by embracing the functions of untouchables and glorifying them in the eyes of his followers.

Ambedkar and other Harijan leaders, however, did not share this vision of equality. They cared more that the scheduled castes able to tear down the occupational barriers that kept them captive to their depressed social and economic conditions. Equality of opportunity must mean state intervention to promote the upward mobility of individuals in scheduled castes and tribes, who would otherwise be incapable of finding dignity and self-respect within these occupational groups. Out of these concerns, Ambedkar developed a conception of equality of opportunity that recognized that individual advancement could result in uplifting the conditions of the group.

The Ambedkar approach to equality in another sense involved a more direct challenge to the concept of *varna,* the unifying force in the traditional social order. It also involved an emphasis on legal and political rights and upward social mobility through the exercise of political power. It recognized that equality of opportunity could flow from an affirmation of the institutions of representative democracy.

The constitutional affirmations of secular equality and the policy instruments that were fashioned to give effect to it are presented in the chapter as a synthesis of the perspectives of Gandhi and Ambedkar. In that sense the constitutional provisions are said to symbolize a reconciliation between the traditional values underlying the social order and the forces of modernity and change. In the affirmation of the liberal concept of equal opportunity and the emphasis on educational preference and political reservations, however, the constitutional provisions appear to favor the Ambedkar approach. They are rooted in the belief that the institutions of representative democracy could bring about a sharing of power and an amelioration of the objective conditions of deprivation. The only concession to the Gandhian approach relates to the abolition of untouchability and the measures directed toward the elimination of ritual disabilities. This, however, was to be achieved through legislative measures and reliance on the judicial process rather than through moral persuasion and righteous conduct.

The impact of the policies of political and educational reservations and the related legislative prohibition against untouchability highlight the continuing dilemmas in the search for equality in India. These policies appear to Dias to have contributed to the depoliticization of the scheduled caste and the loss of caste identity. They appear to have reinforced inequalities and created new structures of discrimination. They have resulted in making the scheduled caste dependent on the paternalistic institutions of the state and have failed to evolve a new social or political consciousness among them. Dias concludes that the policies that were intended as "a strategy of redistribution of power have degenerated into instruments of control by elites of depressed groups." The assessment of the impact of the policies of preference appears to highlight the infirmities inherent in the instruments of state law and the institution of state courts, rather than the content of the social policy that the instruments were designed to advance. Dias also does not assess adequately the perceptions and aspirations of scheduled castes and tribes as they relate to preference policies.

Dias reluctantly concedes that proposals to abolish preference policies or modify their scope are unlikely to be adopted "for obvious political reasons." He appears thereby to concede that scheduled castes and tribes continue to view the sharing of the benefits of development as linked to the opportunities afforded by preference policies for the sharing of power.

Dias implies that equalization policies directed toward a betterment of the conditions of poverty groups in a wider sense could have had a redistributive impact while avoiding the inequities and disparities that have resulted from preference policies. This conclusion is based on the assumption that many of the problems relating to untouchables arise out of "secular rather than ritual deprivation," but Dias gives us little empirical evidence of whether this is necessarily so.

Dias thereupon examines the spontaneous and sporadic growth of the self-help groups that have emerged within scheduled castes and tribes. These groups emphasize redress of historic deprivations and ritual disabilities through the exercise of corporate power and concerted political action. These movements assume that a redistribution of power can be brought about only by participatory processes through which the group forms its values, its identity, and its agenda of social action. Such agenda for social action encompassed not merely the group demands and direct actions to compel enforcement of distributive legislation and policies, but also the creation of institutions and programs to satisfy their material and social needs. Dias thus views the methodology of social change and participatory decision making of these groups as being of wider relevance to the goals of equity-oriented development. It is viewed as an attempt to transform the political system from the bottom up without the human costs of violent change or the disparities and inequities of state-enforced preference policies.

The chapter therefore highlights the need for a complementarity of approaches, reconciling on the one hand the state's obligation to ensure an equitable sharing of power and benefits to all segments of society, and on the other the need to provide space for relatively autonomous and deprived groups collectively to express their identity and satisfy their material needs. Only such a pluralistic strategy could result in a reconciliation of ethical systems underlying "the traditional caste systems, the modern state-sponsored system of egalitarianism, and the emerging self-help groups."

The Malaysian case study illustrates the dilemmas of reconciling ethnic tensions in a plural society. It highlights the dislocations and instabilities that may arise in the process of development where the division of labor and the distribution of wealth and income coincide with ethnic differentiations. Such an argument would offend prevailing conceptions of justice. With the transfer of power to the dormant and historically deprived majority, however, they were no longer morally or legally acceptable. The Malay dilemma was one of articulating conceptions of justice that redress inequities in the opportunity structure while assuring the non-Malay minorities evenhanded implementation of such preference policies. This places a heavy strain on the political and social institutions that seek to give effect to the new conceptions of equality and distributive justice.

The Malaysian study highlights the importance of the historical and social origins of the separate ethnic communities in the shaping of the Malaysian polity. The Malays viewed themselves as the indigenous polity, whereas the Indians and the Chinese were viewed as immigrant communities and as late entrants to Malaysian society. These perceptions were reflected in the political understanding that preceded the grant of independence, wherein Malay privileges were conceded for the grant of citizenship to non-Malays. The national government and the constituent ethnic parties resorted to techniques of political accommodation within the broad framework of this understanding.

Whatever consensus may have existed when these arrangements were brought into effect soon was eroded by disaffection among militant rural Malays and a new generation of Chinese and Indians. The fragmentation of the Malay political base enhanced the representation of the non-Malay communities in certain states, raising the possibilities of at least neutralizing Malay political domination of the electoral process. The fragile political institutions had been founded on the assumption that political power would be consistently retained by the Malay community; when this principle was questioned, the political forms themselves were endangered. The political instability and violence that was the outcome of these elections again illustrates the fragility of institutions when they fail consistently to give effect to dominant conceptions of political justice. The Malaysian response to this challenge was to extend the conception of political justice to the economic sphere with a view to assuaging further the fears of Malay extremism.

The conception of equality that is implicit in the constitutional arrangements is one of proportionality, and thus presupposes that benefits, rewards, and opportunities should be shared by different communities in proportion to their respective populations. Such a policy of proportionality, however, would need to be applied evenhandedly if it is to enjoy the minimal acceptance of the non-Malay communities. It would otherwise be perceived as an effort to consolidate Malay political dominance. The case study thus illustrates some of the tensions inherent in the management of preference policies weighted in favor of a resurgent and politically dominant majority. Such a preference policy must bear a relationship to an ultimate societal vision—an alternative conception of equality that can discipline and constrain the implementation of the preference policies. Such a societal vision would need to recognize the pluralistic character of Malaysian society and the complementary role of distinct communities in defining the Malaysian polity.

There are two forces in Malaysia that appear to have facilitated a containment of ethnic tensions and conflicts within the existing political framework. The first relates to the growth-oriented developmental strat-

egy of the postindependence Malaysian government, and the rich resource base of the Malaysian economy. The relative success of those
policies has permitted a betterment of the economic condition of wide
sections of the society. The policies of ethnic redistribution that discriminated in favor of the Malays were thus implemented in a climate of
increasing economic prosperity. If the development strategy had been
less successful, with a decline in growth rates and employment opportunities, the ethnic crisis would probably have assumed a different and
more complex character.

Another factor relates to the absence of a territorially based minority
in Malaysia, and its inability thereby to launch a political challenge to
the Malay majority from its territorial base. The apparent political importance of the Chinese and Indians relative to their numerical strength
is further related to their self-perception as immigrant communities. Although the political terrorism of the extreme left may in some respects
be related to the frustrations of Chinese youth, it has not yet posed a
threat to the stability of the regime.

The question that surfaces in this context is whether the policies of
Malay preference could be mitigated so as to minimize the inequities
within the Malay community, as well as ameliorate conditions of poverty
that exist outside the Malay community. If not, the New Economic Policy
could contribute toward the very evil against which it is directed—the
coincidence of power and wealth with ethnicity, reappearing in new
forms.

The Sri Lankan and the Philippine case studies present an interesting
contrast in the responses that these two societies have made to the problems of political instability and civil disorder. The chapter on Sri Lanka
analyzes the factors that contributed to the evolution of a democratic
process of development and the extraordinary instruments that were fashioned within this process to deal with the eruptions of violence and threats
to civil order. The Philippine case study examines the processes that
moved in the opposite direction, leading to a breakdown of democratic
institutions and the establishment of an authoritarian regime.

The analysis of the Sri Lankan experience begins by attempting to
identify the attributes of a sociopolitical system that has a high propensity
for violence and discontinuous change. It is argued that systems with a
high degree of inequality and authoritarian processes for political decision
making are characterized by what has been described as *structural violence*—that is, the violence and aggression implicit in the established
system for the enforcement of law and order and the suppression of
opposition. Structural violence has been described in this study as "violence that is internalized in the structures of domination and inequality
in a society—structures that are legitimized by the prevailing juridical

order and sociopolitical and economic institutions.'' As against such
systems, ''societies that have an equity-oriented pattern of development,
with systems that provide space for the expression of conflict and opposition and that evolve mechanisms for negotiated settlement of conflict,
have a relatively low propensity for violence.'' Sri Lanka is presented
as an example of a society that has moved toward the latter societal
pattern, with a relatively low degree of structural violence. The main
elements in this process of development have been the growth of a competitive political system with universal adult franchise, a program of
social welfare that was given a central place in the development strategy
and that helped to mitigate the worst manifestations of poverty, and
programs of economic development that gave high priority to the improvement of living conditions in the rural sector. The analysis suggests
that at a relatively low stage of development, Sri Lanka has been able
to put in place the socioeconomic and political framework of the social-
democratic systems that have evolved in the industrialized societies. To
a significant degree Sri Lanka was able to sustain simultaneity in the
pursuit of development goals of which we spoke in the introduction. It
was able to do this through a political system that resulted in alternations
of power between governments that emphasized growth and stability on
the one hand and those that leaned toward redistribution and structural
change on the other.

The chapter goes on to examine the manifestations of violence,
repression, and total opposition to the system that have continued to occur
within this framework. The Sri Lankan case draws attention to two important lessons. As in most newly independent societies that install democratic systems, in Sri Lanka the democratic processes released and
surfaced the multifaceted conflicts and tensions that were latent in a
society that had been subject to colonial rule. The very loosening of the
authoritarian structures and the efforts to reduce the structural violence
in the system initially produce new types of instability and disorder. The
processes of democratization themselves have generated new conflicts
between equity and growth, which have been difficult to manage. On
the one hand, the social-welfare program has been a major instrument
of reducing social tensions and mitigating inequalities. By this means it
has prevented the polarization of social forces and strengthened the environment for the functioning of the democratic system. On the other
hand, it has generated an entirely new rhythm of aspirations and expectations, which have outpaced the capacity of the economy to satisfy them.
The contradictions implicit in this situation were major contributory causes
in the disturbances that occurred in 1971. Similarly, the increasing political participation of the masses as a result of the relative success with
which the democratic institutions functioned in the country led to differ-

ent types of conflicts and tensions. The new political instruments gave access to power to diverse social groups that in the past had been at the periphery of the system. These shifts in power themselves released a potential for open confrontation and disruption. The very processes of democratization led to a revival of ethnic and cultural identities and posed a new set of problems to the system.

The second lesson of the Sri Lankan case lies in its management of these new tensions and conflicts. In many societies these situations have resulted in the abandonment of democratic institutions. In Sri Lanka, however, the system acquired a capacity to change and adapt to the situations and to bring about the necessary shifts in the balance of power to promote the required changes at a fairly rapid pace while still avoiding violent discontinuities. The ruling elites as well as the masses held firmly to the foundations of the system and tenaciously sought to devise solutions within it. The Sri Lankan case study, however, draws attention to the vulnerability of the system. The potential for violence and discontinuous change remains high. Postelection violence is a major symptom of the cleavages in a society where poverty is still widespread and the allocation of resources by the powerful elites generates tensions that periodically erupt in open violence. The system, which was relatively successful in handling the vertical inequalities between social classes, has not been equally successful in dealing with the horizontal differentiation between ethnic groups. The manner in which emergency rule has been used and the efforts to prolong the life of Parliament have induced fears that elected governments may attempt to retain power through undemocratic means. It needs to be stressed at this point that the choices in Sri Lanka will continue to be exacting ones, and that until the country has been able on the one hand to find effective solutions to the problems of ethnic conflict, and on the other to sustain a rate of economic expansion that can satisfy the growing demand of a rapidly increasing work force, the stability of the system will remain in jeopardy.

As stated earlier, the Philippines study presents a situation that in many respects contrasts sharply with that of Sri Lanka. The Philippines is yet another example of a society in which the democratic institutions put in place during the period of decolonization have broken down under the stress of the development process. The justification given by the Marcos regime for its authoritarian response and the establishment of martial law does not differ significantly from the justifications given by other regimes that have acted in similar situations to dismantle or suspend the working of democratic institutions. In each case the democratic system has been charged with failure to maintain law and order and incapacity to engineer the structural changes essential for development. The democratic process is said to have provided only an arena for latent social conflicts to surface and to produce persistent civil disorder and economic stagnation. A withdrawal from the representative democratic framework and the establishment of a strong authoritarian system with the capacity to mediate between conflicting forces is then seen as the only effective response. Perhaps more than any other similar authoritarian regime, the Marcos regime, particularly through the writings of President Marcos himself, has been able to articulate and elaborate the ideological framework within which it conceptualizes the authoritarian resolution of the problem and defines its development goals and strategies.

In the chapter on the Marcos regime, Alexander Magno examines this ideological framework and explores certain fundamental issues concerning the dilemmas facing Filipino society. First, he attempts to place the specific developments in the Philippines within a more general theoretical interpretation of the crisis of capitalism in developing societies. Next he contrasts the self-image of the Marcos regime and its ideological projections with the social and political reality. The conceptual categories that Magno uses for his analysis are essentially derived from a Marxist approach. He perceives the dilemmas of Philippine society as arising from the crisis of dependent capitalism confronted by its own inherent contradictions as they are manifested in an increasing polarization of social forces. The Marcos regime is then seen as a typical variant of the authoritarian response to such a situation. It is a response that seeks a new coalition of forces, both internally and externally, and attempts to consolidate the capitalist relations of production on partially new foundations.

Magno argues that the regimes of dependent capitalism seek legitimacy through typical ideologies of technocratic and developmental authoritarianism. The ideology of the Marcos regime, he concludes, falls within this category. The roots of this technocratic authoritarianism, according to Magno, lie in bourgeois-liberal theory itself. Here Magno seems to argue that although the bourgeois ideology provides the base for the democratic institutions within the capitalist system, it also contains the roots of the authoritarian ideology. Through its concept of the state as "the guarantor of the general good and the sensitive instrument of society as a whole," it provides the entry to the technocratic-authoritarian path at the stage when the system inevitably generates contradictions that cannot be solved within the democratic framework. The basic assumptions underlying the ideological position adopted by Magno and his theoretical discussion of the state and its role in society cannot be explored fully within the scope of this book. It does, however, impinge on some of the major issues that were raised in the introductory chapter with respect to the fundamental dilemmas that face developing societies in the process of their development. The way these dilemmas themselves are formulated, as we have seen, depends on the ideological presuppositions from which we start.

In the discussions that took place at the seminars and workshops organized in the course of the project, several participants presented a more sympathetic interpretation of the Marcos regime than is given in Magno's analysis. It was an interpretation that conceded that the ideology of the regime is at least in part a genuine expression of the regime's objectives and goals. The dilemma was then posed as a dilemma of the power holder who is confronted on the one hand with the wholesale corruption of the democratic system, which is resulting in increasing lawlessness and civil disorder in the country, and on the other with the inability to move rapidly on the economic front to promote the socio-economic changes needed to improve the well-being of the poor majority in Philippine society, and thereby to create a more stable social and political order. The authoritarian intervention by the Marcos regime projected itself as the ''rebellion of the poor'' and aimed at establishing a new society. As Magno states, it appropriated the terminology of revolution for itself. The analysts who were sympathetic to the Marcos regime argued that the regime attempted to attack the concentrations of private power that were preventing the necessary structural changes. In order to do this, the regime sought to establish its power base on a coalition of interests that cut across classes. The strategy therefore included programs of land reform that reduced the power of the established propertied oligarchy, programs of urban development aimed at improving the conditions of the urban poor, and dynamic economic policies designed to promote high rates of economic growth. These analysts would also argue that the martial-law regime was a transitional instrument to create the necessary conditions for such a pattern of development.

Such an interpretation, however, invites several fundamental criticisms. The intentions of the Marcos regime as declared must be compared with its social and economic performance. Magno argues that the regime has failed to solve any of the critical problems—problems that, it claimed, could not be solved within the democratic framework and required the martial-law framework for their speedy solution. Yet the rates of economic growth have not been significantly higher than they were before the martial-law regime; the benefits of land reform have been limited; the policies that have been pursued appear to have increased inequalities rather than reduced them; the balance of payments has continued to deteriorate, and the Philippine economy has become increasingly dependent on foreign investment and aid. An assessment of the economic performance of the regime, however, does not by itself provide a reliable or adequate basis for an evaluation of the regimes capacity to promote the total well-being of the Philippine society. Supporters of the Marcos regime could argue with some justification that the rates of economic growth that the Philippine economy has been able to sustain during a period of rising oil prices and international economic instability indicate that the regime has done a creditable job of managing the economy. If we pursue this line of argument, we may find ourselves engaged in an interminable battle of statistics and in conflicting evaluations of the Philippine economic performance. Second, even if the regime had performed relatively well on the economic front, we need to inquire into the deeper human consequences of the martial-law regime and what it did to social relations and political institutions in the Philippines.

This brings us to the more basic questions of whether the total suspension of the democratic political process was inevitable. Second, if it was inevitable, could it not have been so managed as to ensure a speedy return to democratic forms of government? The political action taken by the regime calls into question the genuineness of the claim that the authoritarian regime is a transitional phenomenon. In the case of Sri Lanka, the extraordinary instruments that were developed, such as the emergency, were firmly contained within the democratic and parliamentary framework. Built into the operation of these instruments were mechanisms that ensured that they were time bound and that the system itself would revert to normality within a given period. There were no equivalent safeguards in the establishment of martial law under the Marcos regime. The apologists of the regime point out that nevertheless it has been at pains to establish the constitutionality of martial law. This in itself should not be dismissed as a mere face-saving device. The very fact that a regime feels compelled to establish its legitimacy in terms of a prevailing constitution indicates the moral limits it has recognized and within which it has accepted the need to work. It might then be argued that these limits themselves provide a framework of constitutional norms within which the system could be steered back to democratic processes. Recent developments in the Philippines might be cited as evidence of the beginnings of such a process. Martial law has been lifted; electoral processes have been activated, albeit in a limited form; the government has announced its intention to hold national elections in 1984 and has promised the restoration of democratic institutions. Critics of the regime have, however, pointed out that these measures do not result in any significant dismantling of the authoritarian structure. Presidential powers that were assumed under martial law remain virtually intact. The presidential ''proclamations, decrees, orders, and acts remain part of the law of the land.''

Magno's analysis points out that in the composition of the power structure that has been put in place during the martial law regime, there is a strong coalition between the political, economic, bureaucratic, and military elites. This coalition produces the repressive totalitarian order against which citizens cannot independently organize themselves to exercise pressure and articulate their needs. The new power structure that has emerged is likely to hold fast to the present political framework, as any new process of democratization is certain to sweep it away. Internal changes might have been possible if "the rebellion of the poor" had set in motion more participatory processes that would have involved the people more effectively in social decision making. The regime would then have been able to develop a widening social base from which it could have confidently competed for power within a democratic framework. Magno argues that no such base has been created and that in order to retain itself in power, the Marcos regime would have to continue in its denial of democratic freedoms. It would then seem that even if we accept the avowed objectives of the Marcos regime, its methodology of change has made it a permament captive of its own authoritarianism, from which it now finds it difficult to liberate itself.

At this point it would be useful to recall the way in which Magno defines the initial premises on which he develops his critique of the Marcos regime. He clearly rejects the trade-off explanation, which sees authoritarianism as "necessary for the moment as a political precondition for the achievement of progress" and which "legitimizes the suppression of liberty as a requisite political order for development." In his analysis of the situation, however, he does not indicate clearly what alternative path the Philippine society could have taken. In the opening paragraph Magno tentatively defines two broad categories into which the demands for change and development fall—the liberal demand for incremental change and the radical socialist demand for revolutionary change. There is an implication here that a developing society must eventually choose between these two categories. In his interpretation of the Philippine experience, he argues that the liberal demand to alter the political structure "in some way to make it responsive to the needs of development" is essentially an adjustment within the capitalist system that would inevitably lead to the technocratic authoritarian path. By implication, the alternative lies along the radical socialist path, which undoubtedly would move Philippine society speedily in the direction of greater equity. A radical socialist path that required a revolutionary methodology of change would, however, have demanded its own trade-off, resulting in the loss of the democratic values and participatory structures that were part of the goals of Philippine society before the Marcos regime.

One major base for the opposition to the Marcos regime, however, has been its antidemocratic character. Therefore, implicit in the critique of the Marcos regime is also an affirmation of values that comes out strongly in favor of a democratic participatory political system. The dilemma is then one of seeking a methodology of change that itself does not make any compromises leading to a trade-off between either freedom and growth or freedom and equity. The short-term historical task may be one of struggle against an oppressive regime and its overthrow, but the values that govern the methodology of the struggle and the way in which it develops in given historical circumstances will themselves decide what values will eventually inform the new society that is born out of the struggle and what institutions will evolve for restructuring the social relations. The authors of the Sri Lankan study have posed the issues in the following terms:

> In situations of brutal repression, violent opposition might become a historical necessity. The society trapped in such historical conditions, however, will have to bear the inescapable cost of the violent solutions it seeks and finds. The systems that emerge will be flawed by the violent processes that gave birth to them, and that violence will be carried into the structures and institutions that are newly created. . . .

In chapter 1 we attempted to argue that the technocratic ethos and the trade-off between democratic freedoms and structural change are not the ideological expression of any particular economic system, capitalist or socialist. Their roots extend deeper, to fundamental concepts about man and society that underpin both systems. At one level Magno's interpretation of the Philippine experience as an integral part of dependent capitalism suggests that the good intentions and the proclaimed objectives of an elite are in the final analysis not relevant. Even if President Marcos had a deep commitment to his ideology of a new society, in his objective historical role he would inevitably become the instrument of the elite or class that seeks to perpetuate dependent capitalism and consequently create a repressive developmentalism with its concomitant social, political, and economic institutions. Within such an interpretation the ideology itself has no intrinsic validity: it is a falsification of the reality. Right personal action and the moral character of the elites will by themselves have little impact. We can explore this argument a little further in terms of our discussion in chapter 1. Magno's chapter points out that although the ideology of the regime is a falsification of the social reality, it nevertheless has social significance in that it tries to promote a system of values that would help it gain legitimacy with the population as a whole. The ideology would then set up a framework of values by which it would want to be judged and evaluated. In this sense the ideology of a regime becomes the value framework it claims to uphold and will itself provide the criteria and the tools that enable the critics and opponents of the system to expose the reality and focus on the moral order that needs to discipline the political processes. Through such processes the behavior of the ruling elites and their moral quality become public issues. The conscience of a society is thus formed. This process of creating the social conscience and forming the values of a society, however, will require an institutional framework that will enable a wide diversity of social actors to participate in the process, ranging from the intelligentsia, the academic community, and religious bodies, to interest groups and class organizations of various types.

If we are to assign a significant role to the moral order and the personal attributes of the ruling elites, then it would be enlightening to compare the developments in the Philippines with the experiences of other Southeast Asian societies such as Singapore and Indonesia. In both these societies it might be argued that the prevailing systems correspond to the type characterized as developmental authoritarianism, but in each case the social outcomes have been very different from what has taken place in the Philippines. In the case of Singapore the elites have been able to operate a capitalist model and in the process bring about a fairly stable equilibrium between the different goals of growth, equity, and participation. It has carried through a process of structural change that moved its population from conditions of underdevelopment to those that are comparable to the material well-being in developed countries. The historical conditions and the complexity of the problems were of course enormously different. Singapore, as a city-state with no rural hinterland, is by no means representative of the problems of political management that confront the elites in societies such as the Philippines, Indonesia, or even Sri Lanka. Nevertheless, the relative success of Singapore raises a different set of questions, relating to the quality of the elites who hold power and the values that guide them in national decision making. In the case of Singapore the power holders were individuals who gave an example of personal integrity and incorruptibility. The task of safeguarding the national interest and creating an apparatus for the purpose was more readily accomplished by such an elite. Within such a framework a leadership that leans toward authoritarian forms of government and gives high priority to the values of social discipline and technocratic efficiency appears to have been able to instill in the majority of its people a sense of pride in national achievement and to gain a high degree of social acceptance.

The processes of value formation in a society and the evolution of the moral order that governs the relationships between elites and masses requires much deeper historical and social analysis than is available before we can come to any reliable conclusions. What is important here is that the framework of analysis that has been invariably applied to an understanding of development problems and the behavior of the elites has paid little attention to these processes and has made little effort to

evolve a sound methodology for their analysis. A taxonomy of socioeconomic systems according to the dominant pattern of production relations is certainly useful to understand the broad parameters within which
change can take place. This broad classification by itself, however, tells
us little of the numerous variations in the quality of human life in each
of these general categories within which we try to classify human societies. If we use the Marxist taxonomy we would find in the capitalist
category regimes as diverse as the repressive, highly inequitable systems
in parts of Latin America, on the one hand, and the more humane and
equitable social democracies in Western Europe on the other. Even within
the more specific subspecies under these categories, such as dependent
capitalism, one finds the authoritarian regimes on the one hand, and the
more liberal democratic regimes like Sri Lanka on the other. Within the
even more specific variant of developmental authoritarianism itself, we
have the inefficient, corrupt, and highly repressive systems on the one
hand, and the more equitable, highly efficient technocratic systems like
Singapore on the other.

The same would apply to the systems in the socialist category. Here
too the variants would extend from the orthodox, centrally planned systems to the more flexible market systems such as Yugoslavia; from societies that have been highly repressive and violent, such as Kampuchea,
to those that have sought more humane and participatory strategies, such
as China. The present discussion attempts to explore the limitations inherent in an approach that seeks to interpret the complexity of the historical process and the development experience within these broad, general
categories, and within a taxonomy of human societies derived from the
ideologies and models that have emerged out of the experience of industrialized societies. These taxonomies themselves would have to be
taken further, and we would need to explore the historical specificity of
a given society in much greater depth if we are to understand the processes of value formation within it in order to interpret the development
alternatives available to a society and the limits of freedom and responsibility within which its main protagonists can act. In this formulation
we are giving more weight than is normally done to the role of leadership
in historical processes and its capacity to influence these processes. We
are placing greater emphasis on the integrity or lack of it in the ruling
elites and emphasizing the need for the moral evaluation of those in
national positions of power and responsibility.

The South Korean study presents an interesting example of the dilemma of growth and equity. The South Korean experience has to be
evaluated in the light of the unique and special conditions in which its
development took place. The major land reform that was implemented
immediately after World War II resulted in a large-scale redistribution

of assets and created a structure of income distribution that was more equitable than that of most other developing societies. Although the pattern of economic growth within this structure did not produce the high levels of inequality characteristic of capitalist growth in most peripheral countries, still the operation of a competitive market system in which state welfare had a very low priority resulted in conditions of high risk and social insecurity. As South Korea approached the 1980s, it was moving in the direction of increasing inequalities in its structure of income distribution. Although absolute poverty was declining, relative poverty, which is an index of inequality, was rising. Rapid urbanization and industrial growth, accompanied by the steady expansion of wage employment, were creating new demands for social security and state welfare. The problems were aggravated by the fact that the traditional systems of social security through networks of kinship and family had broken down under the stress of modernization.

What is surprising, however, is that South Korean society, with a remarkably high rate of growth and a relatively high level of per capita income, which it has achieved as a result of this exceptional growth, has a relatively poor welfare and social-security system. According to the data provided in Song Mok Suh's analysis, South Korea needs to allocate only 1.1 percent of its national income to provide a system of social security and income support that would raise the disadvantaged segment of the population above the present poverty line. Even with this additional expenditure, the proportion of GNP spent on social security would amount to 2.27, which is still below the proportion spent by countries in the income range between U.S. $500 and $1,000 per capita. The way in which the choices are presented between growth and productivity on the one hand, and social security and welfare on the other, throws light on the value system that guides the development process in South Korea. The South Korean study focuses attention on two sets of problems. First, the need for social security is balanced against the need to maintain a system that provides the maximum resources and the best incentives for productivity and growth. Sang Mok Suh here deals with the familiar problem of allocating resources between social welfare and production.

The dilemma is perceived in terms of the economist's criteria. The opportunity cost of social welfare can be high, given the constraints on the availability of resources for productive investments. It can lead to dependence on state expenditure, create persistent budgetary problems such as deficit financing of government expenditure, and set in motion inflationary processes that may nullify some of the benefits that social-security and welfare programs expect to provide to sections of the population. The second set of problems concerns the technical constraints relating to social-security and welfare programs that limit their capacity to achieve the basic objectives of supporting the social groups that are most in need. The contributory social-security schemes will primarily benefit the sections that are employed in the formal urban sector and are in a relatively better economic condition. The noncontributory welfare programs such as poor relief, aimed at the most disadvantaged groups, may place too heavy a financial burden on the government, besides being subject to the familiar problems of state-administered welfare programs such as waste, inefficiency, corruption, and failure to reach the target groups. The study also refers to a different set of problems that may arise as a result of the expansion of state welfare—the erosion of the traditional system for security through the family and the kinship network.

These dilemmas will assume a different character depending on the social goals that are given priority in any given society. If the eradication or mitigation of present poverty is a major objective, then the problem of present versus future consumption will be resolved in terms of that objective, and the competition between social welfare and productive activities for the scarce resources that are available will be perceived within a framework of values that already has a profound social concern for the reduction of poverty. In chapter 1 we referred incidentally to the protracted and inconclusive debate on the impact of social welfare on the efficiency and productivity of an economy. Given certain assumptions, it would be possible to demonstrate that a large component of social welfare can impair the capacity of an economy to expand and increase real incomes of the population as a whole. On the other hand, it could also be argued that a system that minimizes risk and insecurity and provides for its poor will create conditions for social stability and establish a humane framework of incentives that would have positive consequences for both the economic capability and the quality of life in a society. In the final analysis the choice of strategies for the alleviation of insecurity and poverty cannot be based on their economic rationale. The choice between present and future well-being, and the decision about who should bear the consequences, is a choice that is made in relation to a larger value system. It is a value system that takes into account the quality of human relations in a society and the pattern of moral obligations and civic responsibilities that should form part of that system. As stated in chapter 1, it is a system in which "the time frame is set for the pursuit and achievement of development goals in order to achieve the most humane equilibrium for the present generation."

We would have expected these problems of choice to have become much more manageable in South Korea, as it has reached a general level of well-being and an economic capacity that enables it to look after its poor without any severe strain. Part of the hesitation and doubt may lie in a social ethos that has emphasized qualities of hard work, industry, and self-reliance. The concepts of public welfare, of sharing on a national basis through state-administered programs and policies, as in the case of Sri Lanka, runs counter to such an ethos. In the traditional setting, however, such an ethos would have been complemented by the support given by the family and kinship groups. The study refers to the concern that is frequently expressed, that state welfare will further weaken these traditional support systems. The assumptions underlying this concern can be questioned, however. To begin with, the erosion of these systems has occurred primarily through the processes of urbanization and social changes that have resulted from development. Compensatory state-administered systems seem to be inevitable in such a situation. Second, such state-administered systems by themselves need not further weaken the kinship and community network. If they are organized on a decentralized basis with community participation, giving a central role to the family and household, such programs could in fact underpin and strengthen the family structure.

The South Korean case points to the need for readjustment and reorientation in some of the basic values and the ethos that have guided the development process in the past—a readjustment that would be able to accommodate some of the positive elements of the modern welfare state. In such an approach an intrinsic value has to be assigned to the component that has been described by economists as ''the grant economy''—the public delivery of goods and services and transfers of income that are outside the exchange economy. This grant economy is more than an effort to combat poverty or provide income support. It is the outcome of a social decision to take certain utilities out of the exchange economy and make them available as part of an inalienable civic entitlement. The character and size of the grant economy is an indicator of the quality of life of a society, its capacity for sharing and for enjoying community, and its total value system.

The Singapore case study deals with dilemmas relating to the human cost of the development program in the specific areas of urban development and housing. Both problems, however, are crucially important to Singapore. On the one hand, the need to protect the physical quality of its small vulnerable habitat has made the problems of environmental management a central concern of government. On the other hand, Singapore has had to make optimal use of the limited space to sustain its rapid urban development and satisfy its housing needs. Chia discusses the way in which Singapore has attempted to balance these different goals and objectives in the strategies it has followed. The economic strategy that made Singapore an attractive base for foreign investment might have led to development patterns that could have created grave environmental disequilibria. One can imagine a scenario in which an urban industrial complex could have degraded the environment and aggravated the problems of housing for the population as a whole, while catering to the needs of a small elite. Chia does not analyze the processes of political decision making that produced the favorable outcome in Singapore. For this, we may have to reopen some of the issues raised in the discussion of the Philippine experience and examine them in depth—a task that is beyond the scope of this chapter. Chia concentrates directly on the nature of the programs that were implemented and how these programs handled some of the more specific dilemmas that arose at the micro level. Within a free-market system in which the private sector played the main role in the economic sector, a strong state apparatus laid firm guidelines for the private sector, directed and planned activities in highly vulnerable areas such as urban development and environmental management, and assumed almost the entire responsibility for housing. To achieve the desired outcome, Singapore had to have a system of enforcement that was deterrent, speedy, and efficient, and that acquired some of the characteristics of authoritarian rule.

The discussion in the seminars that were held on the project explored some of the relevant issues and inquired to what extent the values of a highly efficient competitive meritocracy and technocracy have neglected other central human values that find expression in the culture of a society, in its vision of life, in its structures for community, in its institutions for voluntary human relationships such as the family, and finally in the diversity of dissent and opposition that is the substance of freedom. The Singaporean model is a relatively successful imitative model of the Western industrial system. As an immigrant community, it is in a sense at the opposite end of the development spectrum from a country such as Indonesia, with its search for a model of development that rests on Islamic foundations and seeks nourishment from its deep historical roots and its long tradition. Nevertheless, Chia's analysis indicates how within its technocratic ideology Singapore must be sensitive to the issues that go beyond it. The strong commitment of the government to satisfy the mass aspirations for material well-being has also meant a sensitivity to the human costs of its program. Chia examines the way in which housing programs have kept considerations of equity, ethnic relations and national identity, the cohesiveness of family units, neighborhood community, and solidarity within their perspective, and have provided mechanisms to contain the negative effects and promote positive outcomes in these areas. What is important is that within the technocratic framework, these issues are discussed, their importance recognized, and policies adjusted in response to them. But Chia concludes that these concerns are as yet fragmentary and that Singapore is still a long way from reconciling "the hard realities of the international marketplace, on the one hand, and the needs of a society based on cultural values that defend the weak and disadvantaged members. . . ."

In our concluding commentary on the studies in the book, we have been primarily concerned with the way in which a national system has developed or failed to develop a sensitivity and responsiveness to the full range of human values as they pertain to a particular development situation or problem. Within the limits of our brief analysis, we have tried to examine each combination of development problems in relation to selected value components given in the framework discussed in chapter 1.

From what has been said with respect to the contradictory character of development choices, the inexplicable tangle of gain and loss might appear to result in a predicament of dilemma and indecision—an analysis which would then provide little guidance for action and policymaking. The objective of the analysis, however, has been the very opposite. It attempts to show that policymaking and action will always take place within an imperfect development process, just as economic decisions must be taken in an imperfect market. Development strategies will therefore be constrained within imperfect choices. The quality of the development that these choices will produce, however, will, among other things, depend on three crucial factors. First, the system making the imperfect choice must have a clear awareness of the imperfection. Second, there must be a sustained concern within the system for what is lost in human terms or for the good that could not be pursued in any imperfect choice; and third, the system must possess the built-in motivations and drives to restore what is lost in the imperfect choice and to regain the neglected objective. If we examine a national development strategy or a major development program within it and ask to what extent it possesses these three attributes, we would be able to gain some understanding of the value system and the societal vision that guide or set the limits to these strategies and programs. A development strategy therefore must not only define its targets and anticipated positive outcomes. Equally important, it must identify and define the imperfections in the choices that it makes and anticipate the possible losses that might be incurred in relation to any of the three clusters of development goals discussed in chapter 1.

It might appear that the concept of imperfect choices presented here differs little from that of the trade-offs made in the conventional development models. In the latter, too, development choices have to be made between competing objectives. Such choices always involve a willingness to forego a particular development good in order to retain or enhance another development good that becomes more important in the context of the choice. The imperfect choice and the trade-off belong to qualitatively different development models, however. The difference lies in the total framework of values within which the choices are made in each case. In the trade-off model the development strategy is designed and implemented on the basis that trade-offs will have a long duration, and the loss of those values that are traded off will have to be incurred over an indefinite period of time by the society concerned. These are perceived as the inescapable costs of the development strategy chosen if it is to be pursued consistently and yield the anticipated outcomes. What is traded off is generally given lesser value or obliterated in the ideology of the society making the trade-off. The awareness and the perception of the loss does not constantly exert pressure on the total process of social change, as in the case of the imperfect choice. In the imperfect choice the loss or deferment of any component within the total development goal is consciously carried forward in order to be made good. What is excluded in the imperfect choice is all the time recognized as necessary. Therefore, there is a conscious effort to reduce the duration of the loss to the minimum.

The two basic stereotypes of the trade-off models of development are the capitalistic growth model and the socialist model. In the successful case based on the former model, political freedom and equitable distribution would most often be traded off for the rapid expansion of the economy. The socialist model, on the other hand, would be based on a trade-off of political freedom for a mix of growth and equity. Several analysts of the development process have argued that these trade-offs are inescapable in the historical conditions in which development is taking place in most developing countries. The analytical basis for such an inference, however, rests on interpretations of historical processes and on conclusions regarding the limits to the freedom of human action that themselves are highly dogmatic. That the development process in the past has almost invariably been based on costly trade-offs does not establish the inevitability of such trade-offs, just as the fact that poverty always existed in the past does not imply that it can never be eradicated. The analytical approach that we have presented assumes that the processes of social change provide the crucial space for freedom and responsibility; it suggests, therefore, that decisions have to be taken primarily in terms of the value framework and not in terms of a predictive model that dictates a trade-off on the basis that the optimal result could not otherwise be obtained. The choices then have to be directed not to the search for the best trade-off between different development goals—for example, between equity and growth—but rather to creating the conditions in which no costly trade-offs are required between these goals. The condition that compels costly trade-offs result in maldevelopment. In this

sense the normal growth and well-being of a society are not fundamentally dissimilar to the wholeness of human development. A child should
not have to choose between love and food. A condition in which such a
choice becomes inescapable results in a mutilation of the spirit, neurotic
stagnation, withdrawal into nonbeing.

Therefore, one basic task of policymakers and society as a whole is
the constant monitoring and assessment of the development process in
terms of a well-defined framework of values. Only through such an
evaluation can society be steered toward fully human goals of development. The technoeconomic evaluations or the benefit-cost evaluations
are no doubt essential for their specific purposes, but over and above
these the society must acquire the capacity to carry out a more total
development evaluation. A system that is designed for a total development evaluation must be able to motivate and evolve the key development
actors in such a task; a wide variety of social groups with different
relationships to the development process must participate in it. A conscious process of value formation must be set in motion, a process capable of managing the deep value conflicts that arise out of development.

The extent to which a system possesses this capacity would of course
depend on the particular historical forces that have produced it and govern
it in the present. Within these parameters, such capacity will also depend
on the moral being and the creativity of a given society, whatever its
state of historical evolution. We need to remind ourselves that repression
and authoritarianism are the complement of acquiescence and submission
by the masses, the inaction and intellectual passivity of the intelligentsia,
and the failure of groups and institutions such as religious bodies that
have special responsibility for the moral order of society. In the pro-
founder sense, to the extent of our acquiescence and inaction, we also
participate in the act of oppression. When the Iranian masses in revolt
chose martyrdom rather than live under the shah's regime, repression
became powerless before the forces that were unleashed. Here again, the
moral quality of a society is manifested to the degree to which it can
mobilize resistance and opposition to oppression from all sections of
society; the opposition itself must become broad based and participatory
to the fullest extent possible. In this manner it has to ensure that the
profound moral power and authority growing out of that opposition do
not pass into the hands of a minority or a small heroic cadre, which by
that very process will introduce new forms of oppression in place of the
old.

From our discussion of the various themes selected for the study,
participation emerges as one indispensable condition for the development
process in which the different development goals are perceived as an
organic unity and in which there is a simultaneous effort to achieve them.

The full balance sheet of gains and losses in development could best be kept in view when the different social groups who are affected by these gains and losses can organize themselves to articulate their needs and to share in the decision-making power related to the satisfaction of such needs. We have seen how top-down bureaucratic and legalistic schemes for protective discrimination of disadvantaged groups operate only very selectively and have very limited impact. A more participatory approach, which mobilizes these groups and enhances their capacity for self-reliant improvement, would have a more positive outcome, even though it will usually bring to the surface latent social conflicts. In the Philippine case it was argued that the technocratic authoritarian methodology of change was incapable of creating a popular participatory base that might have enabled the regime to retrace its path back to representative democratic institutions. In a struggle for interracial equity, it is easy to slip into conditions where the so-called rights of the majority are asserted in a way in which the minorities are marginalized and their opportunity for participation in the system severely restricted. If proportionality is one of the values that should be a strategy for interracial equity, then the methodology for achieving such proportionality has to be one in which the minorities actively participate, whether it be through forms of decentralization, regional autonomy, or other equally effective participatory mechanisms.

Eventually the scope for participation in any given society will depend on the structure of power and the character of the elites. In our discussion of the conceptual issues relating to violence and development in the Sri Lankan case, we argued that the methodology of change is itself related to the level of structural violence in a given society. A highly repressive authoritarian system may initially provide little or no space for participatory modes of action. The methodologies of change that are developed in response to such a historical situation often rely on centralized control, secrecy, and violence, creating the vicious circle that perpetuates the denial of political freedoms and the nonparticipatory character of the society. In the repressive nonparticipatory framework, therefore, the primary task is to create the initial space that enables the participatory methodology of change to take root and develop. This would be the main historical responsibility of the social groups and the intelligentsia, which can form the social coalition in opposition to the prevailing system.

This task might at first appear to be no more than the bourgeois-democratic task in the Marxist sequence of social evolution, recast in different terminology—an effort essentially directed at dismantling the authoritarian structures of the precapitalist phase and establishing the framework of freedoms to provide for the free mobility of the factors of production for the development of the capitalist system. It is in fact a task intrinsically different in character from the so-called bourgeois-democratic task. It is related to a different phase in history and a different convergence of historical forces. The participatory framework of political, social, and economic decision making becomes both the precondition and the concomitant of the social transformation; it takes society speedily beyond structures wherein the distribution of power is highly unequal and social relations highly asymmetrical. The participatory framework becomes in itself a major force for social change and sets the parameters for the social transformation. The democratic process in Sri Lanka, for all its limitations, illustrates the potential of the participatory framework. The participatory structures have therefore to be evolved very early in the development process and protected against the strong and sometimes violent pressures that will be constantly exerted against these structures from the nondemocratic counterrevolutionary right or extreme left.

The participatory mode is the mode of social action that is intrinsic to the process of development that we have tried to outline in the introduction. It is more than a mere strategy or mode of action, however. Inherent in the participatory mode itself is the release of the full human energy and creative potential of a society, which can shape the social goals and create a new system of social relations. Implicit in the participatory means is a process of value formation that defines and forms the social ends. Within the limits of historical feasibility, in most societies it could therefore provide an alternative to the elite-centered strategy of incremental change within the liberal capitalist model or the conflict-oriented discontinuous and violent change of the revolutionary socialist model. The basic assumption in such an approach is that such an alternative model is historically more relevant to Asian societies than either of the two other models and that the convergence of forces both in the international system and in the internal historical processes within the Asian societies make it a feasible stage of their historical evolution.

Before we can talk meaningfully of a participatory model of development, however, we need to go much further than the normative framework within which we have analyzed the selected development dilemmas in this book. We would have to visualize convincingly the new structures of social relations and modes of production that will be put in place of the existing ones and indicate how they differ significantly from those that might be established under the liberal capitalist or radical socialist models. We would have to identify the participatory constituencies of a society that include and go beyond class formations and that can create the necessary coalition of social forces to act as the midwife to the alternative participatory society. We have to demonstrate that the historical context is favorable for a social transition of this nature. Such an effort poses an immense challenge to the intelligentsia and the main agents of social change in Asian societies. It calls for an intellectual inquiry that goes beyond the existing ideological frontiers of these societies. What this book has attempted to do is to introduce some of the relevant issues. In doing so, it expects to provide a conceptual thrust that would help to initiate a fuller inquiry and promote the alternative social processes it has tried to delineate.

About the Contributors

Chia Lin Sien is senior lecturer in the Department of Geography, National University of Singapore. He received the B.A. from the University of Sydney; the M.Sc. from McGill University; and the Ph.D. from the University of Singapore. He was previously in the Department of Geography, University of Malaysia. He is on the editorial boards of the *Singapore Journal of Tropical Geography, Applied Geography,* and *Maritime Policy and Management.* He has edited, with Colin MacAndrews, *Developing Economics and the Environment: The South-East Asian Experience* (1979), and *South-East Asian Seas: Frontiers for Development* (1981). Dr. Chia has recently been appointed a member of the International Consultative Committee of the Dalhousie Ocean Studies Programme, Dalhousie University, and is the coordinator of the Regional Shipping Project in the Institute of South-East Asian Studies, Singapore. His research emphasis is in maritime geography, with special emphasis on marine transportation in Southeast Asia.

Clarence J. Dias is the president of the International Center for Law in Development, New York. He was formerly reader in the Department of Law, University of Bombay, and visiting professor at the Boston College School of Law. He has contributed several articles to international journals and symposia on law and social change.

Alexander R. Magno is a faculty member of the Department of Political Science and a research fellow of the Third World Studies Center of the University of the Philippines. He writes a weekly column on political affairs in an English-language magazine. He received the bachelor of arts and master's degrees from the University of the Philippines.

Sang Mok Suh is currently a senior fellow at the Korea Development Institute (KDI). He received the B.A. in economics from Amherst College and the doctorate from Stanford University. He worked as an economist with the World Bank for six years. His publications include: *Society Security in Korea* (1980); *Business Indicators* (1981); and *Patterns of Poverty on Anti-Poverty Programmes* (1981).

Viswanathan Selvaratnam is associate professor, Faculty of Economics and Administration, University of Malaya, Kuala Lumpur. He is currently on secondment to the Regional Institute of Higher Education and Development, Singapore.

Abdurrahman Wahid is currently the first secretary to the National Religious Council of the Nahdatul 'Ulama, the largest Islamic movement in Indonesia. He is also a board member of the Asian Cultural Forum on Development, Bangkok; the national chapter of the Society for International Development, Rome; the Institution of Development Studies; and the Indonesian Association for the Advancement of Social Sciences. He was educated at Al-Azhar University, Egypt; and the Baghdad University; and has published two books: *Bunga Rampai Pesantrens* (*Selected Writings on Pesantren,* 1979) and *Muslim Dalam Pergumulan* (*A Muslim in Struggle,* 1981). He is currently working on a book, to be published in English, on the changing values of Indonesian Muslims, which is supported by a Ford Foundation research project.

About the Editors

Godfrey Gunatilleke is a director of the Marga Institute, the Sri Lanka Center for Development Studies, Colombo. He previously held senior posts in the Sri Lanka Civil Service, including that of Director of Plan Implementation. Mr. Gunatilleke writes extensively on development issues in the Third World. He is the regional representative for Asia in the Third World Forum and a member of the Council of IFDA, Switzerland.

Neelan Tiruchelvam is an associate director of the Marga Institute, Sri Lanka; executive director of the Asian Council for Law in Development; a member of the Law Commission; and a board member of the Sri Lanka Foundation and Human Rights Center. An attorney who received the doctorate in law from Harvard University, he has written extensively on sociolegal issues. Dr. Tiruchelvam was recently appointed to the Presidential Commission on Devolution.

Radhika Coomaraswamy is a senior research officer of the Marga Institute. She was a visiting lecturer in international law at the Bandaranaike Center for International Law and is a member of the Women's Bureau. She received the B.A. from Yale University, the J.D. from Columbia University School of Law, and the master's in law from Harvard University.